# Monogram Models

## *2nd Edition*

Thomas Graham

SCHIFFER PUBLISHING®
4880 Lower Valley Road • Atglen, PA 19310

## Disclaimer

Monogram® is a registered trademark of Revell-Monogram, LLC. This book is neither authorized nor approved by Revell-Monogram.

**Other Schiffer Books by the Author:**
*Aurora Model Kits.* ISBN: 0-7643-2018-1. $29.95
*Aurora Slot Cars.* ISBN: 0-7643-1863-2. $29.95
*Box Top Air Power: The Aviation Art of Model Airplane Boxes.* ISBN: 978-0-7643-2964-7. $29.99
*Remembering Revell Model Kits.* ISBN: 978-0-7643-2992-0. $29.99

**Other Schiffer Books on Related Subjects:**
*Flying Models Collectibles & Accessories.* James C. Johnson. ISBN: 0-7643-1979-5. $29.95



Library of Congress Control Number: 2012952503



Modified by Mark David Bowyer
Originally Designed by John P. Cheek
Type set in Americana XBd BT / Humanist 521 BT

ISBN: 978-0-7643-4424-4
Printed in India
5 4 3 2

Schiffer Books are available at special discounts for bulk purchases for sales promotions or premiums. Special editions, including personalized covers, corporate imprints, and excerpts can be created in large quantities for special needs. For more information contact the publisher.

Published by Schiffer Publishing, Ltd.
4880 Lower Valley Road
Atglen, PA 19310
Phone: (610) 593-1777; Fax: (610) 593-2002
E-mail: Info@schifferbooks.com

For the largest selection of fine reference books on this and related subjects, please visit our website at
***www.schifferbooks.com.***
You may also write for a free catalog.

This book may be purchased from the publisher.
Please try your bookstore first.

We are always looking for people to write books on new and related subjects. If you have an idea for a book, please contact us at
***proposals@schifferbooks.com***

# Contents

# Acknowledgments

Writing this book has given me an opportunity to get to know a number of very talented and interesting individuals. I hope that this book is at least partial repayment for the many kindnesses they showed me.

I was privileged to have interviewed Monogram co-founder Jack Besser many years ago, but unfortunately, he was in poor health recently and was unable to contribute more of his memories to this book. Jack Besser passed away in the fall of 2004. Monogram's other co-founder, Bob Reder, on the other hand, was very helpful and willing to spend many hours speaking with me. Also, his book, *A Brief History of Monogram,* was simply indispensable in sorting out the sequence of model kit issues over the years. Thomas Gannon, Jr., Monogram's president in the 1970s and 1980s, was pleased to explain his leadership of the company. Sadly, he passed away on April 15, 2005.

One of Monogram's most veteran executives, Syl Wisniewski, invited me into his home, and we looked at a stack of old Monogram catalogs as he told me about the kits that he had designed over the years. Roger Harney, who long oversaw model development, shepherded me throughout the research process. Model designers and model makers who had great stories to tell about their years at Monogram are Bob Johnson, William Koster, Clark Macomber, Ken Merker, John Odrlin, and Joseph Sojka. Art director John Cather, Sr. explained his aspect of the company. Artists who shared their recollections were Lou Drendel, Thomas Kowal, Richard Locher, Thomas A. Morgan, and Sonny Schug.

Dean Milano served as my guide through the Revell-Monogram plant in Northbridge and also allowed me to photograph many items in his fabulous (but now closed) Car & Toy Museum.

Custom car designers Darryl Starbird and Tom Daniel had great stories to tell about creating both 1/1 scale cars and 1/24 scale cars. Stanley Mouse told about his brief, but memorable, association with Monogram that resulted in the "Happy Monsters."

Without the assistance of some incredibly knowledgeable hobbyists, this book would have been impossible. Fred Stearns of Fred's Model World helped me with the car models and their values, while Dean Sills of Dean's Hobby Stop helped with the rest. Tom Passalaqua contributed his knowledge of early Monogram kits. John Greczula, "Tom Daniel Historian," handled the Tom Daniel kit section with the help of A. J. Ciccarelli and Charlie Eshenbaugh. Others who made valuable contributions were Ben Ballengee, Christian Bryan, Matt Irvine, and Trevor Ylisaari

Model car historian Craig Clements welcomed me to spend a very fruitful day in his home photographing some incredibly nice car models from his collection and also many belonging to his good friend Ron Hanke. Mark Mattei allowed me to set up my camera in his Chicago home, where some rooms are stacked from floor to ceiling with hobby rarities. Dean Milano must have the best-appointed basement museum display in the country, and he let me photograph his models. (Yes. He actually takes vintage collectible kits out of their boxes and builds them!) Most of the photos of Tom Daniel cars come from the collection of my Florida neighbor, Tim Nolan, who gave me free use of his back porch as a photo studio.

Gill Hodges and First Coast IPMS invited me to one of their sessions to shoot some prize-winning models.

To all these people I am deeply indebted. This book is really a joint effort. If I have failed to mention anyone else who helped with this project, I apologize for my forgetfulness. Of course, any errors of fact or judgment contained in this book are solely my responsibility.

This book is also a tribute to the steadfast support I have received from my wife, Susan, who has proven her worth as a photographer's assistant.

Chapter 1

# The Wood Old Days

In 1927, Charles A. Lindberg flew solo across the Atlantic Ocean, and the world went a little bit crazy. The achievement of the shy, blond, midwestern pilot and his silver single-engine monoplane captured the imaginations of people around the world. Nowhere was this connection stronger than in the hearts of adolescent boys, whose thoughts turned to exploits of heroism in the skies every time they saw an airplane pass overhead. Soon there were weekly serials on the radio about the adventures of sky pilots, and pulp magazines like *Air Wonder Stories* supplied pictures to go with the tales of aerial derring-do. Youngsters devoured every bit of information about flying, from whatever source. Any opportunity for approaching a real airplane at an airfield was a tremendous thrill.

Actually flying in an airplane was out of the question for most boys growing up in Depression-era America, but there was a substitute that at least partly filled that craving for the excitement of flying—model airplanes. Boys joined neighborhood clubs with names like the Air Hoppers and the Sky Scrapers. Each weekend they would gather in a local high school gymnasium or armory, or in a park or empty field to launch their hand-made model aircraft into the air. Some were just gliders, but the most popular planes were powered by wound-up elastic bands that spun their propellers. Sometimes there would be fierce competitions that led to bragging rights for the winners and much discussion of the "secrets" to improved flying characteristics in the next plane built.

Construction of new planes went on almost constantly because crack-ups put old favorites out of commission on a regular basis, and sometimes, if you flew out of doors, planes would be lost on rooftops or treetops, and sometimes they caught a thermal updraft and disappeared out of sight completely. If you graduated to gas powered planes, occasionally one would get away, and you would have to climb in a car and chase a silver speck in the sky down country roads until it came down in someone's cow pasture.

Among the flying model enthusiasts in Chicago was Bob Reder, just a ten year old boy when Lindberg made his epic flight. Reder grew up in a Czech family in the neighborhood of Lawndale, just to the east of Al Capone's Cicero. As a youngster he played with kids from all ethnic backgrounds in the neighborhood, sold newspapers on street corners to supplement the family income, sang in the church choir, enjoyed Boy Scouting, and, of course, went to school. When he was thirteen, he and a cousin built a Wanner model airplane from a kit containing balsa wood strips, tissue paper, music wire, and a rubber band. The kit was labeled "ROG"—that is, it took flight by "rising off the ground." When the cousins wound-up the propeller, placed the plane on the ground, and turned it loose—it bumped along for a second and then lifted into flight, just as it was supposed to. "I was hooked!" Reder later declared. "Model building and flying became a part of my life." (Reder 2000, 2)

Jack Besser (left) and Bob Reder wind up a rubber band powered Monogram Prowler flying model typical of planes that flew in the 1930s and '40s. *Hobbycraft Dealer* (October 1946).

## Comet Models

Reder flew models at a number of venues around Chicago. He often found himself squeezing aboard a streetcar or elevated railway with a huge box in his arms containing the model plane he would fly that day. After a few years Reder became well known as a savvy builder of prize-winning models. He often dropped by the workshop of Comet Models, which was located behind the Goldberg family tailor shop, to purchase supplies.

The owners of Comet Models got to know him and hired him to do odd jobs around the place. They also in vited him to build models for use by the company in displays or exhibitions to promote the sale of Comet kits. By the time he graduated from high school in 1934, he had matured into a tall, lean young man with a shock of wavy hair, scholarly-looking wire-rimmed glasses, and a winning, unfailingly courteous personality. The day after his graduation, Reder went to work for Comet full time as a draftsman and model designer.

Comet had been founded in 1929, but older companies had started selling stick-and-tissue model airplane kits soon after the Wright Brothers first took to the skies. By the 1920s there were dozens of mom and pop companies packaging balsa wood and tissue and instruction sheets together as kits. They sold many of their models through mail order, but some department stores and sporting goods shops carried them in their crafts departments. In 1926 Nathan and Irwin Polk opened a hobby department in Bamberger's Department Store in Newark, New Jersey. The enterprising Polk Brothers stocked model trains and boats and Indian beads and an expanding variety of craft products. Soon they had their own hobby shop in New York City and a mail order catalog that circulated nationwide. Perhaps most importantly, they helped people in the hobby business become aware of each other and their products. In 1929, the magazine *Model Airplane News* appeared, with stories, advertisements, and announcements that further defined the outlines of the hobby universe. Then, in 1940, at the national flying model championships in Chicago, hobby companies, hobby product distributors, and hobby shop retailers joined to form the Model Industry Association.

Young Bob Reder stepped right into one small circle of activity in the midst of these historic developments. Comet Model Airplane and Supply Company soon moved from the back of the tailor shop into the Peter Schutler Wagon Works, a huge complex where wagons had once been assembled, but which had since been subdivided to house a variety of manufacturing enterprises. It was a busy place where saws and routers hummed as they cut balsa wood, creating small clouds of sawdust. The plant manager tried to suck the dust into collectors, but four times a day the floors needed sweeping. Growing production in the Comet plant soon ranked it among the largest hobby companies in the country. Comet was owned and operated by a partnership of Sam Goldberg, Bill Bishop, and Louis Kapp. Bishop, whose original name had been Bibichkow, headed the design and drafting area. He took the novice draftsman Reder under his wing. As Reder sat at his drafting table, penciling-in outlines on his instruction sheets, Bishop leaned over his shoulder, giving pointers on the mysteries of model airplane design. Reder learned the value of attention to detail and absolute precision in the model making business.

Most of Comet's models were simple ten and twenty-five cent kits that contained nothing more than a sheet of balsa wood, thin stringers of balsa, tissue paper, and an elaborate instruction sheet. Kids who bought the kits were expected to spread the instruction sheet out on a table, tack it down with straight pins, and then spread wax paper over the instructions and pin that down too. Next began the laborious task of cutting the balsa strips into lengths corresponding to those that could be seen dimly through the wax paper and gluing the wood parts into their proper locations. Once the wing or fuselage assembly had been completed and the glue allowed to dry, the model builder could lift it off the wax paper and start the process of assembling the skeleton of the model and covering it with tissue paper. When the tissue was first glued on, the model looked like a saggy mess, but a light spray of water would shrink the tissue, pulling it taunt over the frame. A final overall brushing of dope sealed the paper. The propeller (hand-carved out of balsa) and landing wheels (attached with metal wire) went on last.

Bishop allowed his designer draftsmen at Comet to sign their names to the instruction sheets of the models they developed—feeling that this would instill pride of workmanship in his staff. By 1935, some of Comet's models bore the "Reder" stamp. It took only about a month to develop one of these simple models, and the eighteen-year-old Reder wasted no time making his mark. Soon both Comet and Reder graduated to building more elaborate, more expensive "scale" models that more closely resembled real airplanes. Within a few years, Bishop turned the design engineering department over to Reder, and Reder assumed supervision of four other young men, among them a newcomer, Syl Wisnewski.

Wisnewski's path to Comet paralleled Reder's. He was a local boy who bought his first Comet model off a drug store shelf and then went on to become a champion builder of gas-

Monogram's first gas engine powered model planes drew upon Reder and Wisneiwski's years of experience designing for Comet. *Model & Hobby Industry* (August 1948).

powered model airplanes—even though turning round-and-round holding a speeding plane on a wire made him dizzy. To pay for his hobby, he built display models for Comet, and then he came on the payroll full-time right out of high school. He took his place at one of the drafting tables—another lean, quiet, and very earnest young man. Years later, commenting on the scholarly German model airplane builder in the movie *Flight of the Phoenix*, he explained that designing a model airplane was not science or math:

> It was mostly trial and error. You'd draw up something and then you would build it and make adjustments. If it didn't fly right, you'd change the dihedral of the wing or do something else to the stabilizer or rudder. So it was trial and error. No engineering involved. Of course, I didn't have an engineering degree. It was just what I picked up by playing around.

Looking back on his days at Comet, Reder would dispute Wisniewski's description of model design a little bit. "It wasn't math, but it wasn't trial and error either. Each new design built upon those that had gone before. A designer had a whole history of what works in his head. However, new designs did require fine tuning." He also added that Wisniewski was "an expert designer ... a very, very clever guy." Everything he developed seemed to work the first time out.

## Trial by War

Overnight, Pearl Harbor changed everything. Two days after the Japanese attack, Reder was called to Washington for instructions on establishing a program to furnish identification models of Allied and Axis aircraft to the armed services. As a major producer of model aircraft, Comet was a natural choice to lead the program. Paul Garber, of the Smithsonian Institution, served as the link between Reder and the military. Comet already had photographs and information on hand of all the pre-war aircraft since it maintained an archive of reference material for models it might bring out. Garber sent additional photos and data as it became available. The government told Reder that it expected plans for twenty planes to be delivered by February 1942, followed by twenty more in April, and another ten in May. Other groups of ten would follow.

Comet's team of draftsmen worked long into the nights rushing to complete designs for the first set of 1/72 scale model planes. When they were finished, the government delivered sets of plans and supplies of wood to American high schools where students constructed the models. Not only did this supply the military with ID models, it also allowed American boys and girls to feel that they were making a meaningful contribution to the war effort.

One notable absence among the models was Japan's mystery plane, the Zero. Nobody had so much as a good photograph of the aircraft. Then, in June 1942, a Zero crashed in the Aleutian Islands. The Navy took photos of the plane and rushed them to Comet. Reder hurried to make plans for the model. He didn't know the size of the Zero; so he just guessed that it was about average fighter size.

*Life* magazine carried a story about youngsters helping the war effort by building identification models. Comet's connection was not acknowledged in any way, except for a tube of Comet brand cement that appears in one photo. *Life* (March 23, 1942).

Altogether Comet drew up assembly instructions for ninety aircraft, and American school children cut, shaped, and assembled more than a half-million wooden models. By 1943, Comet had switched over to designing models for companies that made injection-molded plastic ID models.

Even with a war going on, Comet continued to make model kits for the civilian market, although on a much reduced scale. Since balsa wood was in demand for military uses, Comet had to search for alternatives. "Everybody was scrambling during the war because of the scarcity of supplies," Reder later recalled. Basswood substituted for balsa, but it was heavy and hard to cut. Comet even packaged some ID models for sale in hobby shops.

Like all draft-age young men, Bob Reder wondered if he would be called to service. Bill Bishop assured him that the government would not call him into the military since he was doing important work with the ID models and other military projects like gliders, target kites, and wind tunnels. However, as the war progressed, Reder found himself classified 1A and headed for the Navy. Bishop intervened on his behalf once more, and the draft board relented.

Syl Wisnewski's experience was different. His local draft board gave no one a deferment, and Wisnewski found himself in the Army. He wanted to be a pilot, but the Air Corps said it had enough candidates for pilot training. Then he went to OCS, but the Army washed him out because they thought he was too soft spoken to command troops. In the end, he spent two and a half years in training and never left the country.

Another Comet employee who also left to serve in the US Army was Jack M. Besser. He had joined Comet back in 1936 after dropping out of high school to support his widowed mother. He started as a shipping clerk, and from there he worked his way up to salesman, taught himself the skills of a businessman, and then was promoted to assistant manager of sales. A native of Chicago, born on the west side in 1915, Besser packed a lot of energy and determination into his compact, muscular frame. During the war he married one of the secretaries at Comet, Myrtle Tannenbaum, and then taught close quarters combat for the Army military police. When he ruptured his appendix, the Army discharged him, and Besser returned to Comet as sales manager.

Jack Besser led Monogram Models as its president from 1945 to 1975. *Courtesy of Revell-Monogram.*

## Monogram is Born

After the war, the normally well-oiled Comet organization no longer operated quite so harmoniously as it had earlier. Comet's three owners no longer saw eye-to-eye on some company matters. With the future of Comet uncertain, Jack Besser and Bob Reder began tossing around the idea of launching out on their own with a new company. Both were recently married young men contemplating their career options for the future. They possessed talents that complemented each other. In a new company Reder could handle design and production of products, while Besser would manage the company and promote sales.

Key to their thinking for a new company was the innovative concept of creating model kits with more prefabricated parts that would be easier to build. Most kids wanted to build something themselves, but lacked the patience to stick with construction of a stick-and-tissue airplane. All of the cutting and gluing was just too frustrating, and if they finished a model, it often looked like a lopsided jumble. Although model kits with pre-shaped parts would cost more to produce, boys would have a much better chance of completing a decent-looking model that would at least fly across the room. With more boys buying model kits, sales would increase, and increased sales volume would produce profits that would more than cover the increased costs of producing the kits. It looked like a sound plan.

While continuing their duties with Comet, Besser and Reder carefully laid the groundwork for their enterprise. Working in the evenings and on weekends, Besser searched for machinery to cut and shape balsa parts. Most industrial woodworking machines were too large and clumsy for the precision work model making required, but Delta home workshop tools proved to be a practical solution to the problem. They were relatively inexpensive and, despite wartime shortages, they were available. Reder picked up the required equipment and supplies in his '32 Willys Overland and carried them to his mother's home, where a temporary workshop was established in her basement.

Meanwhile Reder was busy at a drafting table set up in a spare room of his home drawing-up the production designs and instruction sheets for the new company's first products: model ships. Although Reder and Besser's experience had been in model airplanes, they were familiar with the intense competition among well-established companies making flying models. Model ships, on the other hand, represented a relatively open field, and the public had a huge interest in ships made famous during the war. Reder selected an LST, the destroyer USS *Hobby*, and the heavy cruiser USS *Chicago* (B1, B2, B3) as the first three models. He and Besser also decided to design each of the models in an identical sixteen-inch length, rather than building them to a common scale. That way all the ships would fit into a standard-size box and all would retail for the same price. This made it easier for wholesalers to handle the models, and it allowed a small hobby shop to order a carton of assorted ships, rather than a carton of just one kind of ship.

The ships would be fairly basic kits, but with nicely shaped hulls that required only a minimum of sanding and building to make a nice display model. The kits had to be relatively inexpensive to produce because the capitalization of the new company amounted to just the $5,000 that the two founding partners had managed to scrape together. It was a modest foundation for a company, but it proved to be adequate. In coming years Besser and Reder nursed their company along and plowed their profits back into expansion. They would remain sole owners for the next twenty-three years.

Jack Besser and Bob Reder hold Monogram's first two ships, the Cruiser *Chicago* (B3 $75-100) and the LST (B1 $75-100). *Hobbycraft Dealer* (December 1945).

Jack Besser wanted to spread the word among wholesalers about the new company, but first it had to have a name. A list of possible company names was compiled and debated. Finally Reder's wife, Bernice, suggested "Monogram." Reder thought it had the sound of a "mark of distinction," and conveyed the feel of quality that the new company wanted to make a hallmark of its products. The first trademark was a large letter "M" encircled by the words "Monogram Models." With this important decision in place, Besser began a series of "teaser" mailings to distributors who handled hobby products telling them to "Watch for the Big M." (Reder 2000, 8)

Next, Besser and Reder went searching for a rental space in which to set up shop. Their efforts led them to a modest, low-rent third story loft at 2329 South Michigan Avenue with about four thousand square feet of workspace. In back was a large elevator that had been used to lift automobiles into the loft. They partitioned off a small executive office and a design room with one plywood drafting table. The rest of the space contained bales of balsa wood stacked

All five of Monogram's wooden ship models were sixteen inches long and came in a standard size box, making it convenient to ship cartons filled with any combination of kits to dealers (B1-B5 $75-100 each). *Courtesy of Revell-Monogram.*

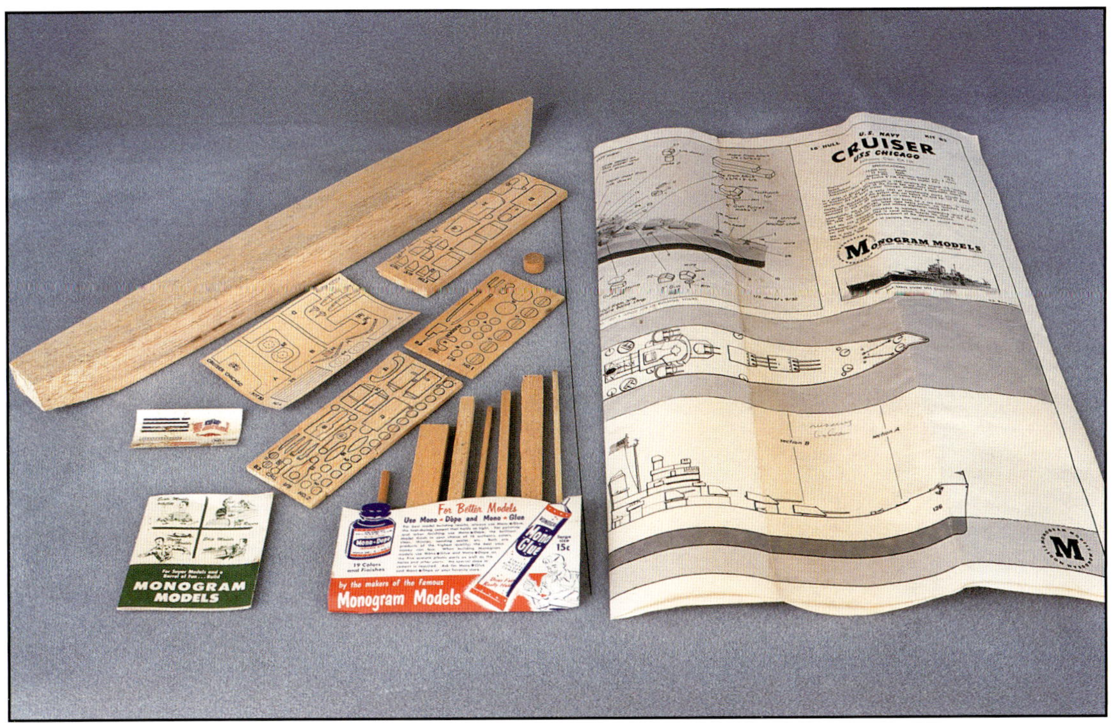


The USS *Chicago* (B3 $75-100) kit gave boys a pre-shaped hull, balsa parts, some wire, a decal sheet, and detailed instructions. Even in the early days Monogram included a mini-catalog of its model kit line. *Author's collection.*

almost to the ceiling, power equipment for shaping the balsa into model parts, storage shelves, and long tables for packaging the parts and instruction sheets into boxes and then into shipping cartons. The total work force consisted of Besser, Reder, one employee for operating the production equipment, and one employee to handle packaging. On November 14, 1945, Monogram's first batch of kits went into cartons ready for shipment.

A few weeks later the staff of Monogram Models celebrated Christmas together. As Jack Besser later recalled:

> We had been in business just a few weeks, and Bob Reder and I, along with two other Monogram coworkers (our entire force), sat down before a makeshift table composed of a number of planks of two-inch balsa, eighteen inches long, supported by two layers of cartons, and enjoyed what was the first Monogram Christmas party. Our Spartan menu consisted of a few sandwiches purchased from the Covered Wagon Restaurant, four Cokes, and one drink of hard liquor each. And we truly enjoyed ourselves at this milestone of having completed six weeks of business.

The next milestone for Monogram came at the annual Model Industry Association convention at Chicago's Hotel Continental in the last week of January 1946. The meeting assembled in the hotel ballroom, where sixty companies in the hobby industry set up display booths in the high-ceilinged room under an elaborate formal chandelier. Companies like Comet, Hawk, Megow, Strombecker, and Testor had their names prominently displayed on large panels behind their booths. Monogram had been born too recently to reserve a space, but MIA convention managers allowed Besser and Reder to set up a display on the narrow mezzanine balcony that surrounded the ballroom. "We were lucky to get in," Reder later recalled, "but the men in the industry knew us." Jack Besser remembered, "Our display consisted of a card table covered by a white table cloth, and our entire line—three $1.00 balsa ship models."

This must certainly be Monogram's first gift set of kits. It dates from around 1950. ($300-400) *Courtesy of Dean Sills.*

From his days as sales manager at Comet, Besser knew all the hobby distributors, and he could estimate about how many kits each ought to order from Monogram. During the five days of the convention, Besser contacted each distributor and made sure that he placed an order. Then, the day after the convention, Monogram started shipping out cartons of model ships from the inventory it had been building up since November. Monogram was on its way.

In May 1946, the company's staff increased to five with the addition of Syl Wisneiwski, who had decided not to return to Comet after his stint in the Army. He knew Besser and had worked under Reder, and he thought they might be starting something big. However, his first impression of the plant was less than overwhelming. "It wasn't fancy at all. They were operating on a shoestring then. ... My first drawing board was just a plywood gismo. It was pretty big, but didn't have any drafting aids like triangles and so on." The stacks of balsa wood arrived in the shop complete with squashed giant cockroaches that had come all the way from South America inside the bundles. The saws and routers didn't have proper sawdust collectors. "The sawdust got in your hair and into your nostrils. You'd get a lot of that stuff in your nostrils."

Years later Monogram's company newsletter, *News & Views* (May 1965), painted this portrait of the operation: "It was a common sight to see Bob Reder sweeping the floor, Syl Wisniewski putting the sawdust in a barrel, and Jack Besser, with his army boots on, jumping on top of the sawdust in the barrel to crush it down so it would be easy to load for the scavenger service." Whenever an order had to be shipped out right away, everyone dropped their usual tasks and pitched in to do whatever needed doing at the moment. However, these young men in T-shirts and blue jeans were working for themselves and willingly put in days that started at seven thirty in the morning and stretched on to eight o'clock in the evening.

During 1946 the roof fell in on the hobby business across the nation, but the little five-man operation on South Michigan Avenue didn't seem to notice the recession. In March, Monogram added the battleship USS *Missouri* (B4) and the aircraft carrier *Shangri-La* (B5) to its model ship line. That same month the Hot Shot (R1) jet racecar appeared. At the time, hobbyists were intrigued by planes, ships, and cars powered by one means or another. CO2 cartridges had been used during the war for purposes such as inflating life vests, and they were very easy to find in a variety of stores. Since they shot out a nice strong stream of compressed air, they were popular as a means of propulsion. All you had to do was slide a cartridge in a chamber in the rear of a car and puncture the cartridge with a needle gun. Syl Wisniewski explained how the cars worked:

> You had to have them on a line because they would veer off in every direction. You had two little eyelets on the bottom of the car. You'd stretch a wire. Then hook the eyelets to the wire. Then shoot the thing and "Whoom." At the end you had a pillow to stop the car.

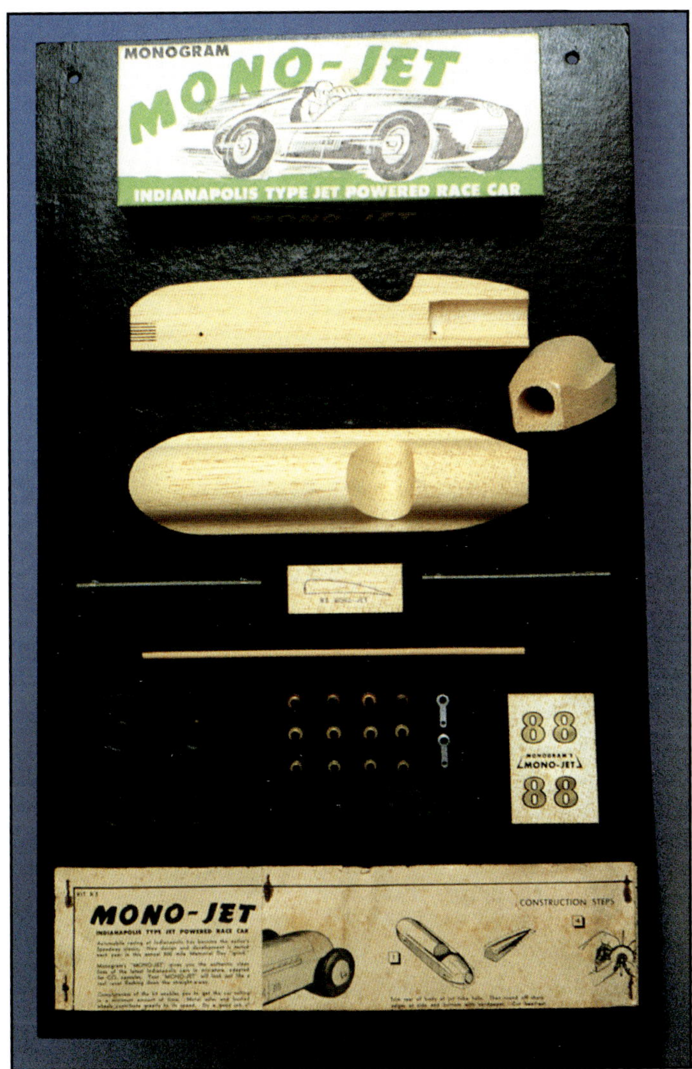

This display board for the Mono-Jet (R3 $75-100) allowed browsers in a hobby shop to see what they would find inside the box—especially the pre-shaped car body. *Courtesy of Mark Mattei.*

The futuristic Hot Shot (R1) came with a partly shaped balsa wood body, rubber wheels, metal axles, and a little clear celluloid canopy. You had to do quite a bit of shaping and sanding to made a streamlined body, but the car was such a successful product that it was joined by the Terra Jet (R2) the next year and the Mono Jet (R3) and Mid Jet (R4) in 1948.

To promote sales of the little race cars, Jack Besser hired an outside vendor to carefully build and paint cars that were then sent out to hobby shops for display. The built-up models showed off the novel features of the kit, letting buyers know that they were getting more than just plans and a box of wood pieces. It cost Monogram about $4.50 for the displays, but they sold them to hobby shops at the discounted price of $2.50 each. (Or, if a store ordered a large enough quantity of kits, the display was free.) Besser explained to hobby shop owners that the displays would pay for themselves by encouraging increased sales. The display models proved so successful that they became the cornerstone of Monogram's point-of-purchase marketing strategy for years to come.

## Monogram Takes Flight

Gas powered engines for model airplanes had been around for years, but improvements in engine performance made them more popular than ever after the war. In the spring and summer of 1946, Reder and Wisneiwski sat down together and designed a plane that would be suitable for gas engine powered flight on the end of a control line. Because the design aimed for speed, they called it the Whirlwind (C1). The sleek, low wing monoplane had hinged doors on top of the fuselage that opened to allow access to the hollow battery compartment inside. The novel aspect of the plane was its prefabricated parts. The wings, fuselage, and tail were all pre-shaped, inside and out. All you had to do was cement the major parts together, and the Whirlwind was ready to fly.

Syl Wisneiwski explained the concept of the product this way: "Although kids were hot on building stuff, they wanted to do it quickly. The kids weren't very patient. That's the reason Bob and Jack got the idea to do as much work for them to start with so that they would complete the project."

Prefabricated parts made construction easy for the hobbyist, but very difficult for the manufacturer. The men at Monogram had to figure out ways to mass-produce parts with many compound curved surfaces. Reder and Wisniewski calculated that each part could be shaped into its final form by passing it through a succession of four or five high-speed spindle shapers, each of which shaved off a little more wood from the original blank piece of balsa wood. Wisneiwski's job was to create the shapes of the cutting blades. The process also had to be as automated as possible so that fresh blanks of balsa could be fed into the machinery as quickly as possible. The Delta units were relatively cheap, but man-hours of production were expensive.

When introduced in the fall, the Whirlwind sold for $7.95. Not too bad for a big model with a thirty-inch wingspan. The Whirlwind also introduced another innovation for Monogram: the propeller, spinner, and canopy were made of injection-molded plastic. Monogram had made an arrangement to produce the parts with Northwest Molded Products in Skokie, a north-central Chicago suburb. Monogram drew up the design specifications for the plastic parts, which Northwest then used to create the production molds and manufacture the parts.

Customer response to the Whirlwind proved to be greater than Reder had anticipated, and Monogram got busy producing additional flying models. The Whirlwind, Jr. (C2), with a nineteen-inch wingspan, appeared in 1947, followed by the Piper Cub (C3), and Aeronca Sedan (C4) in 1948 and 1949. The two Whirlwinds dropped out of the Monogram catalog in the early '50s, but the Cub and Aeronca stayed around through the mid-1950s.

The Whilrwind Junior (C2 $150-175) gave young model builders everything they needed to build a flying model—except the gas engine and control line. *Author's collection.*

When the Model Industry Association annual meeting rolled around in January 1947, Monogram joined the rest of the established hobby companies with a regular booth on the convention floor. At the meeting, all the companies proudly displayed the new products they intended to bring out during the coming year. Monogram's tiny flotilla of wooden warships still represented the core of the company's product offerings; but the Whirlwind and forthcoming Whirlwind, Jr. received prominent display. Jack Besser appeared nattily attired in a double-breasted suit—as befit the president of the company. But Bob Reder seemed to be having more fun, dressed in a Coast Guard life jacket, presiding over demonstrations of Monogram's newest product, the Aqua Jet CO2 powered jet speedboat (B6), as it sped down a twelve-foot long water trough sending up an impressive spray of water. When wholesalers showed up at the booth, Reder would put the life jacket on them and let them fire off the Aquajet. A souvenir Polaroid snapshot of the event served as a reminder to place an order for this amusing product. Over the next dozen years many of them did, and the little jet boat remained a regular fixture on Monogram sales sheets.

The Aqua Jet (B6 $40-70) proved to be a popular selling kit for more than a decade. *Courtesy of Mark Mattei.*

Bob Reder's first love had been rubber-powered free-flight model airplanes; so in the fall of 1947 Monogram brought out the Pirate (F1) and the Prowler (F2). Although competition flying models must be extremely lightweight, Reder and Wisniewski still incorporated a lot of pre-fabricated parts into the models. All the framework parts were pre-cut and ready for assembly into their proper slots and notches. The hobbyist still had to do the gluing and cover the model with tissue paper. One novel feature of the planes was a one-blade propeller attached to a spring that would pull the prop back alongside the fuselage after the rubber band had completely unwound. Once folded back, the prop offered no resistance to the wind and the plane could continue soaring. One of Wisniewski's Prowlers sailed so high that the winds caught it and pushed it twenty miles out into Lake Michigan. A sailor retrieved it and telephoned Wisniewski to tell him that he had found his plane.

Reder thought the flying models were "lots of fun," but he also observed that after a while wholesalers wanted something new in the way of products to offer their customers, and thus a prudent manufacturer needed to plan on cycling-out a product after a few years. The Pirate and Prowler left the Monogram catalog by 1956 to make way for other Monogram models.

With the addition of new products to Monogram's sales line, things were getting decidedly cramped in the tiny third floor plant on South Michigan. Thus, in 1948 Monogram moved to a new location just north and west of central Chicago at 225 North Racine Avenue. The new plant occupied the second floor of a modern brick building and had 10,000 square feet of space—more than twice that of the old loft. This meant more machinery could be installed to increase production, and, as Reder explained, "At last we could order railroad cars of balsa instead of truck loads." (Reder 2000, 13) The move opened up the possibility of big new things—and they weren't long in coming.

Monogram created a sensation at the January 1949 Model Industry Association annual convention. Besser and Reder had combined some of the ideas they had been developing over the previous four years to produce a revolutionary new product: Speedee-Bilt flying model airplanes. These new kits featured completely prefabricated balsa parts that virtually snapped into place. The cowls and propellers of the planes were injection-molded plastic. The planes looked like scale models of real aircraft. They were fairly small in size, with wingspans ranging from a foot to a foot-and-a-half. And they sold for just seventy-five cents. A kid could buy a kit, build it in an evening, fly it, and then go out and buy another one. The potential for mass sales to the growing population of post-war baby boom children was tremendous.

The Speedee-Bilt models featured plastic parts, many pre-shaped balsa parts, and a wing with an airfoil upper surface and routed-out undersurface that would be papered over. *Model & Hobby Industry* (February 1949).

The editor of the hobby industry's trade journal *Model & Hobby Industry* (May 1949) emphatically declared: "Without a shadow of a doubt, Jack Besser, Bob Reder and company have a terrific line of merchandise on their hands. And, as the saying goes, it couldn't have happened to two nicer guys. Here, at last, is a low priced kit anyone can put together."

Comet Models responded to Monogram's lead by jumping into the competition for customers with a similar kit selling for one dollar. Yet, the immediate reaction to the Monogram and Comet models in the hobby marketplace was lukewarm. By summer the editor of *Model & Hobby Industry* (September 1949) had changed his tune. He declared that both the Monogram and Comet kits were selling slowly and contrasted that with alleged brisk sales of five dollar kits. He attributed this situation to hobby shop owners pushing the higher priced kits where profits were greater and to the public's association of low cost kits with low quality.

Monogram vigorously disputed this claim in an advertisement in *Model & Hobby Industry*, declaring that Speedee-Bilts were "Breaking All Sales Records Everywhere!" Monogram's ad also took a swipe at Comet, saying Speedee-Bilts were "The ONLY completely Fabricated Flying Models." Despite this bit of advertising bravado, Reder and Besser were concerned about slower than expected sales of Speedee-Bilts.

Besser's response was an array of creative promotions designed to attract attention to Speedee-Bilts. Display boards were created showing all the finely finished and detailed parts found inside a Speedee-Bilt kit box. Hobby shop owners could pay one dollar for the displays and set them up in their shops to promote sales. Another promotion was a series of advertisements in hobby magazines extolling the virtues of the new kits. The ads centered on the theme: "All of the hard work is done in the Monogram factory. All the fun is left." Monogram also furnished hobby retailers with slingshot gliders, sun visors, flexible metal rulers, and balloons printed with both the name of the hobby shop and Speedee-Bilt. In 1950 Monogram sponsored a national Speedee-Bilt construction contest. Local hobby shops could conduct their own neighborhood competitions by purchasing a ten dollar contest package from Monogram consisting of five model kits, entry blanks, window streamers, a winner's trophy, three medals, and medallions.

Local hobby shops could purchase model contest packets that included trophies, medals, and ribbons as prizes for local boys who entered. *Author's collection.*

Eventually the Speedee-Bilts caught on with America's boys. The line of kits would ultimately reach twenty-one by 1954, and by that time another reason for the slow start of the Speedee-Bilts became clear: All of the original models offered had been of civilian aircraft like the Piper Cub. When Monogram started marketing P-51 Mustangs and other military planes from the World War and Korean War sales took off. Kids found civilian airplanes prosaic, but warplanes stirred up excitement.

Speedee-Bilt models of modern jets and World War II fighters sold better than their civilian companions. *Model & Hobby Industry* (August 1951).

The main drawback of Speedee-Bilts was that they sacrificed flying performance for ease of assembly and good looks. Their all-balsa and plastic construction made them just too heavy for rubber band power to propel through the air. Syl Wisneiwski summed it up: "They were simple to put together, and the kids went for them. I think they satisfied the kids. They weren't tremendous fliers because they were a little heavy for their size. You'd wind it up and you'd throw it, and if it went about thirty yards the kid was satisfied." Indeed, for millions of youngsters it was a matter of great pride that something they had built with their own hands could actually fly across the room.

By the early fifties Monogram had established itself firmly among the manufacturers, distributors, and retailers in the hobby industry. Bob Reder described the company's operating philosophy simply: "Treat others as you would like to be treated." This simple approach earned the Monogram name respect. The editor of *Model & Hobby Industry* (January 1951) expressed a common feeling when he wrote, "In the comparatively short time it has been in existence, this company has built an enviable reputation for quality merchandise, reasonable prices, and fair play. We think we can say without fear of contradiction that when Monogram brings out a new model it is pre-sold by their brand name."

## Superkits

Although flying model aircraft had commanded the interest of most hobbyists throughout the 1930s and '40s, there had always been some demand for "solids" or "shelf models" intended for display. Kits with some partly shaped parts were available in hobby shops, but the least expensive of these solids gave the hobbyist just a block of wood, a sheet of balsa, and instructions with templates for cutting and shaping the wood into a model. Inevitably such kits resulted in a model that ended up looking like a blob. During the war, ID solids contributed to increased interest in display models, and by 1950 Strombecker and Cavacraft had improved the quality of solids by offering partly pre-shaped fuselages and plastic detail parts in their kits.

Superkits combined wood with plastic parts, but the evolution to all-plastic parts was an inevitable next step. (T3 F-84 Thunderjet $50-75, T5 F-86 Sabrejet $75-90). *Courtesy Revell-Monogram.*

During 1951, Bob Reder and his design staff put their heads together to come up with something new in scale display models, and in December Jack Besser put out the word: "A new and revolutionary idea in model building will be introduced by Monogram next month. Preview it at the MIA trade show in Chicago." When distributors visited the Monogram booth at the convention they found "Superkits," the ultimate advancement in wood solids. The Superkits featured sculpted balsa wood fuselages, wings with a nice pre-shaped airfoil, and more than a dozen plastic parts in each kit. The sales pitch ran, "Even a novice can assemble a beautiful super-detailed model in an hour or so." The first three models were a P-51 Mustang, an F4U Corsair, and an F-84 Thunderjet. Each was about six inches long and designed to no particular scale. They were priced as just eighty-nine cents.

Reviewers in the hobby industry liked the kits. Monogram's balsa did entail some sanding to achieve a smooth finish and the soft balsa required careful handling, but it was more fully pre-shaped and easier to carve than Stombecker's pinewood. The Superkits' detail parts had to be punched free from a strip of balsa veneer. But there were plenty of plastic parts like props, wheels, bombs, rockets, and little busts of pilots to go in the cockpits. (Syl Wisniewski confessed: "I made some of the pilot figures myself, but my figures were terrible.")

Production of Superkits presented the same now-familiar problems. Industrial woodworking machines were just too big and clumsy to do the fine cutting required on the little models. Again Reder and Wisneiwski designed their own manufacturing equipment. They came up with a revolving turntable roughly a yard in diameter. Blank blocks of balsa would be clamped around the circumference of the table, and as the table slowly turned, the blocks would pass through a series of shaper heads that formed the fuselage. At the end of one circuit the finished part would drop off and a fresh block would be secured in its place.

Superkits proved to be less popular sellers than Speedee-Bilts, but by the spring of 1954 Monogram celebrated the sale of a pretty impressive one-millionth Superkit. The line expanded to six kits with the addition of a MiG-15, F-86, and P-40 (T4-T6) during 1954, but no more Superkits came on line thereafter. It was a signal of something revolutionary in the wind.

Monogram issued its first Christmas gift set in 1952. This one contains only wood models and thus dates from before 1954. ($400-500) *Courtesy Revell-Monogram.*

## Chapter 2
# Something Revolutionary

In order to set up the Superkit production line, Monogram had to rent more space adjacent to its North Racine Avenue plant. This increased available space to 15,000 square feet, but the additional capacity was obviously inadequate from the start. Thus, another move was in order.

This time Monogram was able to erect its own building, and Reder designed it to the exact needs of the company. It was located at 3421 West 48th Place, farther out to the southwest from downtown Chicago in an area called the Central Manufacturing District. The new plant was built all on one floor and had a railroad siding for delivery of balsa and a loading dock where trucks could back in to pick up cartons of Monogram kits. Once again, the size of the plant more than doubled, this time to 35,000 square feet. In August, Monogram hosted a reception for about one-hundred men in the hobby industry. They inspected the open, airplane-hanger-like production floor, the well-lighted drafting design room, the neat executive office, and—a new innovation—a workers' lunchroom. One feature that improved life for those who worked with the saws and shapers in the "saw room" was a ducted sawdust removal system that sucked the dust away from the machinery and into the furnace. Reder worked with the engineers of the furnace company to formulate a way of burning the dust while it was still suspended in air—without causing an explosion! No longer did bags of sawdust have to be emptied every couple of hours.

Within a few years Monogram extended the back end of the building to add another 20,000 feet of production space. In a move looking toward the future, Monogram installed some injection molding machines to produce plastic parts for its kits. Then the company purchased equipment and hired staff to start producing some of its own production molds for plastic parts. This equipment was located in a shop in the suburb of Niles, but in 1959 an in-house shop was established at the 48th Place plant to repair and maintain the molds.

Ken Merker, who came to work for Monogram in the 1950s, later recalled that there was no parking lot at the new plant, so "you learned to be good at parallel parking." He added, "Bob Reder and Jack Besser ran a very tight ship. It was a very clean operation all the way through. First class. Even though it cost more to do it this way, they felt, 'Let's do it right.'" Like most employees, he found Monogram "a unique place to work."

Two bad boys smoking cigarettes outside the 48th Place plant. Roger Harney and Ken Merker. *Courtesy of Roger Harney.*

Roger Harney added, "We kind of outgrew the 48th Place location pretty fast." The design department had eight drafting tables pushed into corners and up against the walls of its room. Cal Shumate and Roger Harney occupied a small adjacent room used for pattern making. The model makers had only the most basic machine tools to work with: a circular saw, a jig saw, a drill press, a lathe, and a belt sander. That was it. The rest was hand craftsmanship. There was no air conditioning, so in the summer fans were set up to stir around the hot air. But that was state of the art for an industrial plant in the 1950s.

Monogram started the decade with about fifty employees and ended it with about three-hundred. From the beginning, Monogram's work force reflected all the multi-ethnic diversity of Chicago's population, with workers from all backgrounds bumping elbows efficiently as they went about their tasks. Although the company could not afford all the fringe benefits of a major corporation, Besser and Reder tried to make the workers feel appreciated, and they rewarded good service. Female employees were furnished green and white uniforms, while the men wore company-issue shirts and trousers. Anyone with perfect work attendance during a month received a ten dollar bonus. At the annual Thanksgiving dinner, Jack Besser handed out boxed frozen turkeys to everyone, and at the Christmas party everyone received a cash bonus. There was a live band and free alcoholic drinks. Every summer the plant shut down for two weeks in July for vacation, and that became the occasion for another party.

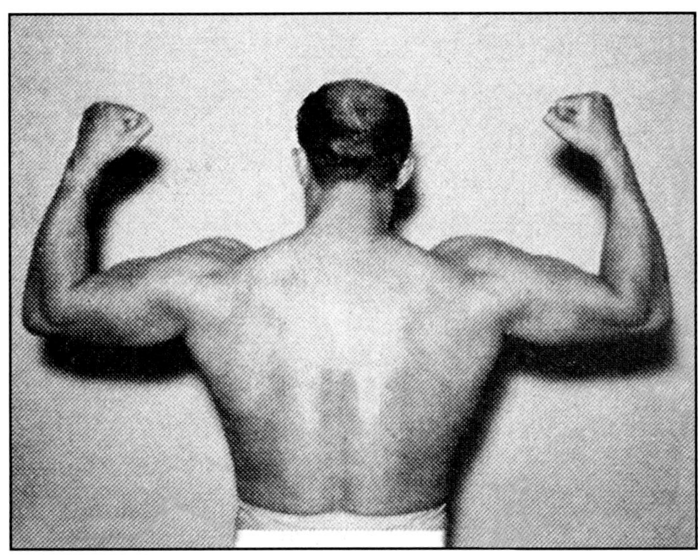

Jack Besser strikes a Charles Atlas pose for his fellow hobby industry associates. *Craft, Model, Hobby Industry* (March 1953).

Bob Reder presents Roger Harney with his five year service pin. *Courtesy of Roger Harney.*

At this gathering women who had worked for the company for five years received a charm bracelet and men got a tie clasp with the Monogram logo. At ten years the awards moved up to wristwatches. The company newsletter, *News & Views,* carried upbeat stories about births and marriages and other human interest items. Loud speakers streamed music into the work areas. Every now and then the company sponsored car building and racing contests among the employees, including the ladies, that were staged in the plant just for fun. Since Jack Besser strongly believed in physical fitness, he encouraged workers to take advantage of the basketball goal attached to the side of the building and the area set aside for volleyball and other exercises. Some employees thought this was carrying the company's paternalistic involvement in people's lives a bit too far, but working for Monogram was good, so they just smiled about it.

Monogram slowly grew and prospered along the way. Its products were well known and respected, and this led ultimately to a sound bottom line on the company ledger books. Monogram always showed a profit at the end of the year.

## Plastic

But in the early 1950s a revolution was underway in the hobby industry that presented both a threat and an opportunity to established model companies. At first men in the hobby world made only oblique references to the situation, discussing it in hushed tones, the way people spoke about cancer in those days. The threat had a name: "plastic." The hobby industry had been built on products made of wood, tin, rubber, paper, and other traditional materials. Plastic threatened to replace these materials as the basic fabric of hobby products. The whole hobby establishment would face revolution, and perhaps some well known companies would perish in the process.

The opening volley of the revolution exploded in 1951 when Revell, Inc. of California, a modest toy company, issued a set of all-plastic model cars under the name Highway Pioneers. Revell's advertising proclaimed: "No Cutting, No Sanding. No special tools or skills required." Anyone could build a really nice looking model simply by cementing together the plastic parts right out of the box. Sales of Highway Pioneers skyrocketed, and it seemed like everybody in America was trying their hand at this new fad.

Actually, all-plastic models were nothing new. Frog in England had originated them back in the 1930s. Hawk Model Company of Chicago had brought out a set of all-plastic racing planes in 1946, but at that time the hobby industry didn't know what to think of them, and they languished in obscurity along with similar plastic kits issued by Lindberg, another Chicago area company. But by 1952 a new company Aurora Plastics of New York was rolling out exciting all-plastic mod-

Bob Reder and Jack Besser show off an industry award at the 1957 HIAA convention for their pioneer use of cello-wrap for model kits. *Craft, Model, Hobby Industry* (April 1957).

els of modern jets and World War II fighters. By 1954 the trickle of plastic kits had become a flood that the leaders of the hobby industry could no longer ignore.

Plastic model kits posed a major challenge to Monogram, which had invested both its financial capital and its brand name reputation in a very sophisticated wood kit line in which plastic parts supplied just the finishing touches. The whole wooden flying model industry appeared to be in jeopardy. Bob Reder served on the Model Industry Association's Aeronautics committee, and in a speech to the 1954 MIA convention he reported the reaction of the makers of wooden models to the plastic revolution. "I have no personal argument with plastics," he explained, "being one of the earlier few to make them a definite part of our merchandise, but I wonder out loud—so to speak—into what direction we are heading, not only as a Model Aeronautics Section, but as an association and industry as a whole." He expressed concern about the loss of building skills and the decrease in knowledge of science and engineering that came with the switch from building flying models to simply assembling the parts of a plastic kit. Would the hobby industry become just a part of the toy industry? "Will our business continue to be an important factor in the character building and education of so many of this nation's youngsters—or will it be 'just business.'"

Jack Besser staunchly defended wood models in his public statements: "More and more fans, after a fling with simple-assembly plastic kits, are coming back to the thrill of more advanced, more interesting, model building, and these [Speedee-Bilts] are the kits they want." Other old-time hobbyists agreed with Besser's sentiments. They said it was OK to lure youngsters into hobby shops with easy-to-build plastic kits, but then hobby retailers should explain to the kids that true "creative" model building required learning to work with wood.

In 1953 and 1954, while other companies were pushing ahead with plastics, Monogram actually expanded its line of wood-and-plastic kits. Sol Kramer, one of the country's leading hobby supply distributors, would talk shop with Reder and Besser at hobby shows. "I told them they were idiots for continuing with wooden kits." However, Monogram's newest wooden kits bucked the trend toward plastics and proved to be very popular items in hobby shops. First came the "DeLuxe" Speedee-Bilt B-25 Mitchell and B-26 Invader (H1, H2), followed by the "Super DeLuxe" Speedee-Bilt Boeing B-17 and B-24 Liberator (H3, H4).

The De Luxe Speedee-Bilts made large display models that were not intended to fly. The B-25 Mitchell (H1 $225-250), B-26 Invader (H2 $225-250). *Courtesy Revell-Monogram.*

The Super De Luxe Speedee-Bilts were Monogram's most elaborate wooden model kits and a fitting climax to the Speedee-Bilts series. The B-17 Flying Fortress (H3 $400-550). *Courtesy Revell-Monogram.*

These kits were intended to be static display models, not fliers. Their wing spans stretched from a foot and a half to almost two feet. The DeLuxe models came in large boxes with colorful art, and inside were a multitude of pre-shaped wood and plastic parts, along with glue, dope, and decals. Plastic kits at the time couldn't compete with these models for sheer size, and these last of the Speedee-Bilts turned out to be big sellers.

Nevertheless, the idea that plastic kits might be just a passing fad vanished as the volume of plastic kit sales continued to surge while that of wood kits faded. However much Reder, Besser, and other hobby veterans may have regretted the hobby industry's turn away from the wooden flying models that they had grown up with and loved, both Reder and Besser recognized that plastic models were the wave of the future. Having witnessed the tidal wave of change in the hobby world, they decided to dive in and ride with the flood.

Thus Monogram began planning to bring out its own all-plastic kits. However, the conversion from wood to plastic would be difficult. The foremost obstacle was the staggering up-front cost of making the tooling necessary to produce an injection molded model. Moreover, a company couldn't issue just one plastic model, it had to have a whole line of plastic kits to offer wholesalers, hobby shops, and customers. High volume sales would eventually pay back the investment in production molds over the long run, but where would the money come from in the short run?

Besser and Reder had always taken care to avoid too much debt, and they maintained a cash reserve on hand to pay company bills immediately as they came due. This close-to-the-vest conservative philosophy had produced slow but solid growth. But now the Monogram team decided to borrow some money to pay for the production tooling for all-plastic kits. The option of taking the company public and selling stock to raise capital was not seriously considered as an option.

In order to service the debt and sustain a cash flow for ongoing operations, Monogram had to continue sales of its existing line of Speedee-Bilts. "We couldn't go to sleep on our old products," as Reder later put it. By continuing to sell wooden models, Monogram bought time to establish a range of all-plastic model kits. Besides, wood kits remained a profitable business.

## The First All-Plastic Kits

Leaders of the hobby industry who gathered at the Model Industry Association's annual convention in Chicago in February 1954 jammed themselves into an exhibit room overflowing with delegates pushing to see the displays. The noise and crowding made it uncomfortable, but there were more serious reasons for discomfort. Although the number of companies hosting booths set a record at 133 (more than double the sixty in 1946), many in attendance were decidedly unhappy. One retailer complained about all the "junk" being exhibited: chenille craft kits, Indian moccasin kits, paint-by-numbers sets, shellcraft, games, toys, "wool to make Mr. Funnyface"—and plastic model kits. Another old timer complained that the new all-plastic kits didn't even belong in a hobby show since they were just "knocked-down toys." During the three years prior to the convention, sales of wooden model kits had stagnated, but any member of the hobby fraternity who openly spoke of the decay in wood kit sales received a stern warning not to discuss it in public.

Yet the transformation of the basic building material in both flying models and static model kits from wood to plastic was obvious at the 1954 convention. Hudson Miniatures, which had done very well selling wooden model car kits, introduced a line of small, plastic model cars that imitated Revell's Highway Pioneers. Comet Models brought out a line of plastic model airplanes. The Monogram booth showcased its now-familiar line of wood-and-plastic aircraft, cars, and ships, but there was something new: a Midget Racer (P1) car in all plastic. Monogram called it "the finest all-plastic model you ever handled ... . Never before such superb, intricate and authentic detail." These bold claims actually possessed real merit. The new plastic model simply outclassed any wooden model in finished appearance.

Right from its first all-plastic kit, Monogram set the industry standard for top quality store displays. The Midget Racer (PC1 $40-60). All prices listed are for the kits, not the store displays, which are very rare and sell for $300 and up. *Courtesy of Dean Milano.*

Soon Monogram had three all-plastic models in the marketplace: the Midget Racer, Hot Rod, and Racing Speedboat (P1, P2, P3). These subjects had been selected by Reder because they would be relatively easy to design, and the molds needed to produce them would be less expensive than those required for more intricate models. Nevertheless, the result was some pretty neat models that were comparable to anything else being offered by other companies in all plastic kits at the time. (Sol Cramer noted that Monogram's new all-plastic models were as good as or better than Revell's.) The shiny red Midget Racer's hood lifted off to show the Offenhouser engine inside. (Interestingly, Monogram's advertisements felt it necessary to stress that it was a "dummy" engine lest hobbyists mistakenly think this new plastic car kit came with a real gas motor, like many of the model cars built by old-time hobbyists.) The bright blue Hot Rod represented a generic '32 Ford. It was not a very accurate model, but—like the real car—proved to be very popular with teenage boys.

An early release Hot Rod before it received decals (PC2 $65-75). *Courtesy of Dean Milano.*

The "Dipsy Doodle" Racing Speedboat was perhaps the best model of the first three. Monogram had used local racer Mat Wyza's Class B hydroplane as the reference for the model and borrowed a ten horsepower motor from Mercury to copy for the motor parts. A sculptor associated with a Chicago museum carved the driver figure that came with the kit.

The following year, 1955, the Model Industry Association moved its annual meeting to Grand Rapids, Michigan, in search of better convention accommodations, and this year it excluded exhibits from some of the companies on the fringes of the hobby industry to please those who had criticized the previous year's crowded convention. In Grand Rapids the exhibit that attracted the most attention was Monogram's booth, with its mammoth, shiny red 1955 Cadillac convertible parked in front. As was its custom, Monogram invited visitors to sit in the driver's seat and have a Polaroid picture snapped. On the partition behind the real car, models of the Cadillac Convertible and Coupe DeVille hardtop (P4, P5) were prominently displayed.

The Dipsy Doodle was a pretty nifty early all-plastic model. Like other car and boat models of the 1950s, it includes a driver figure (PB3 $50-70). *Courtesy of Dean Milano.*

The inspiration for the Cadillac model may have originated with Jack Besser. He liked to tell the story that General Motors originally refused to give Monogram information in advance on its forthcoming car with the innovative tailfins. So in the fall of 1954 Besser and one of the men from the Monogram plant showed up at a local Cadillac dealer for the gala unveiling of the new car models. Besser told the salesman that he loved the car and asked if it would be OK to take some photographs. Then he inquired if he could measure the car "to see if it would fit in the garage." With this mission accomplished, Besser hurried back to the Monogram office to present his ideas to Reder and Wisniewski. They all agreed that Monogram should do the model and that it should be a really spectacular kit. The task of making the pattern for the model was given to Phil Sheldon, who would leave Monogram in 1958 to become chief engineer at AMT.

Reder wanted to have chrome plated parts, like those introduced by Premier Products of Brooklyn in its 1954 line

You couldn't miss the Monogram display parlor at the 1955 hobby trade show! *Craft, Model, Hobby Industry* (April 1955).

of model cars. However, the plastic readily available to Monogram at the time was acetate that melted under the plating process. Monogram's advertising department launched its promotion program for the new model without any mention of chrome-plated parts, but Reder hoped to resolve the chrome problem in time for release of the model. He traveled to Indiana to a shop that specialized in chrome plating. Finding a solution to the problem took a month and a half—partly because the Indiana men insisted on knocking off work every evening to attend basketball games. But eventually a coating was discovered that protected acetate from the corrosive effects of the chrome. The end result was some pretty dull-looking chrome parts, but that still put Monogram on the cutting edge of the industry in chrome plating.

This, plus the real rubber tires, steel axles, and clear plastic windshield, made the Cadillac an exceptional model. It sold for $2.95, compared to ninety-eight cents for Monogram's first three models. (The acetate plastic did betray the DeVille hardtop in one significant way: the large, thin roof part tended to warp at the slightest provocation, such as a little heat or sunshine.)

During development of the Cadillac, Monogram had carefully assembled the pattern and sent Syl Wisniewski off to Detroit to show GM Monogram's handiwork. A bumpy ride in a low-flying DC-3 across Lake Michigan left Wisniewski's stomach in distress, but the executives at GM gave their approval to Monogram's model and so Monogram's ads could honestly state that the model was made "under authorization and control of GMC." Henceforth Monogram would always send display models to the companies that produced the real cars and aircraft as a way of cultivating good relationships. The policy worked, and in the future Monogram often received advanced cooperation from companies when models were being developed.

To promote sales of the Cadillacs, Monogram sponsored a nation-wide contest offering a $5,000 Coup DeVille as the grand prize. An entry blank for the contest could be found in every Cadillac model kit asking contestants to write, in twenty-five words or less, "I like Monogram's All-Plastic Cadillac Models because ..." The entry form also had a place for contestants to write in the name of the hobby shop where they bought the kit. At the end of the contest there would be a drawing and the hobby shop whose name appeared on the blank selected would receive a $500 cash prize. The next nine names drawn received prizes ranging from $100 down to $25 each. If this wasn't incentive enough for hobby shop owners to push the Cadillac models, Monogram pointed out that dealers made a $1.18 profit on the sale of each kit—three times the profit from a ninety-eight cent kit.

Mom, Dad, the family dog, a convertible Cadillac to impress the neighbors in the suburbs—what more could a 1950s American desire? (P4 Cadillac Convertible $120-130). *Courtesy of Dean Milano.*

The defects of acetate plastic are evident in the bumpy windshield and the hardtop, which has warped-off and blown away (P5 Cadillac Coupe $120-130). *Courtesy of Mark Mattei.*

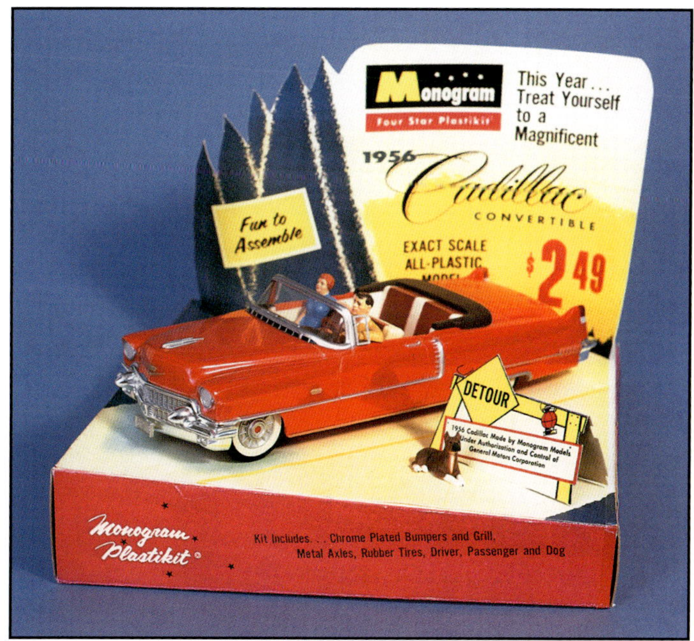


*Right:*
The '56 version of the Cadillac stayed in the catalog for only three years before disappearing forever (PC13 $120-130). The Four Star Plastikit logo was in use from 1955 to the end of the decade. *Courtesy of Dean Milano.*

In 1956 Monogram added a Kurtis Kraft Indianapolis racer to its car kit offerings, but after that automotive efforts stalled. These first four kits would remain the only cars in the Monogram catalog down to 1959. Sales figures showed that aircraft models were the most popular plastic kits, so Besser and Reder got busy building an extensive lineup of airplane models.

The Indy Racer became one of Monogram's all-time best selling cars. (PC12 $70-80) *Courtesy of Mark Mattei.*

The B-25 Mitchell was introduced in 1955 and stayed continuously in the Monogram catalog until 1985 (PA7 $30-40). *Courtesy of Mark Mattei.*

Thus, although the one large Cadillac model headlined Monogram's new kit offerings in 1955, the company also released six model airplane kits. All of these first plastic models were twin-engine aircraft scaled to fit in a standard-size box and retail at the same ninety-eight cent price point established by the first three model cars. The first two planes were the B-26 Invader and B-25 Mitchell (P6, P7) that were selling so well in DeLuxe Speedee-Bilt form. These were followed by the PBY Catalina, Douglas DC-3, and B-66 Destroyer (P8, P9, P10). All were "molded in gleaming aluminum plastic" with "full detail, right down to the last rivet." Actually, these models were relatively simple and would soon be surpassed in accuracy and detail, but they remained on the Monogram sales list for years—ultimately the B-25 became the last of the old stalwarts standing, leaving the catalog only in 1985 after thirty straight years of sales.

Early issues of the PBY Catalina came in silver plastic; later, more common, releases were in blue (PA8 $35-45). *Courtesy of Mark Mattei.*

The real DC-3 has lived a long and storied life—so did Monogram's model of the DC-3 (PA9 $50-75). *Courtesy of Dean Milano.*

The final aircraft kit release for 1955 arrived in December, just in time for Christmas. It was the olive drab military C-47 Skytrain (P11) variant of the DC-3. Monogram's earlier model of the DC-3 represented a civilian TWA airliner with a passenger door that could built open or closed, a loading stairway, and figures of a pilot, co-pilot, hostess, and passenger. The C-47 model had dual cargo doors in its side, a ladder, two crewmen, and four standing paratroopers. How had Monogram managed this transformation? The answer was ingenious, but fairly simple.

Production tooling for injection-molded kits usually consists of several separate steel mold blocks held tightly together in a mold frame. Monogram's mold designers had simply tooled two different blocks for the left fuselage half, doors, ladders, and figures. After the original run of DC-3s had been completed, the molding department merely switched out the civilian mold block and replaced it with the C-47 mold block. Since the runner gates and every other aspect of the blocks had been designed at the same time, the fit remained perfect. There was no need to cut an entirely new second mold. "You had a little more expense up front," explained mold designer Ken Merker, "but the total cost was much less."

Syl Wisniewski recalled bumping into his old boss from Comet, Bill Bishop, one day at an HIA convention. During these meetings the men from the various companies wandered the isles looking at what new products the competition had to offer. Everybody knew everybody else, and there was a more-or-less friendly rivalry among companies—a camaraderie partly fueled by the reality that most companies were growing and earning healthy profits. Bishop expressed amazement that Monogram was making the transition from wood to plastic so seamlessly. "How can you afford to do that?" Careful planning and sound business practices went a long way toward explaining Monogram's success.

By this time Monogram had already established the tradition of offering gift packages of model kits for Christmas.

During World War II the civilian DC-3 became the C-47. Monogram made the same conversion with its popular Skytrain (PA11 $50-70). *Courtesy of Dean Sills.*

The Bag of Kits gift assembly of models was introduced in 1955 and contained all seven of the Monogram all-plastic kits available at the time—not counting the Cadillacs (MGP1 $500-600). *Courtesy of Revell-Monogram.*

These are two of the multitude of gift assortments Monogram put together for Christmas season sales (MGP5, MGP12 $400-500 each). *Courtesy of Revell-Monogram.*

Jack Besser explained that it was a matter of presenting a product to the public in an appropriate way. "We have long had the feeling that the average model building kit is not high priced enough and does not have the glamour required to make it generally acceptable to adults for Christmas giving to kids." Back in 1952, Besser and his sales director made up 250 sets of gift wrapped kits for Christmas and placed them in five hobby shops as a market test. All but three of the gift sets sold. Since the kit boxes were held together simply by thin cardboard sleeves (or later cellophane), the storeowner could easily break up the sets after Christmas and sell them as individual kits. Following the success of this trial, every fall stores came to expect a variety of Monogram model sets to be offered. The number of gift set assortments offered seems to have peaked in 1956 at twelve, but by 1960 the offerings had dwindled to just four and then were issued only sporadically in the 1960s. Perhaps it was indicative that the "glamour" of model kits as a 1950s era novelty was fading in the minds of parents and grandparents.

## Triumphs and Trials

Monogram also had assembled a team of very talented young men to develop and produce their models. Bob Reder, a very hands-on manager, set an example of precision workmanship that filtered down through the ranks of designers, model makers, and tool makers. The men who carved the wooden model patterns were working with very small parts, with tolerances measured in thousandths of an inch. Syl Wisniewski supervised the designers and model makers. He demanded that part fit be exact. "We paid attention to detail. I was a bit fussy about that," he explained. One technique he used to promote precision work was to assign two or more men to work on parts for the same model. Thus each man had to be sure his parts were made to exact specifications or they would not fit with the other man's parts. As Ken Merker explained it: "Syl was a real tough taskmaster. You had to make it right. There was no other way to do it than to make it right. For example, one person made the wing, another made the fuselage using a template to match the airfoil. They worked independently. Tolerances were very precise. It was sure though, but we sure learned how to do it right."

One of the early kits created through this exacting process was the Ford Tri-Motor (P15), a model destined to become a Monogram classic. The model carried the markings of the plane that reached the South Pole in 1929, and it included a dog sled and team of explorers in parkas. Making this model was more of a problem for the mold makers than for the model makers because the men who operated the engraving cutters that had to inscribe the aircraft's corrugated metal wings and fuselage into the steel production mold. Wisliewski recalled that model as one of the toughest assignments of the early plastic era. "The Ford Trimotor: That was a real bitch because it had corrugated sides, and modeling that stuff was a problem."

Even as Monogram's line of all-plastic kits grew, Jack Besser still spoke out in support of old-fashioned wooden model kits. "While necessity forces us into the business, development, and the merchandising of quickie-type items," he declared, "my associates and myself have always belonged to the 'model building' type of school." He asserted modern-day youngsters ought to be challenged to develop the skills necessary to build wooden models. Of course, Besser's opinions were partly self serving because Monogram still sold a lot of wood-and-plastic kits.

Besser also stated that he didn't want the corner hobby shop to be squeezed out of business by large toy stores and department stores. Yet Besser could hardly be characterized as a defender of old fashioned hobby merchandise and the patterns of marketing them. As an aggressive salesman, he was very much interested in seeing Monogram products being sold by chain stores, toy shops, sporting goods stores, and by that most curious of hobby kit dealers, the bicycle shop.

The Ford Tri-Motor has been reissued again and again over the years because of its ungainly but interesting design (PA15 $30-40). *Courtesy of Dean Milano.*

To add new life to its Speedee-Bilt line, in 1957 Monogram revamped the series, giving it a bright new look. The five slowest selling civilian models were dropped from the collection, leaving an even dozen of the more exciting (mostly military) plane models. These went into new "glamour packed" boxes with full color illustrations on top, and each sold for a standard one dollar. Monogram even declared: "There's a growing trend to flying models and more complete model building." This claim combined a dose of advertising puffery with wishful thinking, but the Speedee-Bilts did continue to fly right on into the 1960s.

By the mid-1950s, plastic kits had made model building something that any average boy in the neighborhood could try his hand at. He didn't have to be among a small circle of devoted hobbyists who sought out the obscure hobby shop located on some side street in town. He could bicycle to the local Kresge or Woolworth, buy a sixty-nine cent kit, and assemble the parts while sitting on the floor of his bedroom. All his friends were building models too. *Boys Life* magazine conducted a survey in 1956 and discovered that eighty percent of boys built models, with aircraft leading cars and ships as the most popular subjects. (A similar survey done by *Boys Life* in 1951 had shown that model building trailed stamp collecting and coin collecting as the leading hobby enthusiasms of American boys.)

By the late 1950s, plastic model kits had become so popular that a complaint went up within the hobby industry that there were too many kits on the market. It was alleged that distributors and retailers were overwhelmed and confused by the exploding proliferation of products. Too many companies were bringing out models of the same subjects, spreading profit potentials too thin.

Nonsense, declared Lew Glaser of Revell, the industry's acknowledged leader. Glaser had always aggressively pursued high volume sales, and he saw no need to scale back his efforts. Abe Shikes of Aurora Plastics shared that same forceful attitude. If anything, Aurora excelled Revell in its enthusiasm for new products, often sacrificing model accuracy in its haste to get its latest kits onto store shelves before the competition. By 1959, Aurora was proclaiming: "The largest, most varied collection of hobby products in the world!" Revell responded by asserting, "Revell outsells the next three leading brands combined by 39%!"

The Water Devil Runabout came out of the 1940s-1950s hobby craft tradition and did not last long into the 1960s (PB17 $65-75). *Courtesy of Revell-Monogram.*

The TWA Airliner set was available only for a brief time (MGP-5 $300-400). *Courtesy of Christian Bryan.*

TWA offered its passengers mail-in coupons to purchase Monogram's Lockheed Super G Constellation (PA19 $40-60). *Courtesy of Dean Sills.*

As the battle for sales supremacy raged at the top, Jack Besser maintained a more restrained attitude. Monogram declared itself simply "the finest name in hobbies ... never the most kits, but always the best ... authentic ... perfect part fit ... magnificent detail." Besser explained: "We never crowd the market with too many new kits at one time or bring out new kits too fast. Always a respectable thirty days or more between introductions keeps appetites keen for more." While Revell and Aurora slugged it out over who was "Number One," Monogram claimed only to be "among the top five" in hobby kits. A count of the number of models offered in their respective 1959 catalogs shows that Aurora led with 152 kits. Revell followed with 118, while Monogram trailed with just 64—and twenty of Monogram's kits were wood-and-plastic.

The Blue Angels F11-F Tigers lasted a lot longer as Monogram models than they did in active service with the US Navy (PA29 $50-70). *Courtesy of Dean Sills.*

In the pursuit of sales overseas, Monogram also lagged behind Revell and Aurora, both of which created subsidiary companies abroad. Monogram did sell its products in foreign countries, but relied on hobby product distributors abroad to handle the operations. Thus shoppers could find Revell and Aurora kits in all kinds of stores, but Monogram's kits appeared only in hobby shops.

## The Men Who Made the Models

About this time Monogram was fortunate to hire some key personnel in the plastic model design and development fields who would play important roles in these highly skilled areas over the coming decades. Among these was Ken Merker, a youngster from the Chicago South Side who had built stick-and-tissue model planes as a kid ("All of us did."), but who wanted to become a real aircraft pilot. This dream vanished when a physical disclosed his color blindness. So about as close as he got to aviation was loading baggage for American Airlines. Then a friendly hobby shop owner let him know that Monogram was looking for a model maker. "That sure beats throwing bags on airliners," thought Merker.

The Cessna 180 came out first as an amphibian, but traded its floats for wheels in the 1960s (PA26 $50-70). *Courtesy of Dean Sills.*

The Piper Tri-Pacer was a neat little model that enjoyed more popularity than most civilian general aviation models (PA25 $30-40). *Courtesy of Dean Sills.*

He interviewed with Reder and Wisniewski, who hired him part-time on a trial basis in October 1955. He continued to work for American Airlines five days a week, then put in two days with Monorgam. He was assigned to carve bits and pieces of models, such as the stabilizers and rudder of the Ford Trimotor. After a couple of months, he was put on full time as an apprentice draftsman and model maker. "They started me at a whole dollar and a half an hour," he later recalled. That was a ten cent cut from his pay at American. However, his start at Monogram turned out to be ragged. First the Marine Corps called him up for eight month's service. Then he got married and went into the mink ranching business. "An utter disaster," he later explained. (The mink ranching, that is.) He telephoned Bob Reder and asked for another chance. "Yeah, you can come back," said Reder, and Merker decided that he had better settle down and apply himself to his work. He returned to model making and soon developed into a skillful designer and draftsman. Later in the 1960s, after design was separated from model making, he became head of the renamed engineering department.

Another key player who joined Monogram about this time was Roger Harney. He had been born in the Chicago suburb of Oak Park in 1935, but grew up in the Bohemian neighborhood of Berwyn. During World War II he got his start in modeling by building little Hawk wood solids of the aircraft flying in the war, such as P-40 Warhawks and P-39 Aircobras. A few years later an uncle showed him how to build gas-engine powered control line flying aircraft models. Then as a fifteen year old he earned a chance to compete in the Plymouth-sponsored national model championship in Detroit. He finished third in his first try, but won the senior scale flying model competition for the next two years, entering a large Spad fighter that he had built by scaling-up some three views by the popular aircraft design expert William Wylam. The wooden framework of the model was faithful to the real aircraft, and it had nice metal louver panels and machine guns fabricated from sheet metal.

Meanwhile Harney had graduated from high school, attended junior college for two years, quit modeling, and was earning money working at a gas station, while spending money on cars as a member of a hot rod club. His first big project was to pull the engine from his '52 Olds Super 88 and "warm it up a little bit." When he broke up with his girlfriend about this time, she gave him a parting admonition to make something more of himself than a gas station attendant. Following her advice to seek employment as a "lab technician," he scanned down the employment want ads and happened across a listing for "model airplane builder." He couldn't believe it! He arranged an interview with Bob Reder—to which he carried his award-winning Spad—and was offered a position as a model maker. The first day on the job he walked into the model shop and was shown the wooden pattern of Phil Sheldon's T-28 (PA14). "Gosh," he thought, "I can never make this!" But he was taken under the wings of Syl Wisniewski and Calvin Shumate (a black man from South Chicago who had been hired a year earlier) and went to work learning the ropes.

The Auto Racing Trio first appeared as an assortment of kits in a thin cardboard sleeve (MGP-7 $300-400) and then as a boxed gift set (MGP-8 $300-400). *Courtesy of Mark Mattei.*

The T-28 Trainer first appeared in yellow plastic as a Navy B version (PA14 $35-45), then in silver plastic as an Air Force A variant (PA28 $30-40), and finally as a gray T-28D from the Vietnam War (PA121 $20-30). *Courtesy of Dean Sills.*

The designers and model makers all shared the same small room at the West 48th Place plant. It was crowded with about eight or ten men, their drafting boards almost touching. At the time most of the men were expected to handle both drafting of plans and carving of patterns. Occasionally one person could design and carve almost all of a model. On his first project Harney worked with Ken Merker to carve the pattern for the Cessna 180 (PA26). Harney began with the water skis held by the girl figure, then went on to the floats, wings, and stabilizers. Merker did the fuselage. He was given more responsibility on the Piper Tri-Pacer (PA25). Harney carved all of the airplane, while Shumate did the engine. Harney and Shumate teamed up again on the Gulfhawk II (PA58).

Harney's carving efforts were particularly difficult because Monogram had just changed the way it made patterns. Prior to his arrival the model makers had carved their patterns twice the size intended for the finished model kit. When they had finished their work, the wooden patterns would be sent to a tool and die company that would copy directly from the wood parts, using a pantograph machine to reduce the scale to half size when milling the steel mold. Some small parts were cut directly from the engineering drawings, without use of a wood pattern. But then the tool shop Monogram was using acquired machinery that copied patterns directly, one-to-one. This meant that Harney and his colleagues had to carve in smaller size. After they had done their work, the wood parts would be cast in epoxy to make molds that the toolmaker could use for tool cutting. This one-to-one carving lasted only for about a year, and then Monogram went back to two-to-one production of the patterns. In these early years the wood used was box elder, but later the model makers used basswood. Both woods had very fine grain that polished to a smooth surface.

The design shop at Monogram's 48th Place plant. *Courtesy of Syl Wisniewski.*

*Below:*
The orange Gulf Oil Gulfhawk II (PA58) was a favorite of Bob Reder, who had designed a model of one for Comet Models back in the 1930s. Its military version, the F3F-3 (PA70) had a different cowl with machine gun ports. *Courtesy of Dean Sills.*

At this point Harney asked Reder to give him a chance at model designing. Reder said OK, and Wisniewski, who Harney regarded as a super teacher, showed him the finer points of drafting plans. He worked on a few small projects, but then was given the assignment of drafting the design for a '32 Ford Sport Coupe (PC57). This proved to be too much of a challenge for Harney's limited drafting experience at the time. When another model carving project came up, he asked to go back to being primarily a model maker. To his relief, Syl said OK. The move back to the model shop suited Harney just fine. "It was one of the happiest times of my life. Just heaven. All I was doing was making models, and I couldn't wait to get to work."

Another model maker who couldn't wait to get to work was Joseph Sojka, who had joined Monogram about a year after Harney. Sojka's life story followed a familiar pattern. He grew up in Cicero, the Italian-American/Polish neighborhood next door to Harney's Berwyn. He started building model airplanes when he was "real young," then got into model railroading and sketching as a high schooler. He went on to receive advanced training in technical illustration and engineering at Chicago Aeronautical University, but found upon graduation that nobody was hiring—except Monogram. Bob Reder put him on at the standard $1.50 an hour, with a five cent raise in three months. Syl Wisniewski brought him along in model making. Sojka discovered that Wisniewski was "pretty fussy" and vigilantly sought out any flaw in the model carving. But he liked working in the cramped model/drafting room. He found that most of the other men in the model shop were also hobbyists who just loved what they were doing. Sojka started coming in an hour early just to work on his own personal modeling projects for fun before commencing his company modeling work for pay. Model making was a great job—you got paid to do what you did anyway just for pleasure.

The '32 Ford Sport Coupe (PC57 $180-200) went out of the Monogram catalog in the mid-1960s and was never reissued. *Courtesy of Craig Clements and Ron Hanke.*

The original Hot Rod (P2) took on a new look as the '32 Ford Deuce Roadster (PC55 $95-105). Jack Besser saw Fred Allen's "Devil Deuce" on the cover of *Rod Builder & Customizer* magazine (November 1957) and said Monogram had to have one too. *Author's collection.*

The same newspaper advertisement that attracted Joe Sojka to Monogram also brought John Odrlin. At age thirty-five Odrlin stood out as a senior citizen among his fellow design and model making coworkers. He had been born in 1923 and grew up in Chicago doing the usual things boys did, including flying rubber powered model airplanes on Sunday afternoons. His talent for drawing earned him two scholarships to the Art Institute of Chicago, and this pointed him down a path leading to a career in mechanical engineering. When the company he was working for laid him off in 1958, he answered Monogram's newspaper ad. Odrlin brought a model ship to his interview with Bob Reder, but Reder did not want him as a model builder. His mechanical engineering credentials were impressive enough that Reder hired him on the spot and put him to work as a model designer. One of his first projects was taking over design of the '32 Sport Coupe from Harney. He tacked the usual tasks of turning a stack of photographs and measurements into precise engineering drawings of model parts. "Reder kept careful watch to see if we knew which end of the pencil to hold," he later recalled. Sometimes the boys from the model shop would bring a design drawing back to drafting for "enlightenment" on what a part was supposed to look like. The job of carving the '32 Sport Coupe pattern ended up with Roger Harney—so the story of that model's development had a happy ending.

Thus, by the late 1950s, Monogram had put together a critical core of very talented model designers and pattern carvers, most of whom would stick with the company for the next three decades. The combination of Reder and Wisniewski's policy of uncompromisingly high quality standards and a proficient staff that could execute all phase of model development resulted in Monogram models that set industry standards for excellence.

The Slingshot Dragster (PC49 $105-115) could be powered by a $CO^2$ canister, blurring the line between a scale model and a toy. *Courtesy of Craig Clements and Gib Grayless.*

The Jet Firebolt (PC51 $95-105) was an all-plastic successor to the earlier wood $CO^2$ powered racers. *Courtesy of Dean Milano.*

## Chapter 3

# Four Star Plastikits

Giving customers an easy-to-build model had always been a critical part of Monogram's strategy. Besser and Reder knew very well that many model kits purchased in stores were never completed because youngsters either lost interest or lacked the skills to finish the model. When this happened, chances of a repeat sale dropped precipitously. Thus it was decided that Monogram's models had to be designed simply enough to be completed within the short attention span of an average kid. As Ken Merker put it, "The original idea was to make a relatively simple model that would go together easily and would look good when you were done—and you'd go and buy another one." The design department helped model builders by planning the slots, tabs, and locater pins so that there was only one way the parts could be fit together. No backward wings or upside-down stabilizers.

Yet advanced model builders demanded more. Reder understood the serious modeler's mentality since he was one of them, but he also knew that a hobby company could not achieve financial success if it attempted to satisfy the enthusiast's desire for models of obscure aircraft or what Reder called the "nit picker's" passion for absolute authenticity and minute detail. So an attempt was made to reach a happy medium. One way to do this was to keep the part count in a model down, but build as much detail as possible into those parts.

The executives at the top of the company pyramid played their upper level roles with the same enthusiasm as the boys in the model shop. Bob Reder was, in Sojka's words, "a long time model builder who knew what it was all about." Jack Besser was not a model builder at all, but he still regularly walked through the model shop to see how everybody was doing and chat with the model makers. He knew every Monogram employee by their first name. Harney thought Besser set a good example for all the workers down the chain of command. "He was a great guy." Besser worked very hard, treated Monogram as his own personal domain, and committed himself to making the company a success.

Although Monogram had grown quite a bit from its early days, the company was still run in a simple, straightforward manner. Jack Besser handled sales, finances, and manufacturing. Reder dealt with engineering, tooling, quality control, and cost accounting. Reder maintained meticulous records relating to every phase of producing a model. For example, the time put in by the designers and model makers was tabulated to determine labor costs and to aid in projecting the cost and development timetable of future models. Reder firmly believed that his company worked very well, "without any hot shot MBAs."

The Albatross Amphibian (PA20 $30-40) came with two crashed-at-sea survivors in a life raft. *Courtesy of Dean Sills.*

Monogram labeled its model of the Wright Flier the Kitty Hawk (PA30 $25-35) because that has an appealing ring to it. *Courtesy of Dean Milano.*

In the late 1950s Besser and Reder had to make some critical decisions about Monogram's long term product line. One significant choice was, in Reder's words, "to steer away from ships." This would mean an obvious hole in the company's model kit lineup, but as Reder later explained it, there were three good reasons to avoid ships: First, Revell had already covered the ship market with models that were "pretty darn well done." Secondly, ship models, with all their small detail parts, were expensive to develop. And, lastly, the demand for ship model was not nearly as broad as for aircraft and automobiles.

The Frogmen (PB48 $80-100) was the first of several box covers Tom Kowal painted in the late 1950s and early 1960s. "I was whacking those darn things out," he later recalled. *Courtesy of Revell-Monogram.*

An area that the whole model industry jumped into with enthusiasm in 1957 was Army tanks and military vehicles. Nothing had been done in this area earlier in the decade, so the field was wide open. Aurora introduced a line of 1/48 scale tanks and cannon. Revell offered 1/40 scale armor, and Monogram came in with a collection of awkward 1/32 and 1/35 scale Army tracked and wheeled vehicles. The 1/35 scale may have come about simply by accident because that size made the kits about right for a standard box. Perhaps it was this lack of consistency in scale across the industry that confused the hobby marketplace, but neither Aurora, Revell, or Monogram seemed to have found large numbers of willing purchasers. Monogram stopped adding to its line of Army models after its nice 1/35 scale Patton tank (PM37) appeared in December 1958. An M-56 self-propelled 90mm gun was announced, but never came into production. Those kits already in existence stayed on the sales lists, but Monogram would not expand the military armor line again until the end of the 1960s.

Aircraft models were another matter. Monogram was committed to being an aircraft model company—and, besides, Reder and Besser's first love was model airplanes. For a while Monogram built "play value" into some of its airplane models by incorporating working features into them. This started with the B-66 Destroyer (PA10), which had a little button on top of the fuselage that opened the bomb bay doors and dropped a bomb. The kit became—and remained for many years—a good seller, even though the boys in the design and model shop who had made it considered the B-66 sort of a joke. But you didn't argue with success, so the TBF Avenger (PA31) launched its torpedo, the B-58 (PA32) dropped its weapons pod, the Vigilante (PA53) fired a bomb out its tail, and the F-105 (PA33) violently ejected its pilot right toward the eyes of curious onlookers. However, by the early 1960s, toy-like working parts went out of vogue, and thereafter Monogram's moving parts were those features that appealed to more serious modelers. Things like opening hoods on cars and operating flaps on aircraft.

The Jeep and Gun (PM21 $40-50) is a mini-diorama. *Courtesy of Mark Mattei.*

Like the rest of Monogram's early Army vehicles, the Weasel (PM24 $20-30) continued to be a popular kit down through the 1980s. *Courtesy of Mark Mattei.*

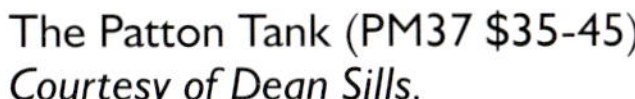

The Patton Tank (PM37 $35-45). *Courtesy of Dean Sills.*

Note that the box illustration for the Patton Tank (PM37 $35-45) includes the profile art for the box side panels. *Courtesy of Revell-Monogram.*

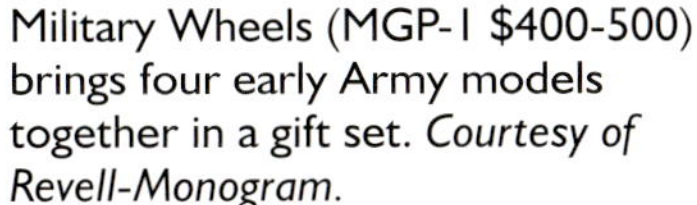

Military Wheels (MGP-1 $400-500) brings four early Army models together in a gift set. *Courtesy of Revell-Monogram.*

Serious modelers ridiculed the B-66 (PA10 $30-40) model's bomb dropping capabilities, but kids were intrigued by the idea.

About the time that operating play features started to fade, Reder decided that it was time to get serious about making truly accurate scale models. Up to this time Monogram (and Revell, too) had built its aircraft models to "box scale"—that is to fit into a standard size box. Reder knew that the Europeans—Airfix, Frog, and Heller—were committed to 1/72 scale, but he felt that fighter planes produced in that scale were just too small. You couldn't get in much detail. On the other hand, some American companies had been selling 1/48 scale aircraft for years, starting with Hawk and Lindberg back in the 1940s. Aurora had also settled on 1/48 since the early 1950s. So if Monogram went with 1/48 scale, hobbyists had the opportunity to build extensive collections of model airplanes that crossed company lines. Therefore 1/48 became the scale of Monogram's new generation of aircraft models.

A second big decision was to concentrate on World War II aircraft, which were known to be popular subjects. So far in the 1950s Monogram had been all over the place in its aircraft selection, including some modern jets, but during the decade of the 1960s all of its new airplane models, with a few exceptions, would be from the Second World War. The third ingredient in Monogram's aircraft strategy was to begin with models of US Navy planes from the Pacific Theater. This would generally avoid duplication of models that had already received attention from other model companies.

The A3J Vigilante (PA53 $30-40).

The B-58 Hustler (PA32 $30-40) epitomized the modern technology of the 1950s Air Force.

Monogram already had one Navy plane in its catalog, a T-28B trainer (PA28) in box size that scaled out at 1/51—close enough to 1/48. Reder had gone to nearby Glenview Naval Air Station on one bone-chilling cold winter day to photograph a T-28 for the model design plans. (A half century later, after Glenview had closed, Reder would be deeply involved in setting up a museum at Glenview to preserve memories of the now closed Naval Air Station.) This nice model was followed by a TBF Avenger (PA31) with all those working features that were a short-lived fad in the modeling world at the end of the 1950s. It had bomb bay doors that opened to drop a torpedo, retractable landing gear, folding wings, and a turret that rotated. However, it was Monogram's third Navy plane that ratcheted the quality level up another level. The SBD Douglass Dauntless (PA54) was another neglected model subject. True, Hawk had been selling its very nice 1/72 scale Dauntless for many years, but a 1/48 scale Dauntless would find a whole new market.

Ken Merker did the design for the kit, including the operating flaps, retractable landing gear, and working bomb release. He was a bit unhappy about having to prescribe grooves in the sides of the bomb so that it would fall free from the bomb cradle mechanism, but he concluded that the Dauntless was, nevertheless, "one of my better things." Joe Sojka, fresh off his first solo job of carving the Quarter Midget Racer (PC63), sculpted the parts of the Dauntless by himself. The two men did their work very well. Twenty years later *Scale Modeler* magazine (October 1980) would declare the kit "revolutionary at the time" for its high quality, excellent part fit, and working features. The magazine writer observed that the Dauntless proved to be "a harbinger of things to come from Monogram for the next twenty years."

The Air Force Patrol (MGP-7 $400-500) is one of Monogram's most attractively packaged gift sets. *Courtesy Revell-Monogram.*

The TBF Avenger (PA31 $25-35) and SBD Dauntless (PA54 $30-40) began Monogram's collection of US Navy aircraft of World War II. *Courtesy of Dean Sills.*

During the heyday of models with operating features, Monogram produced a model that far exceeded the ordinary standards of toy-like moving parts—the Phantom Mustang (PA67). This model was Syl Wisniewski's baby. "The P-51. I loved that plane," he said warmly. When making a model of the Mustang was brought up for discussion in the new products committee, it turned out everyone loved the Mustang. Bob Reder thought it had that elegant shape, a great-sounding name, and a memorable history from World War II. All the things to make it a successful model. To separate Monogram's Mustang from all the other P-51s on the market, it was decided to make it in big 1/32 scale, mold it in clear plastic so you could see the insides, and motorize it with operating elements.

Wisniewski got busy on the project. "I designed the whole works. How the parts work and so on. I had a job designing it. I had to beef up the airfoil shape to fit in some of the workings. We had little cams in there to operate the landing gear and doors." Ken Merker did the detailing and part drawings, and Hans Jernstrom carved the pattern. By the fall of 1961 their handiwork was ready for the hobby shops.

The Phantom Mustang came mounted on a red remote control pylon that held two D batteries and an electric motor to raise the landing gear. Just push a button and all three gear, including the tail wheel, retracted. Push another button and the motor inside the plane's engine spun the propeller. Two levers near the top of the pylon released the two bombs from under the wings. Parts inside the clear shell were molded in red, green, silver, and black—so you didn't have to do any painting. It cost a pretty hefty $4.98, but its working features really did work. It became an immediate sales success and enjoyed enduring popularity over the years. For many hobbyists, the Phantom Mustang remains the quintessential Monogram model.

Another line of kits that Monogram introduced in the late 1950s that seemed at the time to have great potential were models of the missiles and rockets appearing on the nation's TV screens on the evening news. Bob Reder kept up with the latest developments in rocketry in *Aviation Week*, and he thought missiles might be a whole new untapped field for model kits. Reder picked out the Snark (PD27) as the first subject for a Monogram model. The Snark was an air-breathing, jet propelled unmanned bomber with lots of possibilities for creating excitement in hobby shops. It was painted bright red, with white stripes along and around its fuselage, and it was launched in a billowing cloud of smoke from its rocket-assist canisters. Monogram hurried to get it into production, basing the model solely on photographs that had been published of the missile. Except for the wings and fuselage patterns, development went directly from the design drawings to the mold shop, skipping over the normal step of making pattern models for most of the parts.

Speed paid big dividends. Monogram got its model into stores in late January 1958, before Revell and Aurora had their versions of the Snark on the market. It helped that President Eisenhower mentioned the Snark as one of America's entries into the space race with the Russians. Sales were, in Reder's words, "fantastic!" In six months Monogram sold a half-million kits. The presses in the Monogram plant worked round the clock pumping out parts. Soon the Snark was joined by the Little John, Regulus II, Rascal, and a set of the Vanguard and Jupiter C satellite launchers (PD38, PD39, PD41, PD42).

The Phantom Mustang (PA67 $100-140) epitomizes the ingenuity and quality of Monogram's models. *Courtesy of Dean Sills.*

The Snark (PD27 $125-150), Regulus II (PD39 $160-190), and Rascal (PD42 $190-220) enjoyed brief popularity before crashing and burning. *Courtesy of Dean Sills.*

To give Monogram guidance on rockets and space, it hired one of the nation's leading experts on space technology, Willy Ley, a German missile developer who came to the United States after the war. He became a well known writer and lecturer who toured the country promoting US space programs. Bob Reder arranged to meet him in Chicago after one of his presentations and invited him home to have a drink of Scotch. In the living room of Reder's home, his four children tried out their school language skills on Ley, and he managed quite well in German, French, Russian, and Spanish. "He and the kids were having a ball," Reder later remembered. Then Ley said, "Now, I'll have that Scotch you promised." Reder found Ley a pleasant man with an amazing breadth of knowledge.

Willy Ley's imaginary TV Orbiter (PS44 $130-150) stands next to the real Vanguard and Jupiter C earth satellite launchers (PD41 $190-240). *Courtesy of Dean Sills.*

Willy Ley and Jack Besser pose for a publicity shot with two of the space exploration models Ley designed for Monogram. *American Modeler* (April 1959).

The Space Taxi (PS45 $50-60) is the most recognizable of Ley's model creations. *Courtesy of Dean Sills.*

You could fly from New York to London in one hour on Willy Ley's Passenger Rocket (PS47 $75-90) *Courtesy of Dean Sills.*

Ley brought with him some sketches of designs for space vehicles that he thought might make good subjects for model kits. The design group turned these concepts into plan drawings that Reder mailed to Ley in his New York home for revision. The four models produced for Ley all presaged actual spacecraft. The T. V. Orbiter (PS44) that would transmit pictures of the earth's atmosphere soon became reality in weather satellites. The Space Taxi (PS45) workshop in space looked much like subsequent space stations. And the Orbital Rocket/Passenger Rocket (PS46, PS47) employed the basic elements of the Space Shuttle. Ley was delighted with the attention Monogram paid to his ideas, and he used Monogram's models as displays in his public presentations. The problem was that these 1950s vintage concept spacecraft were quickly superceded by the real things in the 1960s, and that made Ley's models look old fashioned almost as soon as they were released.

Lots of American boys bought the US Missile Arsenal (PD40 $190-240) to learn about modern rockets. *Courtesy of Dean Sills.*

Monogram's most ambitious entry in the space race was the US Missile Arsenal (PS40), a collection of thirty-one missiles mounted on a clear base with a cardboard insert that identified each missile. Monogram took out a four-page advertisement in *Craft, Model, Hobby Industry* magazine to introduce the model to the hobby industry: "The most important hobby kit produced in the Space Age! Ready now at the height of the world's consciousness and anxiety over the use of missiles and men in space. ... They are authentic in every way but do not violate any restricted information." Behind this last statement was a story.

Before release of this kit, Monogram sent a public relations man to Washington to present a built model to a high ranking general in the Air Force. This publicity opportunity turned into a fiasco when the general spotted the tiny model of the Genie air-to-air atomic missile on the display. The general declared that Monogram could not release a model that included this top secret missile. Monogram already had built up a stockpile of 100,000 kits to send to distributors and was producing hundreds more kits daily. So Reder and the company attorney flew to Washington to try to put out the fire. They were bounced around from the Air Force to the State Department to the Atomic Energy Commission, each time explaining that Monogram had acquired information on the supposedly secret Genie from a photo in a general circulation aviation magazine. Nobody wanted to take responsibility for giving an OK to the model. Disappointed, Reder flew home and telephoned Ley for his advice. Ley considered the question and declared: "Ship the kits." Besser and Reder thought it over, then decided to go ahead and release the kit. Within a few weeks several stories on the Genie appeared in magazines and newspapers, and the issue never came up again.

As it turned out, models of missiles proved to be a disappointment in the hobby marketplace, and the companies that enthusiastically brought out missiles in 1958 and 1959 began dropping them from their sales lists soon after the end of the decade. Many of the models—the Snark being the prime example—were of missiles that quickly became obsolete and vanished from the news headlines. Also, it turned out that for many people rockets in space were just not that engaging. A boy could imagine himself piloting an airplane, but missiles had no pilots; they were just hardware.

Roger Harney expressed the opinion of other men in the model shop when he said, "Rockets were not very exciting. All they looked like was a stick."

Harney, however, had a bias. He wanted Monogram to make more car models. He had been pestering Reder to develop a 1940 Ford, but instead energy and development money were invested in the Ley space models. Harney later remembered visiting the 1960 HIAA annual show and walking over to the AMT parlor. His heart sank when he spotted AMT's nice new 1940 Ford model on display.

At the time AMT, a newcomer to the hobby field, was shaking up the modeling world. Throughout the 1950s AMT Corporation of Michigan had been making fully-assembled promotional models of the Detroit auto makers' annual releases. Then in 1958 AMT threw the unassembled parts of some annual promotionals, along with some extra accessory parts, into model kit boxes and called them 3-in-1 customizing kits. Perhaps most importantly, these model cars were made in 1/25 scale (not the prevailing smaller 1/32 scale), and they had one-piece bodies that made them easy to build. American boys went for these relatively primitive kits in a big way. Monogram's sales representatives reported what was happening in the stores back to headquarters in Chicago, and Monogram decided to get busy with a line of cars of its own. Car models were soon on their way to edging out aircraft models as the best selling model kits, both in America and at Monogram.

Ten Missiles (MP3 $45-55) was one of the very few Monogram models to be sold in a plastic bag with a header card. *Courtesy of Dean Sills.*

The store display for the Regulus II (PD39 $160-190).

Monogram got back into model cars in 1959 with some improved, but still fairly unsophisticated car models, the Slingshot Dragster, Firebolt speed car, and—most significantly—the '32 Ford Sport Coupe (PC49, PC51, PC57). These were followed in 1960 by some enduringly popular models, the Long John dragster, Black Widow, and Green Hornet hot rods (PC59, PC60, PC61). Each of these models was designed simply from photographs in magazines, and they were made to no particular scale. Also, the Sport Coupe, Long John, and Black Widow had to be designed around a Mabuchi electric motor and two AA batteries so they could be run on the floor as toys. (This made the Long John a fat little dragster.)

The box art for the Long John dragster (PC59 $95-105) was done by Bob Korta, who did many of Monogram's early illustrations, as well as pictures for the Dick and Jane readers. *Courtesy of Craig Clements.*

The Black Widow (PC60 $105-115) is a much beloved little hot rod. *Courtesy of Craig Clements and Ron Hanke.*

If you had the Black Widow, you also had to have the Green Hornet (PC61 $70-80). *Courtesy of Craig Clements and Ron Hanke.*

Around 1960 every American model company had some motorized model kits in its catalog. (PC212M $70-80, PC259M $95-105, PC260M $105-115). *Courtesy of Dean Sills.*

However, 1960 marked a turning point that revolutionized Monogram's approach to model cars. Bob Reder located a meticulously restored 1930 Ford in the Chicago area. He and a staffer went out to measure and photograph the car so that the designers would have solid reference material to work with. The resulting 1930 Ford Phaeton (PC64) was issued just after New Year's in 1961, and it was a dandy. The Phaeton excelled AMT by giving hobbyists enough extra parts to build it four ways: Stock, Street Rod, Jalopy, and Drag Rod. The chassis was molded in black, while the body came in tan. The part count reached 125, so it was a pretty expensive kit at $1.98. The only regret Monogram later had about the model was that it committed the company to the international 1/24 scale, while AMT, Revell, and most of the American industry went with 1/25.

By this time Roger Harney had established himself as Monogram's in-house expert on cars, although he would not officially join the New Products Committee until 1963. Reder and Wisniewski looked to him for recommendations on the next car models that Monogram should add to its offerings. AMT had the new car market sewn up, so Harney steered Monogram along the path it had already been following: vintage cars with hot rod and customizing potential. Harney explained: "I knew what was going on in the full size car scene." He read all the hot rod magazines, attended many of the custom car shows, and even asked the guys in his hot rod club, "What car would you like to see Monogram make a model of?" Reder thoroughly endorsed the hot rod orientation, declaring that the popularity of custom rods was "growing like crazy" at the time, and this showed up in healthy sales of the model kits.

With the release of the Customizing Ford A (PC64 $85-95), the quality of Monogram's car kits went up a notch. *Courtesy of Dean Sills.*

Roger Harney looks through the company's collection of automotive books for reference material. *Courtesy of Roger Harney.*

*Below:*
The Customizing Dragster (PC65 $155-165) could be built in three basic variations—or any way a kid could dream up. *Courtesy of Craig Clements, Ron Hanke, and Gib Grayless.*

Harney suggested that the '30 Ford Phaeton be followed up with a '36 Ford (PC68) and a '34 Ford (PC72). Creating the '36 Ford broke new ground for the model shop: it was the first pattern attempted totally in clay. Hans Jernstrom, a free-spirited, very talented Swede whose usual task was sculpting the human figures that went with the models, got a chance to try his hand doing the '36 Ford pattern in all clay. It turned out to be a bad idea, so Monogram's first clay pattern also became its last. But the Fords were a great success. All the Fords had customizing parts, and the parts that came with one kit could be used with the other Ford models, giving hobbyists a wide range of building options.

The Customizing '36 Ford (PC68 $95-105). *Courtesy of Craig Clements.*

Parts from the Customizing '30 Ford (PC71 $95-105) were interchangeable with parts from other customizing kits. *Courtesy of Craig Clements.*

Monogram's next automotive project was something a bit different, and in the long run it would unexpectedly pave the way for a whole new line of model kits. Reder thought that a working model of an automobile engine might appeal to boys who were mechanically inclined, but too young to work on the real things. Roger Harney was the natural choice to head the venture, and Ken Merker was assigned to work with him. It dawned on Harney that it might be possible create a model just by copying an actual engine, so he asked the tool shop if they could pantograph from parts that were eight times the size intended for the model. When the tool men said that was doable, Harney went shopping at junkyards and speed shops looking for manifolds, rocker covers, and other parts that could be employed in the engine. The idea was to have lots of customizing options for builders to choose from. Reder contributed the idea of attaching the customizing parts with large pins split down the middle so that they could be pressed into place and then popped out to make another configuration. Plywood tables were built and spread with wax paper. The car parts were greased-up and then coated with plaster to take castings. Sometimes the plaster stuck to the parts and didn't want to come off. It was all "a sloppy mess," in the words of Harney and Merker. However, the grubby hard work paid off, and they ended up with some very precise model patterns that could not have been produced from design drawings. Only the block, pan, bell housing, and a Merker-designed blower had to be done by the usual progression from design drawings to wooden pattern. "It sure came out so nice," concluded Harney.

The Wright Cyclone engine (PE52 $120-130) appealed to mechanically-minded youngsters. *Author's collection.*

The Customizing Auto Engine (PE62 $80-90) received an elaborate store display to show all the separate customizing parts. *Courtesy of Mark Mattei.*

The Chevy 283 V-8 engine (PC62) was destined to become a Monogram classic, but another project from the same time turned out to be a dead end. Monogram, like other model companies, thought from time to time about creating some kind of product that would appeal to girls. "Potentially, it was a huge market," explained Reder. Aurora had tried Guys and Gals of All Nations, Revell had offered Perri the Squirrel and Dr. Seuss's fanciful animals. Reder wanted Monogram to try Artorama, a framed relief diorama of African animals. Hans Jernstrom sculpted figures of giraffes, lions, and zebras; then he painted backgrounds on plastic that would be vacuum-formed to give some depth to the dioramas. It was a novel idea and pioneered vacuum-form technology. Roger Harney thought they were "neater than hell." However, Artorama just did not sell. An elephant scene was in the works, but was cancelled when the others failed in the stores. Reder noted philosophically that it was worth a try, and development costs had been minimal, so it was no great loss. Aurora and Revell also found that their efforts to attract female modelers led to nothing.

Art-O-Rama gave hobbyists a vacuum-formed shadow box, injection molded animals, cement, and paints. *Author's collection.*

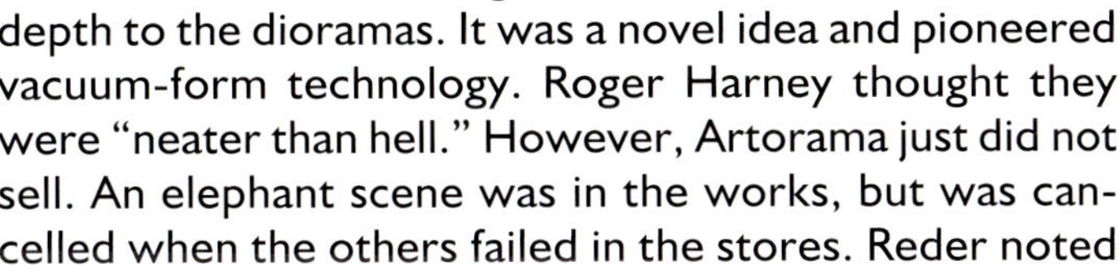

The box art for the Kitty Hawk (PA30 $25-35) has a light, airy feel appropriate for the fragile subject. *Courtesy of Revell-Monogram.*

All this activity had Monogram jam packed into its manufacturing plant on West 48th Place. There was no more room to grow, and, in addition, Monogram was burdened with a widely separated sales office in Skokie and a mold production shop in Niles. Bob Reder began searching for a new plant site and found the answer when a neighbor put him on to a nine acre tract north of Chicago in Morton Grove. The property was surrounded by both residential subdivisions and businesses. An empty field on Waukegan Road had a scenic little creek running through its center that drained into Forest Preserve park at its rear. Ever the engineer and planner, Reder drafted the layout for a large, one-story building, with underground conduits for the cooling water pipes and electrical outlets that served the plastic injection molding machines. (The little creek got its own drain culvert.) For an outlay of one and a quarter million dollars, Monogram bought 120,000 square feet of work space where all its operations could be consolidated. It was all brick and steel, with no widows, except in front. Inside, the building held all new equipment and modern furniture. Each of the departments received spacious, efficient rooms—some were even air conditioned. As a final touch, framed box art went up on the walls of the public areas.

On November 11, 1961, five-hundred invited guests from the hobby industry and news media received a grand tour of the building and enjoyed a buffet dinner in the lunch room. The next day it was the company's 350 employees who took the tour. There were clowns and balloons. Bob Reder was very satisfied with the new facility and figured Monogram was set for the next hundred years.

When the move was made to the new plant north of Chicago, Besser and Reder were concerned about the fate of their loyal employees, whom they liked to call "coworkers." Besser talked with the staff and invited them to continue working for Monogram at its new location. Besser told the workers: "I'd like very much to have you come with us ... I know it's not possible, but you can't blame me for wishing and hoping." Monogram offered to provide a bus from the end of the public transportation line to the Morton Grove plant, but neither Besser nor Reder really expected many to take them up on the offer, or, if they did, to continue riding the bus for long. To their surprise, not only did many workers accept the offer, but after a year's time even more employees were riding the bus. The bus from the city would continue for years before finally being abandoned.

The Iroquois helicopter (PA50 $30-40) was a pretty basic kit, yet it remained a popular model for many years and went through several transformations. *Courtesy of Dean Sills.*

The Red Chariot (PC75 $95-105) just made young boys happy. *Courtesy of Craig Clements and Ron Hanke.*

The model shop in the new Morton Grove plant gave the model makers spacious quarters in which to work. *Courtesy of Roger Harney.*

The Yellow Jacket (PC76 $120-130) appeared in this issue only and thus is very rare today. *Courtesy of Dean Sills.*

One department that received its own room in the new plant was the display studio. This unit of about thirty women—"girls" in that day's parlance—was responsible for building and boxing the point-of-purchase display models that went to hobby shops. Each model was attached to a cardboard base and background that was part diorama and part billboard. The women worked in assembly-line fashion to paint and assemble about 5,000 displays for each newly introduced model. That totaled about 50,000 to 60,000 units a year. Bob Reder recalled that packaging the fragile displays posed quite a challenge. Test runs would be made in which boxed displays were dropped to see what broke, and then adjustments would be made to ensure that the displays arrived at stores intact. Monogram's store displays were unsurpassed in the hobby industry at the time and are highly collectible today.

Another aspect of sales promotion was the art that went on Monogram's kit boxes. When a youngster looked at a shelf stacked high with model kits, he had no idea what quality model might emerge from the jumble of parts inside the box—but he could plainly see the pictures on the outside of the box. Jack Besser explained Monogram's artistic philosophy in a 1957 interview. "Our packaging today must jump off the shelves and counters and right into the consumer's imagination." He said that while planning its box art Monogram's staff had to decide what depiction of a car or plane would have "the most visual appeal ... the greatest sales impact."

Every model company in the 1960s had to have a model that tapped into the youthful surf 'n rock culture. The Blue Beetle (PC93 $120-130). *Courtesy of Dean Milano.*

Air Power (PA56 $225-275) displayed some nice little models in a dramatic fashion. *Courtesy of Dean Sills.*

Fred Wellman and his son, Fred, Jr., were responsible for both advertising and box art at Monogram. They employed several Chicago area artists to paint the illustrations that went on the kit packages. Shortly before the move to Morton Grove, Fred Wellman, Jr. received a visit from an artist who showed up with a portfolio of some of his work. It was Richard Locher, who explained that he had done the illustrations for the *Buck Rogers* comic strip, assisted Chester Gould with *Dick Tracy*, and had also been painting box art for Comet Models. Most recently he had been doing Comet's rockets: the Snark, Atlas, Regulus, and Jupiter C. Fred Wellman liked what he saw and gave Locher his first assignment, the Curtiss Helldiver (PA69).

Dick Locher's first box art for Monogram appeared on the Curtiss Helldiver (PA69 $25-35). *Courtesy of Revell-Monogram.*

Monogram's new artist had been born in 1929 in Dubuque, Iowa, where he grew up. From about the age of five he knew that he wanted to be an artist some day. He recalled that early in his schooling he made a huge chalk drawing of an ocean liner that covered the length of a blackboard, turned a corner, and continued on another blackboard. His teacher was impressed enough to call in the school principal to admire the work. From there it was a progression to the Chicago Academy of Fine Arts, where he studied magazine illustration and did some cartooning on the side. During his service in the Air Force in the early 'fifties he flew F-94Cs. His involvement in aircraft engineering work on the XB-58 at Wright-Patterson in Dayton gave him a chance to eat lunch in the cafeteria with a group of expatriate German designers who had worked on glide bombs and radio controlled bombs during World War II. While in the service Locher did some one-panel cartoons for the military newspaper *Stars & Stripes* that tried to present a view of life in the modern Air Force in the same spirit Bill Maulden had employed during World War II. Locher emerged into civilian life to study briefly at the Art Center for Design in Los Angeles and then take a place at an artist's table among the hundreds of commercial illustrators working for the many Chicago area studios that created illustrations for mass circulation magazines like *Colliers* and the *Saturday Evening Post*. His studio, Feldkamp & Malloy, served clients as varied as Hertz car rental and US Steel. He learned to stretch the images of Chevrolets and Fords so they appeared sleek and stylish in advertisements.

Locher felt that a realistic depiction of a spinning prop was the mark of a good piece of aircraft art. The F3F-3 (PA70 $40-60). *Courtesy of Revell-Monogram.*

Locher's ME-109 (PA74 $20-25), like all of Monogram's painted box art, omits the swastika from the tail fin, but it is included on the decal sheet. *Courtesy of Revell-Monogram.*

In 1955, Locher started illustrating box covers for Comet, as well as drafting plans for some of their flying models. The managers at Comet instructed him to keep the backgrounds of his box art compositions clear so that the aircraft would stand out. His success with Comet led him to his meeting with Fred Wellman, Jr. at Monogram.

By the early 1960s, Monogram's method of producing box art had already been established and would remain basically the same for years to come. The art director would drop in on new product meetings to learn what models were going to be produced. As soon as a subject was decided upon, he would select an artist to do the box art. Monogram did not have an artist on staff; instead it used several freelance artists. Some artists were better at some subjects and others were better at other things. A phone call to the chosen artist would get the ball rolling. Sometimes Monogram could supply the artist with a built-up model and some reference materials, but often the artist was required to call upon his own resources or Monogram's reference library to find pictures of the plane or car being modeled. Monogram would also give the artist the decal sheet for the plane or car, and the decal images had to be strictly followed for the box art.

The Grumman Hellcat (PA80 $20-25) by Locher. *Courtesy of Revell-Monogram.*

Next the artist would create three to six tight pencil sketches of the plane or car, each from a different angle. (Locher submitted his sketches in color.) Monogram would pick which pose showed off the model to its best advantage. Then the artist would do a more refined sketch that would be checked over by Monogram's engineering department to make sure it accurately portrayed Monogram's model. This occasionally raised the hackles of the artists. Locher felt that sometimes this "fine tuning" spoiled the artistic spirit of the composition—"took away some flavor." Artists had long realized that too much attention to detail can lead to a dead, static image. Nevertheless, Locher felt that all-in-all the process usually went smoothly, and the artist felt free to produce a fine, artistic creation to grace the top of another Monogram box.

Dick Locher submitted this preliminary thumbnail color sketch to Monogram for approval before proceeding with the final illustration. The C-47 (5603 $30-35). *Courtesy of Dick Locher.*

Locher enjoyed working with Monogram over the following years. He usually worked in the studio downtown, but to meet a deadline he sometimes took a painting home to finish over the weekend. He learned that the company was receptive to new ideas and welcomed contributions from anyone. When Locher suggested that the F7F Tigercat (PA163) be pictured flying upside down, Monogram said sure, go ahead. He created his illustrations on artists board, working at about twice the size of the box panel. Like most commercial illustrators, Locher painted with designer watercolors, sometimes called gouache, or with milk based poster paint. Both were easy to work with and dried quickly.

Locher painted the F7F Tigercat (PA163 $10-12) flying upside down, but Monogram did not have nerve enough to print it that way on the box. *Author's collection.*

Most of the time Locher traced the outline of a plane from a photograph on transparent paper, then transferred the image to the art board. He had to carefully position the plane in relation to the ground so that it took a realistic flying attitude. Then he would begin in the top left-hand corner, painting both the background and plane at the same time since the two had to harmonize with each other. For example, a cloud might reflect off the fuselage of the plane. He did not want the plane's lines to be too precise because that would make it look like a cutout of a toy plane on a poster. Sometimes he would blur the trailing edge of a tail fin to suggest speed—although he did not have "speed lines" trailing after his planes the way his favorite old-time artist Jo Kotula did. In the end he wanted an evocative composition that drew the viewer into the action. "Customers don't buy the product," the old advertising adage went, "they buy the anticipation of the product."

In 1964 Locher was joined by another artist, Tom Morgan, and together their illustrations helped to define the look of the Monogram kit line for the rest of the decade of the 1960s. Morgan had been born in Chatham, Ontario, Canada and grew up drawing Spitfires and Messerschmitts during the war years. One of his best friends was a boy from an English refugee family who had witnessed the real thing over the skies of England. He and the neighbor boys all built balsa flying models. "We used to hang out in the model shop and wait for the next shipment of kits to come in. When plastic propellers and wheels showed up, they were like manna from heaven."

In 1948 Morgan joined the Royal Canadian Air Force, but a leg injury kept him out of flight school, so he trained as a photographer and then as an artist. By the time he left the Air Force in 1953, he'd decided to make his living as an artist. This choice took him to the Chicago Academy of Fine Arts where Locher had recently studied, and it was there that he fulfilled his lifelong dream to become a commercial illustrator. He drew inspiration from the everyday advertisements that appeared in magazines. He analyzed the techniques artists used to illustrate beverage bottles, with their rich colors and illusions of wet water droplets trickling down the sides of the bottle. "I thought it was so amazing they could do that." He learned to work in all media, including opaque watercolors, the commercial artist's standard medium. Morgan was pleased to find that it just seemed made for his talents.

After graduation, Morgan went to work for Feldkamp & Malloy, where he met and gained valuable help from a number of other talented artists. "It was a great learning time for me," Morgan recalled. Among the artists he worked alongside was Dick Locher. When one of Morgan's illustrations for Trans-Canada Airlines won an award, he decided to specialize in aviation art. Since Chicago was a center for model companies, and they needed lots of pictures of airplanes, this became a rich source for commissions. He started as a freelance artist with a small, well equipped studio of his own in downtown Chicago. He entered the world of hobby art by doing a set of forty small color illustrations that went on flying aircraft models made by Comet.

Tom Morgan's Mosquito (PA129 $25-35) flies through a colorful blaze of action. *Courtesy of Revell-Monogram.*

One day Morgan heard that Monogram might be looking for an artist, so he simply telephoned Monogram to offer his services. His initial interview with Fred Wellman, Jr. took place in the new Morton Grove plant. The folks at Monogram liked his work, and soon he received his first assignment, the Hawker Hurricane (PA90).

Morgan went through Monogram's standard development steps in the production of his box art, although after a while the Monogram folks came to trust his judgment on how an airplane or car ought to be posed. "I usually hit it the first time." Morgan decided on the pose of an aircraft after holding the model and examining it from all angles to find that one view that struck him as right. He would first send in a small thumbnail sketch, and when that was approved, he would follow up with a detailed pencil sketch to be approved by the engineering department, but also to be used by the art department to begin pasting-up the box graphics layout. Morgan, just like Locher, chafed a bit at the engineering department's suggestions for changes to his art. "Go for the effect, not for the nuts and bolts," he maintained. Bill Koster was one of those engineering guys who thought in terms of a 1/1000 standard of precision—and he admitted that his department's critiques of the box art was "kind of harsh sometimes." Finally, Besser and Reder eased the finicky engineering guys out of the art development picture, and the art department ran the whole show independently. Fundamentally, there really wasn't much disagreement among the Monogram team because everyone wanted realism in the models, both inside and outside the package.

The F8F Bearcat (PA144 $6-8) by Morgan. *Courtesy of Revell-Monogram.*

Tom Morgan usually liked to have two depictions of an aircraft in his art, each from a different angle. The Dornier Do 17Z (PA214 $10-12). *Courtesy of Revell-Monogram.*

Morgan had no formula for doing a painting. "By this time I had enough art experience to rely on my training and subject knowledge. I also had a private pilot license, which helped me develop a 'feel' for flight, so I was comfortable with my paintings." First he did a pencil sketch of the plane on the art board, and then quickly painted in the background, fitting it to the attitude of the aircraft. Then he would do the plane section by section, usually starting from the nose and working toward the back. As a last touch, "I'd have fun with the details. Over the years, the more I did, the more subtle I became. What I left out was as important as what I put in."

In those days the finished art was sold by the artist to the company, and the artist lost his claim to the art. A standard commission in the 1960s might net the artist $350, although that would go up for a more complicated piece. This was a reasonable cost for the company, and it provided the artists with a decent income as well. After all, this was commercial art, not fine art, and once a piece was done the artist left it behind and moved on to his next job. (This changed later on when a law was passed allowing artists to retain rights to their art.)

For Morgan, the next assignments often came from other model companies. When Ray Gaedke retired from doing Lindberg's art, Morgan pick up their work, signing it T.A.M. When Hawk's main artist took another position, Hawk hired Morgan to paint their box illustrations, this time signed with a simple TM. All three model companies wanted brilliant color effects on the packaging—red, yellow, orange skies. Especially Hawk. They asked for "lots of burning aircraft, bullet holes, battle weary craft. ... I'm not sure how the 'bullet hole' genre started. I put them in one painting, and suddenly it became some kind of trademark for my work."

Model designer Bill Koster also painted a few pieces of box art. His depiction of the FW-190 (PA107 $15-20) lets youngsters see the pilot's face. *Author's Collection.*

One department that did not expand with the move to Morton Grove was the wood shop. Wooden models were not considered a growth area, even though Monogram had introduced a new concept in wooden flying models called Bild 'n Fly in 1960. They were developed in house by Eugene Shapp, a designer who produced very crisp engineering drawings that were the envy of other draftsmen in the shop. He was also a free flight model hobbyist who competed in international contests. The set included the famous Goodyear pylon racers Mr. Mulligan and Cosmic Wind, plus the Air Force L-20 Beaver utility plane (F1, F2, F3). Monogram touted them as "The first flying model improvement in 12 years." Actually, Bild 'n Fly was more an update of the basic rubber powered balsa fliers that had been around since the 1920s. The kits consisted of thin balsa parts laminated with colored paper imprinted with the plane's markings. You simply assembled the parts and fixed them in place with white glue. The propeller, cowl, canopy, and wheels were plastic. The wings consisted of just flat strips of balsa, not the ingenious pre-formed airfoils of the Speedee-Bilts. But the simple construction of Bild 'n Fly models did make them very light weight and thus superior fliers. No dedicated flying hobbyist would take them seriously, but they might have appeal to a dad walking into a hobby shop looking for something to take home and fly with junior in the back yard. However, not many dads opened their wallets for Bild 'n Fly; so they quickly disappeared from the scene.

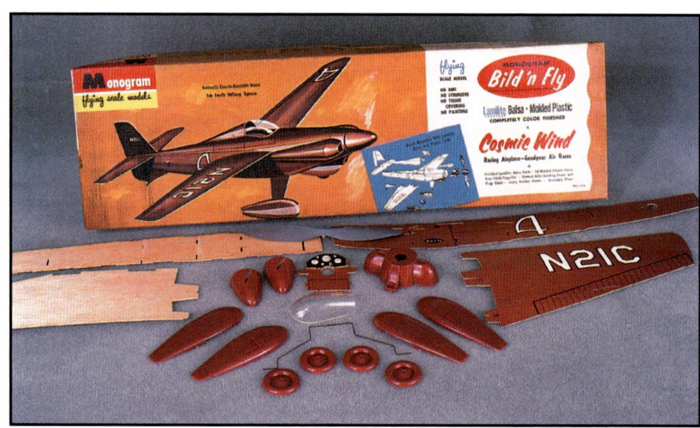


The Cosmic Wind (F3 $125-150) had balsa parts laminated with colored paper on one side—plus plastic detail parts. *Author's collection.*

The rest of the wood-and-plastic models eventually disappeared as well. The venerable Hot Shot jet car and Aquajet speedboat last appeared in the 1960 catalog. The four big "DeLuxe" bomber kits went out of the catalog after 1961, but the rest of the Speedee-Bilts stuck around until 1965—well over a decade into the age of plastics. To mark the passing of the Speedee-Bilts, Monogram's in-house newspaper, *News & Views,* ran a story with a photograph of Jesse Jefferson putting a padlock on the door to the wood shop. Jefferson was one of the "old stalwarts" of the company who had started work back in 1947 operating shapers to form wooden ship hulls. The story concluded with this epitaph: "Now the Speedee-Bilts no longer rule the air. Some say this is the price of progress. But to the people who developed, worked, nurtured and watched the industry grow, it is the sad end of an era."

## Chapter 4
# Custom Cars by Starbird

The move to Morton Grove confirmed the arrival of a new era in high quality plastic model kits. Ken Merker and Roger Harney had been responsible for moving miscellaneous design and modeling stuff from the 48th Place plant. They took great care with the elements of projects that were underway at the time, and they also took great care with the doorbell that had been used to chime the beginning and end of break periods. Everyone understood that it was important for all the design and modeling guys to take a break simultaneously, so that if one person needed the help of another they could count on finding them at their work place. But the door bell reigned as an irritant over some of the more free-spirited boys in the shop. Thus Merker and Harney took pains to see that the doorbell was packed in the bottom of a crate, under a heavy iron vice, and a weight of other debris. Thus, in the new shop everyone still took breaks together, but the tyranny of the doorbell's chime had been squashed. (Also, after a petition by Merker and Harney, the company finally relented and allowed designers and model makers to bring cups of coffee into the work place. Cigarette smoking, of course, had always been permitted and the air in the shop was often hazy with smoke.) Soon after the move, design drafting and model making became separate divisions, with the design shop receiving the more exalted name "engineering" department. Each worker received a larger work space and eventually a cubicle all his own in which to work and decorate with personal flourishes like built models, photos, and box art.

One of the in-progress projects that made the move to Morton Grove was something everyone just called the Big T, which had grown out of an unexpected response to the big Chevy V-8 engine. Car modelers told hobby shop owners that they wanted a big 1/8 scale car model in which to place the engine. When word got back to the men at Monogram, their first thought was to make a car model with nothing under the hood and ask model builders to buy the Chevy engine separately. However, after some discussion, it was decided to make a complete 1/8 scale car with a new, less complex motor. Reder asked Harney what car they should make, and Harney came up with the idea of a T bucket, which was the latest sensation on the hot rod scene. One appeared on the TV show "77 Sunset Strip," and Tommy Ivo's modified T body car had just made the cover of *Hot Rod* magazine. Naturally, Harney became head of the project and did some of the design and carving, but several other of his colleagues were called upon to lend their assistance and expertise. To finish off the model, Harney created the decal sheet.

The Big T (PC78 $115-125) came with a trophy. *Courtesy of Craig Clements.*

Monogram introduced the Big T to the model industry world at the February 1962 Hobby Industry Association convention, showing off a plastic, wood, epoxy, and metal display model handmade for the show by Roger Harney. The big 1/8 scale model attracted quite a bit of attention from everyone in the hobby industry, and that was very satisfying since it meant that the distributors who served hobby shops and big retailers would be placing orders for the Big T when it came out later that summer. The boys from Monogram also cruised the big hobby fair to scout what the competition was up to. At these shows one staffer was responsible for gathering up the brochures from all the model companies to take back to Monogram headquarters for further analysis. The annual HIAA show was a way of taking the pulse of the hobby industry.

One thing the Monogram representatives noted as they sized-up the competition was a developing trend among its competitors in the model auto field to hire celebrity show car designers whose names and faces were attached to the model kit lines of companies. Revell had Ed "Big Daddy" Roth's exotic Outlaw hot rod parked in its parlor, while over at the AMT display they were showing a '58 Thunderbird model specially customized for AMT by George Barris, their star personality custom car creator.

The popularity of the Big T led Monogram to bring out the Little T (PC92 $95-105). *Courtesy of Craig Clements.*

The men at Monogram decided that they needed a custom car luminary to promote their products as well. As it happened, the March issue of *Car Craft* magazine carried a feature article on how Monogram made its model kits, and as Jack Besser perused the magazine, he noted a car designed by Darryl Starbird on its cover. Why not Starbird? He operated out of the Star Kustom Shop in not-too-distant Wichita, but his cars were exhibited in shows from coast to coast, giving him national exposure. Bob Reder liked Starbird's unusual name and thought it would be easy for youngsters to remember. So Jack Besser gave him a phone call, "out of the blue," as Starbird recalled it, and asked if he would like to work for Monogram. Starbird thought it over and decided it was a great idea. The consulting fee Monogram offered would bring in much needed income, while Monogram's model kits would be free publicity for Starbird's handiwork. From Monogram's perspective, Starbird's show cars would promote the Monogram name every time they went on display in public. So Monogram and Starbird signed a two year contract in the summer of 1962 (which would be renewed in the summer of '64).

Monogram's new star spokesman had been born in Topeka, Kansas, in 1933. The Starbird family name came from Old England, not Native America as some assumed. At an early age he caught the car customizing bug, and by his junior year in high school he had modified his first car. He went on to study design at Wichita University and then started working for Boeing aircraft, but all the while he spent his evenings hammering auto body sheet metal into unique shapes in his garage. In 1954 he went into business full time with the Star Kustom Shop. It was tough going. Most custom car action took place in California, while Starbird was located in the Midwest, where—in his words—"nothing happens." One way he supplemented his income was by taking photos of his custom jobs as they went along and then writing how-to stories for car magazines. That earned him a couple hundred dollars for the custom work and another couple hundred for the magazine story. Eventually people started to take notice, and his cars began to appear at shows, and their photos made the magazine pages. When his sensational Predicta debuted at the Oakland Roadster Show in 1960, Starbird's standing in the ranks of car customizers soared. And that brought him to his rendezvous with Monogram.

Darryl Starbird created the full size Big T to publicize Monogram's model. *Courtesy Darryl Starbird.*

Starbird's relationship with Monogram involved flying to Chicago for a couple days at a time and working with the Monogram staff on development of new model cars. Although Besser had contacted him, it was Reder who became his prime connection at Monogram. Reder developed a close relationship with Starbird, finding him "a nice guy to work with." Starbird observed that Besser was the "go getter" of the company, while Reder was more the one who said, "Let's make sure this will work first."

Many of Starbird's design efforts were done with Roger Harney. They would sit down together with preliminary design drawings for proposed car models. Starbird admitted that he was no artist, so most of his contribution consisted of rough sketches—"ideas mostly." His primary concern was the custom parts that would be added to stock car models. For example, he would design a bubble top that could easily replace the stock roof of a car. Harney and John Odrlin from engineering would translate these ideas and sketches into more polished drawings. Then these drawings would be sent over to Ken Marker in engineering for further refining. "We would take it from there," declared Merker. Some of Starbird's ideas proved to be too radical for practical manufacture. So some back and forth took place until a workable design emerged. Problems that came up later on could usually be worked out over the telephone. Starbird noted with pleasure that the Monogram's model kits that emerged from this process were superior in quality to those of the main competition, AMT, and they came in rich colored plastic that didn't require painting.

Besser and Reder came up with the idea of building a full-size adaptation of the Big T model car for use in promotions and publicity. Starbird was given the assignment of creating the upscale version of the Big T-reversing the normal procedure of scaling down a full size car into a model. Harney wondered if this reverse engineering could be pulled off since he had designed the model from little more than inspiration and drawings on paper. However, he needn't have worried since Starbird found the model fairly easy to copy. "Harney had done an excellent job," Starbird later explained. Of course, some changes had to be made for practical reasons, but the full size T-rod that emerged was, in Starbird's words, "very, very close to the model car." Starbird liked the Big T since it was a fresh concept in T-buckets at the time. Monogram's advertising department credited both the real car and the model car to Starbird, leaving Harney completely out of the equation. But this had been explained to Harney in advance, and he understood that it was Starbird, with his cool good looks, skinny necktie, and sharp sports jacket, who would play the role of custom styling expert for the public.

The full size Big T turned out to be a hit for Monogram's promotions. Sales representatives would load-up the bed with model kits and take the car to shopping centers in the Midwest, where the car would be parked in front of a hobby shop. It always attracted big crowds. The salesmen would set up a display of Monogram kits and answer a barrage of questions about the car. The Big T won a prize at the Labor Day NHRA National Show in Indianapolis. In December 1962, it drove in Chicago's State Street Christmas Parade, displaying the Monogram name to a million onlookers. Its spot in the parade line came just before Santa's sleigh, and the car's red and white color scheme fit in just fine for the occasion. Robert Reder, Jr.—beaming from ear to ear—was at the wheel, while Jack Besser's daughter Donna waved to the crowd from the passenger seat. As Jack Besser once said, "We're selling pleasure, and it is a happy business." (About 1971 Monogram sold the Big T to California car designer Tom Daniel, who resold it to a friend a short time later. Then it disappeared from sight.)

By the time the '55 Chevy (PC83 $125-135) came out in the early 1960s, Monogram had a distinctive logo for its car kits. *Courtesy of Dean Sills.*

The '58 Thunderbird customizing kit (PC89 $125-135). *Courtesy of Dean Milano.*

You had a choice of body colors in the Customizing Thunderbird (PC89 $125-135). *Courtesy of Craig Clements and Ron Hanke.*

The Big Drag (PC84 $250-270). *Courtesy of Craig Clements.*

The '40 Ford Pickup (PC91 $95-105) incorporated operating features like opening doors. *Courtesy of Dean Sills.*

Monogram sold a quarter-million Big T model kits during its first year on the market—at $10.95 a pop. The opportunity to extend this success was too good to miss, so three more big scale models were added that utilized the '24 Ford chassis and Chevy V-8 engine. The Big Drag (PC84) replaced the interior with one center-mounted driver's seat, then added a roll bar, Moon gas tank out front, and a turtle deck in back. There was a 1/8 scale crash helmet, too. The Big Rod (PC85) had a '32 Ford grille in front, a Ford-embossed cylinder gas tank in back, and a custom canvas top. The Big Tub (PC86) added a bench rear seat inside a Phaeton body. These three follow-on kits sold well and remained on the Monogram sales lists through the rest of the 1960s, but only the original Big T would be reissued in the succeeding decades.

The Big Rod (PC85 $250-270). *Courtesy of Craig Clements.*

The Big Tub (PC86 $250-270). *Courtesy of Craig Clements.*

Monogram employed Starbird for another major effort at a big-scale classic hot rod, the Big Deuce (PC88). Monogram also paid Starbird to build a full-size '32 Ford custom roadster—the epitome of hot rods. Starbird found this task to be simpler than upsizing the Big T because he had complete creative control over building the car. While he was working on the 1/1 scale car in Wichita, Monogram's Roger Harney led a team of model makers working on the 1/8 scale edition of the same car back in Morton Grove. Both cars were completed about the same time at the end of the summer in 1963. When the Big Deuce model was introduced, *Craft, Model, Hobby Industry* magazine (October 1963) judged it "Monogram's finest kit." *Car Model* (May 1964) went one better and declared it: "the most magnificent car model ever made."

It was magnificent. The model had battery-powered operating lights, opening doors, an opening trunk, a windshield that folded down, and front wheels that steered. There was a new big Pontiac engine. You could build it as either a full-fendered roadster or leave off the fenders and have a highboy. The part count totaled 284, with more than half of those being chrome plated. It came in two different packages, molded in either red or yellow. However, to get all this you had to pay $14.98—four dollars more than for the Big T. And this spelled trouble for the Big Deuce in the stores. Its first year's sales did not come up to the level of initial sales of the Big T. That was disappointing, but good enough to keep it on the market.

One of the major problems with the Big Scale cars was that a boy quickly ran out of space in his bedroom to display his handiwork. The Big T was sixteen inches long, and the Big Deuce was twenty inches long. Most boys discovered that smaller, less expensive car models gave them a chance to buy, build, and display a larger number and wider variety of cars. Monogram found that sales of the big scale models were better in the large retail stores, where grandma bought the big expensive kits as appropriate gifts for birthdays or Christmas.

Meanwhile, Starbird offered to sell his Predicta to Monogram and allow them to make a model of it. It was an expensive proposal for Monogram since Starbird's custom cars were, in his words, "high dollar cars for their day." But Besser and Reder thought it would be a good investment and agreed to the deal. Starbird quickly got busy refurbishing the car before delivering it to Monogram. He thought that the three year old car was "getting a little shabby," and he wanted to update the look by enlarging the wheel wells and replacing the old bullet grille with horizontal louvers. Jack Besser had only one request for the revision: paint it red, because red car models sell best. So the original blue finish went red. When Starbird showed up in Morton Grove

The Big Deuce (PC88 $120-130) came in either red or yellow plastic. *Courtesy of Craig Clements and Ron Hanke.*

Popular hot rods in 1/24 scale. The Little T (PC92 $95-105), Woody Wagon (PC103 $85-95), and Little Deuce (PC132 $85-95). *Courtesy of Craig Clements.*

Darryl Starbird's Predicta (PC95 $70-80) became an enduringly popular show car. *Courtesy of Dean Milano.*

with the revised Predicta, Besser was a bit upset because design work for the model had already begun based on the car's old look. However, nothing had gone beyond the paperwork stage yet, so revisions to the tooling drawings were reasonably easy to accomplish.

The Predicta model (PC95) came out in 1964 and immediately established itself as one of those gold standard models by which other custom car models are judged. The Predicta's origins as a junkyard '56 Thunderbird were not evident under the complete restyling Starbird had given the original vehicle. The model had a hood that opened to show the Chrysler engine, opening doors, a bubble top that flipped open, and front wheels that turned when you pushed the driver's control stick. The first issue included a little booklet by Starbird entitled *From Carbs to Customizing* that gave youngsters a lexicon of customizing jargon. The original issue came in red plastic, but a later issue used a pearl red that was soon discontinued because it was difficult to keep the pearl powder mixed evenly in the injection molding process.

Starbird's next car came about because of a challenge sent out by Oakland's Roadster Show to the twenty-one members of its Hall of Fame. Each member designer would be allowed to enter one totally new car in the 1963 show's Tournament of Fame. Starbird telephoned Jack Besser and asked if Monogram would finance a car for the competition. The men at Monogram first asked Starbird for some concept sketches and then gave their OK, telling Starbird he had complete creative freedom from there on in. It took only three or four months—and $15,000 dollars—to complete the car, which was appropriately dubbed "Futurista" (PC108). The car's delta shape, flat profile, and dual bubble canopy did indeed make it look like a craft from either outer space or the future. It had just three wheels and a Volkswagen spyder engine under the Lucite top in back. The interior was plush red velvet and everything worked by push button. For the show Starbird had even devised an innovative audio tape activated sound system that played a thirty minute loop of commentary on the car and tripped switches to open the top, turn on the lights, and activate other features of the car. The Monogram name appeared alongside Starbird's name on the display.

Despite its novel design and innovative details, the Futurista lost out in the competition to Bill Cusenbery's Silhouette. As the only non-West Coast member of the Hall of Fame, Starbird thought there might have been a geographic tilt to the judging, but perhaps it was just that Cusenbery's muscular Silhouette with its menacing jet fighter look had more manly appeal than the more refined Futurista. And, as it turned out, AMT's model of the Silhouette enjoyed better long term fame as a model kit than did Monogram's model of the Futurista—which disappeared from the Monogram catalog in 1970, never to reappear. (Which, of course, today makes the Futurista one of the most desirable of collectible kits.)

The Futurista (PC108 $135-145) somehow didn't excite young model car builders. *Courtesy of Dean Milano.*

The final vehicle Starbird designed and sold to Monogram was a stocky sort-of pickup that he called the Ultra Truk, but which Monogram dubbed the Orange Hauler (PC131). This custom creation had a radically altered '62 Chevy small truck body riding on top of a '55 Chevy frame, powered by a '56 Buick engine. As could be expected, there was a clear bubble roof. Monogram featured it as the top prize in a national contest intended to call attention to the model.

By the time the Orange Hauler appeared in 1966, the landscape of American auto design had changed drastically. Detroit was bringing out muscle cars with the appeal of a custom car, and the body shops that did specialty customizing for clients suffered a sharp decline in patronage. This change was reflected in the parallel universe of model cars. Mustangs, Camaros, and Firebirds ruled both the roads and the hobby shop counter tops. Custom cars entered what Starbird called the "freak car" stage, epitomized by creations such as the Boot Hill Express (PC188) and Bathtub Buggy (PC223). Starbird was not about to turn away from his trademark futuristic, streamline styling for such weirdness.

Jack Besser, who kept his finger on the pulse of the model marketplace, saw what was happening and did not renew Starbird's contract. Although Starbird's side excursion into the world of model cars had ended, he continued to follow the art form that he had selected for his life's work. Today travelers may visit Starbird's National Rod & Custom Car Hall of Fame in the Ozark Mountains of eastern Oklahoma where they will find a newly minted clone of the Big T and the original Predicta, now restored to its original glory and blue color scheme.

Starbird's idea of a pickup truck, the Orange Hauler (PC131 $70-80). *Courtesy of Dean Sills.*

About the time Starbird introduced Monogram to futuristic cars, the company decided to establish a line of new plastic model kits that consciously looked back to a bygone era: the 1930s age of vintage luxury cars. Monogram's advertisements for the Classic Cars pictured a mature father figure, pipe in hand, admiring the distinctive styling and sculptured lines of Monogram's models of these automobiles, but the kits had appeal for some youngsters, too. "Those old cars really had character," Syl Wisniewski declared. Bob Reder discovered that George Lamberson, who lived in the upscale neighborhood of Hinsdale, owned one of the three 1934 SJ Torpedo Phaeton Duesenbergs (PC81) ever made. Reder and Roger Harney ventured inside Lamberson's large, steam heated garage one winter day to measure and photograph the car. Back at the plant Ken Merker's design team and the modeling boys went to work making an excellent model. It was produced in rich, shiny tan and black plastic that, combined with the chrome details and white plastic inserts for the whitewall tires, made a near museum quality model without even painting it. After the kit's release, Lamberson drove his Duesenberg to the Morton Grove plant to receive a built model of his car in a ceremony on the loading dock. The magnificent Deusey stopped traffic on Waukegan Road as it majestically turned into the parking lot. Monogram's employees were released from work to watch the presentation. "It was a neat occasion," Harney remembered.

The Duesenberg (PC81 $30-40) led off a very successful lineup of vintage luxury cars. *Courtesy of Mark Mattei.*

A Mercedes Benz 540K convertible (PC87)—another Merker design—quickly followed, joined a couple of years later by a Rolls Royce Phantom II and Cord 812 (PC109, PC130). Because of their detail and features, these car models were expensive. They sold for three dollars apiece, compared to two dollars for Monogram's most expensive customizing cars, a dollar fifty for most cars, and one dollar for the old 1950s kits that continued in the catalog. In succeeding years the Classic Car line would be extender further. "We loved them, and we loved doing the models," said Reder. Syl Wisniewski agreed, and felt that the models were a great combination of style, accuracy, detail, and ease of assembly. "We did a pretty good job on them," he affirmed. Quite an understatement.

The Mercedes 540K (PC87 $30-40). *Courtesy of Dean Sills.*

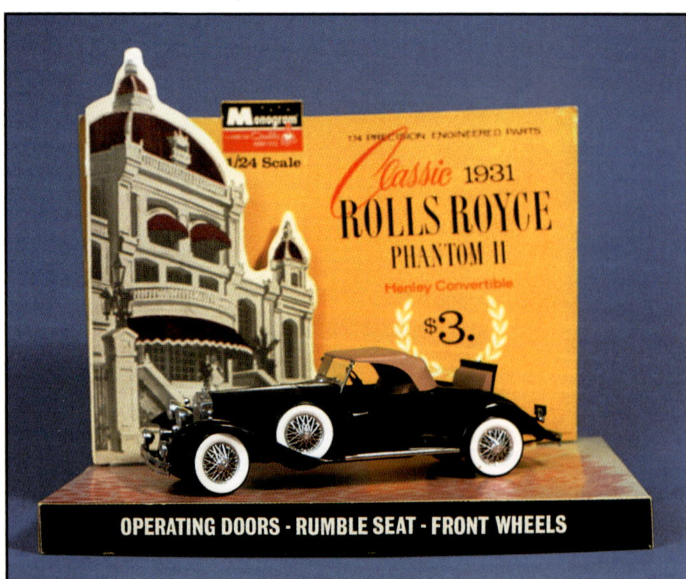


The Rolls Royce II (PC109 $25-35) had a sporty rumble seat that opened. *Courtesy of Dean Milano.*

The Cord 812 (PC130 $25-35) was way ahead of its time in styling. *Courtesy of Joe Hanner.*

The classic cars possessed enduring elegance, but in 1963 Hawk Model Company came up with something from the lower end of the sophistication spectrum: Weird-Ohs—bizarre characters driving outlandish hot rod vehicles. Revell responded to Hawk's creations with its own Ed Roth Rat Fink monsters manhandling hot rods. Roger Harney, who served on Monogram's new products committee, saw that the Weird-Ohs kits were "flying off the shelves. Selling very, very well." So Monogram figured that it had to enter the hot rod monster fray too. One day at a car show in Detroit a writer for a modeling magazine introduced the men in the Monogram display booth to a fellow who occupied his own stand, spray painting hot rod art on sweat shirts: Stanley "Mouse" Miller. Mouse was a pleasant young man who wore outrageous pointed hats that he created by stretching old fedoras over a baseball bat. Harney and Bob Reder knew who Mouse was, of course, since his T-shirt art was prominently advertised in the same car magazines that Monogram advertised in, and at car shows hot rod aficionados always crowded around his booth to watch hot rod monster art being created before their eyes.

Stanley Miller had been born into an artistic family in Southern California in 1940. His dad made a living as an animation artist for Walt Disney and had worked on the movie *Snow White*. When World War II came along, the family moved to Detroit, and it was there that Stanley grew into a teenager, reading *Mad* magazine, listening to black rhythm and blues on the radio, and inhaling the auto culture of Motor City. Soon he was driving a hot rod to juke joints and earning a little money pinstriping and flaming cars in his driveway. Then he discovered the air brush. "As far as I am concerned," Roger Harney later declared, "he really started the air brushed T-shirt craze of monster type things driving crazy, distorted cars, and the rest of the sweat shirt painters copied him." By 1959 Mouse's whole family was involved in a booming mail order T-shirt business.

In 1964 Monogram invited Miller to Morton Grove and put him up in a motel along with a sculptor Miller brought along, Tad Lukancic. A talented auto body sculptor, Lukancic had become, in Miller's words, "an escapee from GM" after a dispute with the auto design folks. Miller also brought along a bundle of sketches and ideas for models. The Monogram staff asked him what were his best selling artistic motifs, and he replied that pictures of hot rodders running over cops sold best. "Cop Killer" and "Fuzz Destroyer." Oh my! Monogram said that would never do. "So," Miller explained, "we did a switch-aroo." The first Fred Flypogger Happy Monster became Super Fuzz (MM104) a friendly lawman running his "prowl rod" over a prisoner. Monogram's designers worked with Miller's sketches to help Lukancic create a sculpture out of automotive styling clay that could be used as the pattern for the Freddy figure. Joe Sojka carved the T-bucket rod and the smoke spun-up by the rear wheels. The smoke was the most difficult part. "How do you carve smoke?" Harney asked. Miller finished-up the total package by painting the box art and drafting the instruction sheet—full of "beatnik jargon."

Flip Out the surfer and Speed Shift the hot rodder (MM105, MM106) joined Super Fuzz in the Monogram display parlor at the 1965 HIAA trade show. Monogram staffers wore little Mouse lapel pins fashioned from the tiny mouse figure that came with each of the Happy Monsters. To promote sales Monogram sponsored a nation-wide contest that asked entrants to suggest another model in the Fred Flypogger series. Inside the Morton Grove plant the "old Monogram custom" of an employee contest was revived, with Mouse sweatshirts and hand-painted Mouse Hulley-Gully hats going to the best model builders. Contestants' handiwork went on display in the cafeteria before the judging.

Alas, however, the Happy Monster line never progressed beyond the original three kits. Monogram set a sculptor to work on another Miller character "Moustang," but he never saw the light of day. The monster-rodder fad played out as quickly as it arose. "Our stuff was the best," Harney judged, "but it came out too late." Besides, just at this time, as Stanley Mouse explained, "I left town." He departed for San Francisco where he had heard there was "a mellow scene happening." He started doing poster art for the psychedelic tribal gathering rock concerts in the Fillmore Auditorium and Avalon Ballroom. Then he created some soon-to-be classic album covers for the Grateful Dead. Today he runs Mouse Studio in Occidental, California, where Fred Flypogger and the Grateful Dead continue to thrive in blissful harmony.

Stanley Mouse painted the hot rod art for the box of his Happy Monster Super Fuzz (MM104 $180-200). *Courtesy of Dean Milano.*

Super Fuzz (MM104 $180-200). *Courtesy of Tim Nolan.*

Monogram issued the simple little Forty-Niner kits to appeal to younger kids. The Corvette (PC404 $35-45), Sprite (PC406 $45-55), Pick-Up (PC410 $45-55), Rail Dragster (PC411 $85-95), Ford Roadster (PC412 $55-65). *Courtesy of Dean Sills.*

The Happy Monster in-house model building contest was just one example of the continuing efforts by Besser and Reder to build a company spirit among the employees. Work went on at Waukegan Road twenty-four hours a day. Most of the staff worked a normal eight to four-thirty day, but to keep the injection molding machines running, there were two shifts of night workers. Muzak continued to fill the building to keep the work space pleasant. Everything was neat and orderly. "Jack Besser kept it real clean," recalled Roger Harney. "He was a fanatic about that." Also, Besser still believed in "healthful physical activity." There was a gymnasium space with weights and other exercise equipment. Monogram fielded teams in a golf league at a local course and at Classic Bowl, the bowling alley just across the street. Bowlers proudly wore Monogram team shirts. In the shipping area there was a court where aggressive games of volleyball and basketball were contested. Sometimes people got hurt. Ken Merker observed, "If we get a rifle team here, we're going to kill people!" But the effort to build cohesion and morale worked, and many Monogram workers developed a fierce loyalty to their company.

Monogram's product line of model kits was the life blood of the company, and continually offering new kits to the public infused renewed energy into the business. The selection of fresh subjects for models was the responsibility of the New Products Committee. The committee consisted of Jack Besser, Bob Reder, Sly Wisniewski, and Roger Harney, plus representatives from manufacturing, advertising, sales, and public relations. The salesman could present their take on what kinds of model kits were being requested by the big retailers and by the distributors who served the hobby shops. Hobbyists were constantly sending in letters to request new models, but that was an uncertain barometer of the actual sales potential of a kit. Bob Reder's opinion counted most on the committee, and he admitted that it was always a judgment call on whether a new model would sell or not. As Wisniewski put it, "We had round table meetings, and we'd say 'Yeah, this would go over pretty good.' And we'd decide we'd go ahead with it."

The men on the New Product Committee kept an eye on what was in the newspapers and on television. Would a new Air Force jet excite boys shopping in the stores? And, if so, would that jet plane still be in the news a year in the future, because the lead-in time for development of a new model kit was about a year. Reder used to keep an eye on the development of new aircraft, and if it looked like an experimental plane might go into production, he would instruct the staff to start collecting material on the plane. Monogram would go to the aircraft, automobile, and truck companies with requests for data on their newest products, telling them that a scale model by Monogram would be good advertising for their company's goods. This argument usually worked. Reder recalled, for example, going to Mack Truck for information on their classic Bulldog truck (7537). It turned out that the company executive he dealt with was a Boy Scout master, like Reder, and that he was only too happy to supply the materials needed to develop the model.

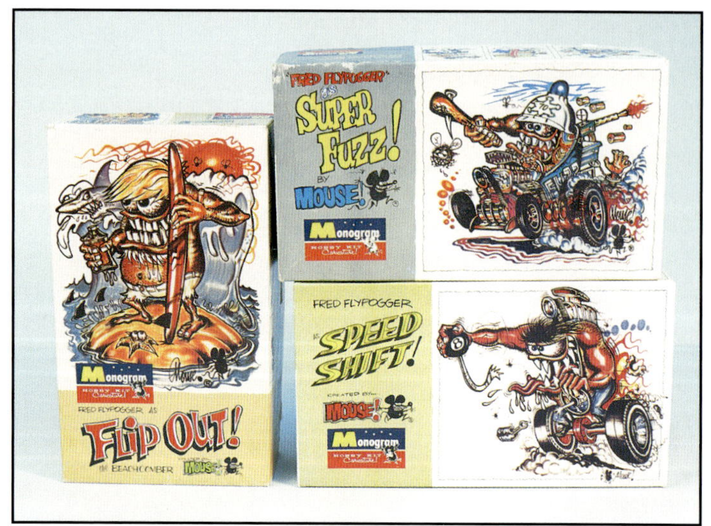

All three Mouse Happy Monsters: Super Fuzz (MM104 $180-200), Flip Out (MM105 $200-220), and Speed Shift (MM106 $200-220). *Courtesy of Dean Sills.*

Monogram continued to produce Christmas gift assortments down into the 1960s, although not in such large numbers as the 1950s. (GP-5053 $150-175). *Courtesy of Dean Sills.*

Both the Wildcat (PA66 $25-35) and Helldiver (PA69 $25-35) have landing gear that retract and wings that fold. *Courtesy of Dean Sills.*

The Zero (PA73 $25-35) and the Hellcat (PA80 $20-25) made a natural pair for young model builders. *Courtesy of Dean Sills.*

Back in the 1950s it was common to develop a model just from photographs that could be found in books, magazines, and newspapers. "The Snark was done completely from photographs," explained Wisniewski. But by the 1960s standards of accuracy had risen and the normal way to gather research material for a model was to find an example of a subject in a museum or elsewhere and carefully photograph it from dozens of different angles that would be useful to the Engineering Department. Once in the development pipeline, a model would be given a project number by which it would identified thereafter. The identity of a forthcoming model was considered a top secret that should be kept out of the hands of competing model companies. Nobody was allowed to enter the Engineering or Model Shops unless they had clearance from Reder or Wisneiwski. Whenever an outside VIP received a tour of the plant, new projects on the workbenches were covered up.

Monogram's Forty Niner aircraft set consisted of just three kits. The F-101 Voodoo (PA401 $10-12), P-40N (PA402 $10-12), and Russian Tu-16 Badger (PA403 $20-25). *Courtesy of Dean Sills.*

Ken Merker, who ran the Engineering Department for many years, explained that for all its precision, model design remained an art. Even photographs were not to be trusted for precise accuracy. "You used the eyeball method because photos do foreshorten," he explained. To begin a design, three-view or four-view "general aspect drawings" of a proposed model would be done. Then Merker had to decide how to break down the model into its separate parts. A separate preliminary drawing would be made for every part.

During the pattern making process Monogram would mold epoxy casts of a car's body and then made sure that the wooden engine pattern would fit snugly inside. *Courtesy of Joe Sojka.*

At this point Reder would hold a conference to see how things were developing and to make an estimate of how much this new model was going to cost to produce and manufacture. Sometimes the model shop boys would present a handmade mock-up model to examine. If a model was intended to sell at two dollars, then a determination had to be made if it would be practical to manufacture the model as it had been designed.

Often the message Reder gently conveyed to Merker was that his enthusiastic designers had produced something that would be very appealing to hobby elitists like themselves, but would be too expensive for Monogram to produce and too complex for Monogram's typical youthful customers to assemble. So it would be back to the drawing board. The solution was usually to combine some parts for easier molding and assembly.

Merker knew that some compromises had to be made for the sake of cost efficiency, even when your goal was a faithful scale model. The fundamental fact of design was, he explained, "No matter how pretty it is, if you can't tool it and manufacture it, it's worthless." Distortions were usually small, but some were unavoidable. For example, slender parts simply had to be beefed-up so that they could be molded and so that the finished parts would not break when a ten-year-old was handling them. The roofs of cars had to have a slight bulge because a flat roof would appear concave on a finished model. Some details of a model had to be exaggerated slightly. "At the time you're doing it on paper," mused Merker, "you think, 'Oh boy, this looks terrible,' because you know what it should look like, but once its done and you get the first parts, you've forgotten all about it and you don't even notice."

Once the design engineers had completed their plans, they would be sent to Roger Harney and the model makers to carve their wooden patterns and then copy the patterns into the epoxy molds. These tooling casts would go to the machinists who constructed the steel molds used to produce the actual plastic kit.

The Porsche 904 (PC127 $35-45) and Chaparral 2D (PC142 $45-55) were popular subjects for both static models and racing slot cars. Monogram designed its models to serve both purposes. *Courtesy of Dean Sills.*

Bob Reder had learned the art of mold making by doing it—starting back in the 1940s with the auxiliary parts for the Speedee-Bilt wooden kits. Mold production, he concluded was "very, very tricky. There are a wealth of problems. Everyone has their own theories. ... You learn what works and what doesn't." The complexity of a model kit, with its dozens of small parts of widely varying sizes makes the layout of the parts in the mold exceedingly intricate. Molten plastic must flow into all the remotest parts of the mold almost simultaneously and must completely fill every tiny recess of the mold.

The Woody Wagon (PC103 $85-95) obviously belonged on a California beach. *Courtesy of Revell-Monogram.*

Although Monogram had been making its own molds since the time it set up its own shop in Niles, Monogram never had the capacity to make all of its own molds. It had to rely on several mold shops in the Chicago area to handle all its needs. No one shop was large enough to do it all. Reder worked hard to cultivate good relationships with these mold shops over the years because only the highest quality molds would do. Monogram insisted on delicate engraving and a mirror-like finish to its molds. To achieve this finish it was necessary to go through a number of time consuming and expensive steps, polishing the mold with ever-finer abrasives and finishing with a diamond paste to produce a mirror luster. Monogram intended to mold its kits in rich colored plastic that didn't require painting, so the plastic parts had to come out of the mold with a flawless finish.

The Woody Wagon (PC103 $85-95) didn't require much painting to look neat. *Courtesy of Dean Milano.*

One topic of continuing debate—"a constant fight," according to Reder—among the staff at Monogram was the treatment of panel lines and rivets on its models. The techniques Monogram ordinarily used in the development of its molds did not permit recessed panel lines and rivets. To some modelers, like Joe Sojka, this was no problem. He liked the raised detail because it allowed him to bring out the highlights on a finished model by just lightly sandpapering over the raised lines and rivets. Reder knew that panel lines and rivets were necessary to give models a detailed, realistic appearance. He would request that the toolmaker inscribe delicate rivets into a mold "in the right size for effect." However, sometimes when the mold arrived, he found that the rivets had been cut in at three times the requested size. However, in the vast majority of cases Monogram's models emerged with elegantly refined details that a jeweler could be proud of.

The arrival of a new mold at the Morton Grove plant was an event of high anticipation because the result of a year's work was about to be revealed. The steel mold would be wheeled into place on a heavy-duty fork lift and fitted into one of the injection molding machines; then test shots would be made, using whatever plastic happened to be in the machine at the time. Usually it fell to Wisniewski or Merker to assemble the new model to see how it all fit together, and usually the test shot would reveal several defects in the mold. Reder observed that sometimes the list of recommendations for modifications to the mold might run to twenty pages. After that, it might take another four or five rounds of test shots before all the kinks had been ironed out and the mold could be readied for a production run.

Charles Spear did not paint much box art for Monogram, but his '36 Ford Coupe (PC118 $85-95) illustration is marvelous. *Courtesy of Dean Milano.*

The Bugatti 35B (PC133 $35-40) has a plastic base and hay bales to create a mini-diorama. *Courtesy of Revell-Monogram.*

Ken Merker found that checking test shots helped improve his skills at the front end of the model development process because he saw how flaws in the original design of a model resulted in problems in production at the end of the process. He also learned that you have to be very careful when you check out a new mold. When the Model A went into one of its conversions for reissue, he failed to note that the mounting pins on the new dash board did not match up with the existing holes in the body. Three days into the production run somebody tried to assemble one of the kits and discovered the glitch. Merker was called in to Reder's office, where he received a calm but firm lecture on the importance of precise work. Then Reder ground-up three days worth of plastic kit production and started the run over again. He might have let the kits go out to stores with the defect, but that was not Monogr起's way of doing business.

Production of the parts for Monogram's kits was done in the hot, noisy molding room, where fifteen machines pumped out trees of plastic parts. The manufacturing process was geared toward rapid production at low cost. Typically the cycle for molding a kit was about twenty-five seconds. A large part, such as the body of a 1/8 scale car, might take as long as eighty seconds. Most of that time was spent in the cooling cycle because parts had to harden before they were pulled from the molds. A few large parts continued to cure some more after they had been ejected from the machine, and these were sometimes clamped into fixtures to prevent them from warping.

The '30 Ford Coupe (PC120 $85-95). *Courtesy of Dean Sills.*

The '30 Ford Phaeton (PC116 $85-95). *Courtesy of Dean Sills.*

Monogram did not have the capability to mold all of its kits in its own machines. In fact, it didn't even desire one-hundred percent capacity because the volume of production rose and fell with the seasons, and Monogram did not want to have expensive machinery standing idle during the slack summer months. So roughly twenty percent of Monogram's molding was hired out to mold shops in the Chicago area. Because Monogram lacked a really big injection molding machine, some models, such as the 1/8 scale cars and, later on, the big 1/48 scale bombers, had to be molded by outside vendors.

The Ferrari GP (PC137 $45-55) and Lotus 33 (PC138 $45-55) were typical road racers of the 1960s slot car craze era. *Courtesy of Dean Sills.*

Odd little home-built drag strip racers were popular cars—and models—in the 1960s. The '40 Willys (PC139 $55-65), '34 Ford (PC140 $55-65), and '37 Fiat (PC141 $55-65). *Courtesy of Dean Sills.*

Bob Reder watched the production process carefully and checked to see that the parts were coming out of the machine in perfect condition. One of the telltale signs of an improperly working mold was flash—thin ridges of plastic that were formed on the edges of parts when some of the molten plastic seeped into the seams between mold halves.

"When a mold started flashing," observed Reder, "you knew it would get worse." Sometimes he would tolerate a little flash just to complete a run, but then the mold would be sent off to the mold shop to be repaired.

However, Monogram had a zero tolerance policy on another bane of model builders—the missing part. This often resulted when a part remained stuck in the mold and did not eject with the rest of the tree. Sometimes parts fell off the trees and were lost on the floor. Other companies such as Revell and Aurora had quality control checks, but packaged their kits right at the machines to save time and money. This resulted in some kits going out with missing parts. So both companies had departments that mailed replacement parts to customers who requested them. Monogram took a different approach.

Monogram double-checked every kit before it was sealed for delivery. The first inspection took place at the molding machine by the operator and her supervisor. But then the actual packaging of the parts took place in a separate room, under a separate department, where women in an assembly line operation placed the component parts of a kit into the boxes. Each worker checked the parts again carefully. "We had a real good crew," stated Reder. He asked the ladies, "How would you like it if you bought a pair of stockings and opened the package and found a run in them? That's how a kid feels when he finds a part missing."

As a final step, Monogram cello wrapped its kits to prevent accidents or pilferage in the stores. Monogram led the way in the model industry in cellophane sealing, beginning this practice back in 1955. Still, some slip-ups happened—and Monogram did mail out replacement parts—but Monogram had the best quality control in the industry, and this became part of the company's reputation for producing a superior product. Jack Besser told his employees: "There are model companies that are bigger, that produce more kits, but there is **no** company that can produce a finer product, with such loving attention as those made by Monogram co-workers."

Before a kit could be shipped out, two other key ingredients had to be packaged in the box: the instruction and decal sheets. "One day Reder was walking around pulling his hair out," remembered John Odrlin. "The guy who had been doing instruction sheets just quit." You couldn't send out kits without instruction sheets, so the abrupt departure of the instruction sheet designer dropped a large monkey wrench into the model development process. Odrlin, who was working in model design, volunteered to try his hand with the instruction sheets. "I did instruction sheets that day," he later recalled. And he would continue performing this vital role for Monogram for the next two decades and more.

Monogram followed a philosophy on instruction sheets that said they should be so clear that a novice builder could assemble a model as expertly as a veteran hobbyist. The drawings on the instruction sheets had be so uncomplicated that a youngster could easily see which way a landing gear strut was supposed to be oriented. Odrlin carefully watched all phases of the model development process to gain an overall sense of what was being produced. Often he had to develop the instruction sheet at the same time that the model makers and mold cutters were completing their tasks. This meant visualizing what finished model parts would look like just by looking at the design drawings.

Usually, however, he had the parts from the first test shots of a model to work from while making the illustrations for the instruction sheets. To add a three-dimensional look to the pictures, Odrlin used a transparent sheet of paper with shading preprinted on it and a beeswax coating on the back. He would lay a piece of this paper over the drawing of a model part, cut out the shading he wanted with a blade, and then rub the shaded paper firmly in place with a plastic tool. *Voila*! Instant depth to an illustration. He also had to decide on the sequence of assembly so that the parts went together smoothly without one assembly step becoming an obstacle to the next step.

Odrlin and the men who worked for him felt confident in their assignments, but they also realized the sometimes things that were obvious to those who had developed a model might not be so obvious to an outsider. So every now and then a bunch of youngsters—usually a Boy Scout troop—would be brought in and given kits, cement, and paint. The staff men observed the activity and sometimes were surprised to discover that the boys did things that were totally unexpected. This led to some rethinking and feedback into the whole development process.

The '41 Lincoln Continental (PC174 $20-25). *Courtesy of Dean Sills.*

Dick Locher painted the box art for the P-51B (PA136 $10-15).

Tom Morgan's box art for the Duesenberg Town Car (PC185 $30-40) looks wet to the touch. *Courtesy of Revell-Monogram.*

The 1958 Fort Thunderbird (PC89 $125-135) could be built four ways, including as a convertible.

# Chapter 5
# Into the Wild Blue Skies

In the early sixties Monogram decided to expand its collection of World War II aircraft models beyond its array of US Navy planes. The first subjects chosen were the familiar Japanese Zero and German Messerschmitt Me-109 fighters (PA73, PA74). This meant that Monogram would be duplicating models that were already in the lines of several other model companies. Bob Reder was fully aware of the danger of saturating the market for Zeroes and Messerschmitts, but he felt that Monogram simply had to have a model of a popular airplane in its catalog, even if other companies had it too. However, as Reder explained, you tried to do something a little different with your company's model. "Ice cream comes in chocolate, vanilla, and strawberry." Of course, Monogram also intended to make the best quality model on the market. A good example of this strategy was Monogram's Curtiss P-40 (PA96).

Reder well knew that the P-40 had long been a favorite of modelers, and he consciously decided on bringing out the early B variant that flew in China before Pearl Harbor. The Flying Tigers had blazed a celebrated story that everyone recognized, and the plane had that grinning shark's mouth nose art. Reder, who thought names sold kits, called it the "Tiger Shark." It had, in Reder's opinion, that priceless element—"romance." When the model came out, *Scale Modeler* (January 1965) explained the genius of Monogram's kit precisely: "This is ironic in the fact that the P-40B was the most illustrious of all the P-40s, yet other manufacturers have insisted on producing every type of P-40 except the B, thus making Monogram's neophyte not only unique but also the most accurate and detailed of all the P-40 kits on the market."

The aircraft that followed the Flying Tiger was another favorite modelers' subject with an heroic story behind it: the Lockheed P-38 Lightning (PA97). This model stepped-up the complexity level another notch. It appeared as a $1.98 kit with 114 parts and could be built in four variants, including the two-seat P-38M radar-equipped night fighter. It also pioneered a model element that would become a common feature on future Monogram models. A panel on the nose could be removed to show the interior of the gun bay. The bay's interior detail was molded right into the fuselage and didn't require any extra building by the hobbyist. Thus you had the illusion of intricacy without giving the modeler any extra headaches, except perhaps painting and highlighting the interior elements.

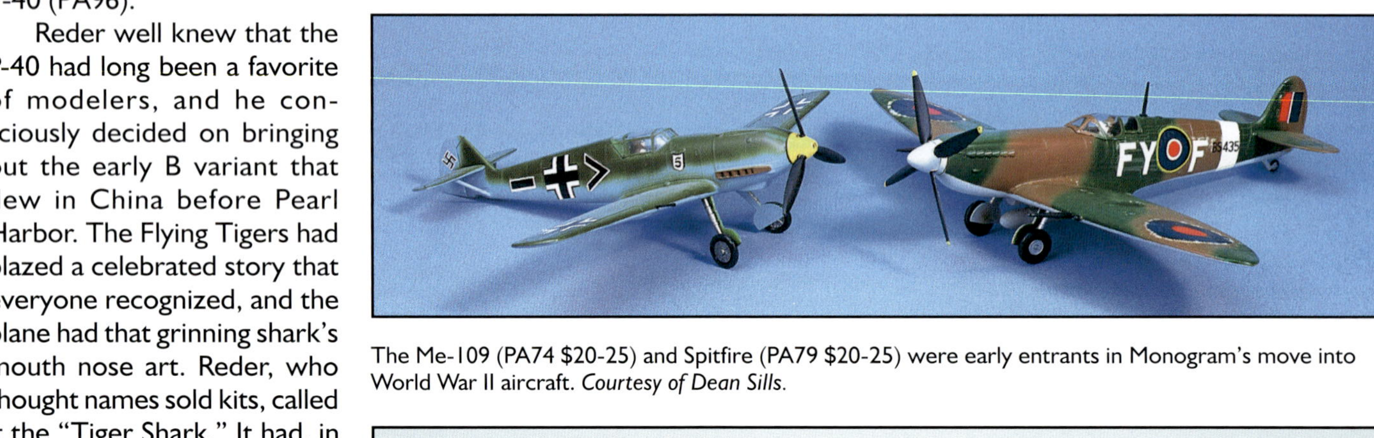

The Me-109 (PA74 $20-25) and Spitfire (PA79 $20-25) were early entrants in Monogram's move into World War II aircraft. *Courtesy of Dean Sills.*

The Hurricane (PA90 $10-15) and Curtiss P-40 (PA96 $20-25) gave model builders a choice of several ways to build the model. *Courtesy of Dean Sills.*

The P-38 was the first model designed for Monogram by Bill Koster, a newcomer to the Morton Grove staff, but someone who would go on to design more than sixty kits for Monogram over the coming decades. Most of Monogram's designers and model makers were local boys, but Koster grew up on Long Island, New York. He served in the Army as a paratrooper, including a short tour in Korea; then went on to the prestigious Pratt Institute of Brooklyn, from which he graduated in 1957 with a degree in industrial design. He worked for several companies, including Magnavox television, where he designed TV cabinets. Each new job carried him farther west, until he ended up in St. Charles, Illinois, where the company he was working for laid him off.

The P-38 (PA97 $40-65) could be built as this two-seat night fighter version. The Corsair (PA82 $20-25) could be built as this Korean War fighter-bomber. *Courtesy of Dean Sills.*

The Focke Wulf (PA107 $15-20) and Mosquito (PA129 $25-35). *Courtesy of Dean Sills.*

The P-47 Thunderbolt (PA187 $10-15) and P-51B Mustang (PA136 $10-15) made a timeless pair in the skies over Europe during World War II— and as Monogram models. *Courtesy of Dean Sills.*

From this point, Koster's story takes a familiar turn. He saw an advertisement placed in the newspaper by Monogram for a model designer. "I thought, 'This is not exactly industrial design, but it is a job and my hobby is building flying model airplanes,' so I went to take a look." Reder hired him and Wisniewski got him busy on aircraft design. After proving himself with components of several models, he got to do the P-38 (PA97) all on his own. Koster thought a lot about questions such as part breakdown. After looking at some old Airfix kits with lots of tiny parts, he tried to decide how some parts might be combined into one. As a model builder himself, he thought, "How would I like the parts to be?" By this time Monogram's rule on kit design was pretty well set: "Ease of construction, with maximum amount of detail."

Koster thought Monogram might increase the appeal of its models for advanced modelers by adding extra parts to its aircraft kits—just carrying the ideas of the P-38 kit a little further. He brought this concept up, and when Monogram turned him down, he decided to go ahead on his own. About 1965 he started a little garage company called Koster Aero Enterprises to make specialty parts for hobbyists who wanted to tinker with the mass produced kits sold by the big mainstream model companies. While moonlighting with KAE, he carried on with his day job at Monogram, but KAE continued as well and is still in the parts business today.

Although Koster did his work with pen and ink on paper, he firmly believed that Monogram's process of going from design drawings to hand-built pattern model and then to mold cutting resulted in a superior model. Of course, Monogram did send some parts directly from design blueprint to tooling, but these were just routine pieces. When Koster examined other companies' models, he could see when parts had been done directly from drawings. They had a too-uniform, mechanical look. Monogram's three-step process resulted in a more realistic model.

One Saturday morning in the mid-sixties Jack Besser, Bob Reder, Syl Wisniewski, and Roger Harney sat down for a talk about new products. Besser had been thinking about the Vietnam War. "I don't like to do this," he said, "but we don't have a choice. We have to make models of things being used in the Vietnam war." It was agreed that some of Monogram's kits would be given new identities and Vietnamese war-themed box art. For example, the old T-28 Trojan trainer (PA14) became a T-28D fighter bomber (PA121) with underwing ordinance added and decals for the South Vietnamese Air Force. The Iroquois hospital helicopter (PA50) became a Rescue Chopper (PA152) and, armed with machine guns, the Huey Armed Chopper (PA151). The kits came in new boxes blazing with combat scenes. The peaceful DC-3 (PA9) of the 1950s became the camouflaged AC-47 gun ship "Puff the Magic Dragon" (PA203). All the Army vehicle kits received new box art that placed them in the terrain of Southeast Asia.

The F-105 Thunderchief (PA33 $35-45) was first issued in the 1950s in silver plastic, and then came out during the Vietnam War era with pre-painted camouflage (PA150 $20-25). *Courtesy of Dean Sills.*

The old DC-3/C47 model of the 1950s was reissued as a Spooky Vulcan Cannon gunship (PA148 $20-25) in the mid-1960s. *Author's collection.*

Monogram's Army vehicles came in green border boxes in the mid-1960s with Vietnam-themed box art. The Patton Tank (PM159 $20-25). *Author's collection.*

Some new models were created specifically for the Vietnam War. Jack Besser had read about Colonel Bernard Fisher, who landed his A-1E Skyraider while under fire to rescue of a downed fellow pilot. Besser thought that daring exploit merited recognition with a Monogram model (PA146) to go with Fisher's Congressional Medal of Honor. The big 1/24 scale Phantom Huey (6839) replicated one of the most familiar aircraft of the war—one seen on television coverage of the war every day. The naval war being fought on Vietnam's inland waters led Monogram to issue its first boat models in many years: the River Assault RAG Boat, Swift Patrol Boat, and Command Junk (PB179, PB180, PB181). The Huey Cobra Team (6839), which came out in 1971, just about wound-up the war for Monogram.

The A1-E Skyraider (PA146 $10-12) was issued because it was making headlines in Vietnam. *Courtesy of Revell-Monogram.*

The Huey Cobra Combat Team (PA191 $30-40). *Courtesy of Dean Sills.*

The Swift Boat (PB180 $15-20) and Command Junk (PB181 $15-20) were Monogram's first new ship models in years. *Courtesy of Dean Sills.*

However, the most significant Vietnam era model was the giant Boeing B-52 Stratofortress, which—with its thirty-inch wingspan—became the world's largest plastic model airplane. It had 250 parts that were scattered over five production molds. Its bomb bay doors opened to display thirty-three bombs. Its flaps and spoilers moved. The tail gun swiveled. But even with all these remarkable attributes, the thing that set this model apart was its unique "jet engine sound" feature.

The big 1/24 scale Phantom Huey Chopper (PA226 $300-350) was an impressive model, but not a big seller. Thus it is hard to find today. *Courtesy of Revell-Monogram.*

This noise maker element had been the special project of Jack Behrends, one of the engineers. He consulted with some outside university experts on how to make an appropriate jet engine sound for a model. As Syl Wisneiwski recalled, "We had one of our guys experiment with that sound. Boy, it was annoying to listen to that day after day 'til he got the right pitch." Most of the hobbyists who built the B-52 would dispute the conclusion that the pitch was right. The sound was compared to fingernails on chalkboard. (However, one can ponder just what a 1/72 scale Pratt &

Whitney turbojet would sound like.) *Scale Modeler* (January 1969) pronounced the noise maker "Mickey Mouse." The magazine also judged the model only "good," not "excellent." Nevertheless, the B-52 became a landmark model for Monogram and the pathfinder for future large size bomber models.

With the exception of the Phantom Huey, the models from the Vietnam War experienced good sales. Despite the nation-rending controversies over the war, boys still wanted to build models from the fighting, just as they had for World War II and the Korean Conflict. "We sold the right products at the right time," concluded Harney.

The second release of the B-52 with Jet Engine Sound (PA215 $55-65) came with Dick Locher box art. *Courtesy of Dean Sills.*

Bob Reder thought the time was right again for another venture into the sphere of rocketry since the Apollo Program was attracting public attention to the effort to land men on the moon. Reder traveled to Houston and arranged for NASA to furnish Monogram with drawings of the Saturn V rocket and Apollo moon craft. This enabled Monogram to get the first Saturn model (PS193) into stores, but it had the downside that the kit's details represented the vehicles used in the preliminary flights, not the ones that actually went to the moon. The model was done in the smaller 1/144 scale used for airliners, but this still meant that the finished model stood an impressive thirty inches tall. Since the Saturn V was basically just a big tube, except for its uppermost stage, the engineering department had no problem developing the kit, and it proved to be a very good seller among Americans following NASA's voyages to the moon.

Monogram followed up the Saturn with models of the Apollo Command and Service Modules (6873) and First Lunar Landing (6872), which depicted Apollo 11's Eagle lunar lander on a moonscape base. The 1/32 scale Command and Service Modules had transparent side panels to show the details of the interiors. The Lunar Landing model included two astronaut figures, assorted scientific equipment to place on the landscape base, a little American flag, and a booklet on the exploits of Apollo 11. Like the Saturn, these models appealed to Americans following the astronauts' flights to the moon. "We hit it just right on those," explained Ken Merker. "They sold very well. We couldn't keep them in stock." However, public interest in space flight models faded just as quickly this time around as it had back in the late 1950s. By 1971, after a short three-year run, all Monogram's Apollo Program models went out of the catalog.

The old Missile Arsenal (PD40) was updated in 1969 to U. S. Space Missiles (PS221 $60-70) to capitalize on interest generated by the Apollo Program. *Courtesy of Dean Sills.*

Dick Locher painted a fantastic scene for the First Lunar Landing (6872 $25-35). *Courtesy of Revell-Monogram.*

The day after the first men landed on the moon, July 21, 1969, John Cather started work for Monogram as art director, replacing the retiring Fred Wellman, Jr. Cather had grown up in the Chicago neighborhood of South Shore during the Great Depression, but, as he put it, "We didn't know we were poor." He got to build lots of balsa model airplanes as he grew up because his dad worked as a draftsman for Joe Ott model airplane company and brought home kits for his family. One of the elder Cather's jobs was designing the box graphics for the Joe Ott kits. John showed an aptitude for creative arts from an early age and after high school went to the University of Illinois to study architecture. He was better at illustration than at engineering, so the next stop in his education was the American Academy of Art in Chicago. From there he went into the printing and photography trade. By 1969, he found himself worn out by the hectic life of working at a printing company and answered an advertisement in the newspaper for an art director. By a strange coincidence, he discovered that the company seeking an art director was Monogram, the chief client of his current employer! Cather found the switch in positions a very positive change. He still worked long hours, but the labor was engaging. "Monogram was a great place to work."

He learned that Monogram had the atmosphere of a big family. Every morning at 10 the heads of departments would assemble in the lunch room for a break. They drank coffee and ate pastries—except now and then when it was White Castle Day and everyone would down lots of little hamburgers. The rule of the morning break was that anything could be discussed, except business. When someone's birthday came up, that became the excuse for a minor celebration.

The Pylon Racers (PA218 $20-30) makes a nice display of two Reno racers. The 1/72 scale P-51 and Bearcat. *Courtesy of Dean Sills.*

By the latter part of the 1960s, Monogram was issuing some very accurate scale models. The Typhoon (PA213 $10-12), Stuka (PA207 $10-15), Kingfisher (PA135 $25-35). *Courtesy of Dean Sills.*

Cather reported directly to Jack Besser because box art was considered an aspect of sales promotion. Monogram furnished the art department with top quality equipment. At first Cather was pretty much a one man show, but over the years his staff grew to about a dozen. It was up to them to design the graphics and layout of the kit boxes. This involved decisions about the style of type face to be used, cropping of the box art, and placement of the Monogram logo and text. He also oversaw the art work on the store displays and the layout of the annual catalog. Cather even had a bit to do with promotions, such as the sweepstakes Monogram sponsored. He recalled the Predicta contest that was won by a fellow named Darrell Zipp—who turned out to be a model maker for Revell. So after the contest, lamented Cather, "We were not able to do too much promotion on that one."

The box art for the Predicta (PC95 $70-80) was an early Tom Morgan effort. *Courtesy of Christian Bryan.*

Monogram's 1/72 Tomcat (5992 $4-6) was not a particularly good model, but Tom Morgan gave it an attractive box illustration. *Courtesy of Revell-Monogram.*

Meanwhile during the sixties Monogram had continued to expand its line of model cars. The big 1/8 scale hot rods had done well enough to justify further ventures in oversize car models. The sleek, ultramodern Jaguar XK-E sports car (PC98) was chosen for an experiment with a powered, steerable model. As a test bed for the system, Joe Sojka and Syl Wisniewski designed a "breadboard" with wheels, motor, batteries, steering mechanism, and an umbilical cord leading to a control box. It demonstrated that the system had possibilities, but ultimately the powered concept was dropped and the XK-E became just a static display model, but one with lots and lots of working features and intricate elements.

The resulting model was quite impressive, but it suffered from many problems. For starters, the design drawings and patterns were done in the same 1/8 scale as the model kit. This meant that tolerances in the fit had to be exact. In Merker's words, the process was "less forgiving of mistakes." Then there were simply all those component parts, including tiny hinges for the opening doors and side windows that actually rolled down when you turned the crank. The front wheels were steerable and the front suspension had working springs. Molding presented problems all its own. The front end was in a separate mold from the rest of the car body. This meant that the process of molding had to be managed very carefully to ensure that the two halves of the car came out of the molding machines in identical shades of red. If the mix of color pellets was off or if one machine ran hotter than the other, then the colors would not match. All the problems were overcome, but it was one big continuing expensive headache.

Dick Locher gave the 1/8 scale Jaguar XK-E (PC98 $95-105) an exciting box cover. *Courtesy of Craig Clements and Ron Hanke.*

Learning from the XK-E experience, Monogram designed the next 1/8 scale car, the Corvette Stingray (PC126), to be like a standard 1/24 scale model. More simple. No opening doors this time. Less troublesome to assemble. And the blue plastic was easier for the molding department to match up. However, there were still opening/retracting headlights, steerable front wheels, and a hood that opened to show an engine detailed with flexible hoses and wirings.

The Corvette Stingray (PC126 $145-155) brought in a new era in automotive styling. *Courtesy of Craig Clements and Ron Hanke.*

During the 1960s Monogram also added to its line of custom cars. The National Hot Rod Association's Custom Car Show was held in Indianapolis over Labor Day weekend in 1962, and it turned out to be quite an event for Monogram. The full size Big T made its public debut, parked in front of a display wall filled with photos of Monogram's car models. Monogram's new styling consultant, Darryl Starbird, won a seven-foot tall trophy for Best Custom with a bubble-top '58 Chevy. Best Rod in the show went to Larry Faber's Li'l Coffin, a custom job that had originally been done by Dave Stuckey, who worked for Starbird, but the car had received addition restyling by Faber. While Roger Harney was admiring the car, Jack Besser walked up and asked, "What do you think of it." Harney replied, "It's the wildest hot rod I've ever seen," and Besser responded, "That's good to know because I just bought it." Actually, explained Bob Reder, Monogram Models, Inc. bought it.

The Li'l Coffin was brought back to headquarters at Morton Grove to serve as reference for the model, and later it went on display in the Better Living Pavilion at the New York World's Fair. Joe Sojka did most of the design and pattern making all on his own, and it turned out to be quite a project for a really special car. Professional architect and model kit historian Craig Clements later described the car's salient aspects in terms that an architect could appreciate: It was "a severely chopped and channeled '32 Ford Sedan. It hugged the Midwestern landscape like a Frank Lloyd Wright prairie home, replete with cantilevered roof." Just as Wright's forward-looking homes suffered from problems like leaky roofs, the Li'l Coffin model had one big difficulty: It was just too complex, with lots of fiddly parts. The doors opened, the front wheels were posable. "It was tedious to build," explained Harney, "but it made a very good looking model." Ken Merker paid tribute to hobbyists who could turn the kit into a finished model. "Anybody who could put that together was good—real good." Nevertheless, many a boy rose to the challenge, and the Li'l Coffin became one of Monogram's all-time best sellers.

For many youngsters the Li'l Coffin (PC94 $75-85) was their all-time favorite model car. *Courtesy of Craig Clements.*

Monogram's next show rod took quite a different path to development. California show rod designer Steve Scott contacted Bob Reder and asked if Monogram would like to bring out a model of his award-winning car, the Uncertain T. Scott and Reder worked out a deal whereby Scott would supply the reference material for the car, rather than having Monogram do its own research. When the packet of reference data arrived at Morton Grove, the boys in engineering were very impressed. In addition to photos of the car, there were elegant engineering drawings done by Steve Swaja, the designer of *Hot Rod* magazine's radical XR6 car. Ken Merker adjusted Swaja's design drawings to suit Monogram's molding requirements, and the Uncertain T model went on to production without anyone at Monogram ever laying eyes on the real car.

Steve Scott's Uncertain T (PC134 $190-210) was a trophy winner in real life. *Courtesy of Craig Clements and Gib Grayless.*

Design of the next two show car models fell to airplane enthusiast Bill Koster. He had already done some work on slot cars, including a ready-to-run "thingie" with a vacuum-formed body called "The Snake." ("That was kinda fun.") However, he and automobiles did not get along together. Roger Harney could sympathize, although his modeling preferences ran in just the opposite direction. "Koster was always a fabulous designer, but his heart was not in these cars." The first car, Boot Hill Express (PC188), was Ray Farhner's car, based on a real 1800s hearse, with a chrome V-8 engine in back where the coffin should be. Koster and the rest of the development team did a fine job on it, and Boot Hill Express went on to be a very popular model kit for Monogram. However, the Bathtub Buggy (PC223) cast a pall of gloom over the engineering and model shops. Bob Reder had made a deal with noted car customizer George Barris to produce the Bathtub Buggy, but Harney spoke for the staff when he declared: "We all hated it. It was just dreadful. And it didn't sell well. It was a waste of money. We were used to making the neat stuff." Years later when asked if he had designed the Bathtub Buggy, Koster replied: "I hate to admit it. I was in agony on those funny cars. I didn't like any part of them."

"Mr. Bones" came back for a second appearance in Boot Hill Express (PC188 $45-55). *Courtesy of Craig Clements and Gib Grayless.*

In 1969 Monogram assigned him a project that he did enjoy. Japanese companies were experiencing robust sales of tanks and other armored fighting vehicles, so Monogram decided to bring out its first new armor models in more than a decade. Menacing German subjects were popular; thus the first model would be the Panzer IV. This tank was selected because it could

Bill Koster designed the German Assault Tank (6861 $20-30) and also painted the art for the box. The burning building in his original painting was replaced by an intact building in the box art. *Author's Collection.*

be reissued in several variants. Bill Koster, who had just completed work on the German Dornier Do 17Z (PA214), tackled the assignment with gusto. Monogram flew Koster to the US Army Ordinance Museum at Aberdeen, Maryland, to measure and photograph the Panzer tank, although Koster recalled that Monogram was so "tight fisted" with its expense money that he had to fly in during the morning, squeeze in all his work during the day, and fly home again in the evening. But it was valuable work, and the reference material he brought back would be used in four Panzer tank models. Koster even had the pleasure of doing the box art for the Sturmgeschutz IV (6861), although he was a little unhappy that Jack Besser ordered the background rubble replaced by an intact farm house to tidy up the landscape. Perhaps appropriately, the steel production molds for the German tanks were cut in Germany by Peter Hoppner.

The same chassis was used on all the German tanks. The Flakpanzer (8219 $20-25) and Sturmgeschuetz IV (8220 $20-25). *Courtesy of Revell-Monogram.*

During the 1960s electric powered slot cars zoomed onto the hobby scene, and boys across America enthusiastically learned the skills of miniature auto racing. They either enjoyed friendly races with kids from the neighborhood on the floor at home, using cars and track from a boxed race set, or they moved up to the more intense competition found in commercial slot car parlors that sprang up around the country. Soon almost every major hobby company in the United States was irresistibly drawn into the action to satisfy a seemingly insatiable demand for more and better cars and equipment. (See Schiffer Books' *Aurora Slot Cars*.) Hobby distributors began asking why Monogram didn't have any products to offer in this rapidly growing arena.

Actually Bob Reder had been keeping an eye on developments in slot cars ever since they appeared on the scene. Syl Wisnewski explained, "The fad started in California, as many fads do. Bob and I flew out there and toured the place to see what was going on." Jack Besser witnessed what was happening to slot car sales and decided that Monogram simply had to enter the market: "The fantastic growth of slot racing and model car racing more than has determined the course we shall follow. Slot racing activity around store tracks and on club courses has skyrocketed." Monogram hired a West Coast slot car consultant to direct its efforts in this new enterprise.

When Monogram entered the competition, it found itself already a couple of laps behind the rest of the field. While it developed its own cars, running gear, and accessories, Monogram bought time by selling some cars that were quick reworks of bodies from existing model kits. Familiar 1/24 scale cars such as the '36 Ford Coupe, the '58 Thunderbird, and even the Duesenberg were offered as slot racers. They ran on purchased chassis, powered by Mabuchi motors imported from Japan—and, predictably, they proved unable to keep up with the rest of the pack on the racetrack. Soon Monogram had some more appropriate cars for slot car layouts: GT racers like Porches and Ferraris. Ken Merker recalled that the emphasis was on speed in getting these new car bodies developed. Accuracy took a back seat. "We'd just crank them out quickly and put them into the model shops."

By this time Monogram also offered a wide array of slot car parts and accessories, such as soft sponge tires, gears, and motors—all packaged under the "Tiger" logo. Most of this was purchased from outside vendors. Probably the best product Monogram developed was a set of very nice 1/32 scale injection-molded scenery kits that could be used to give a race atmosphere to a slot car track layout. There were things like bleachers, spectator figures, and a Dunlop bridge to span the track. These sold well. It looked like Monogram was firmly in the slot now and ready to race.

Then abruptly slot racing ran into a brick wall. Literally overnight slot car fever died. Toward the end of 1967 it suddenly dawned on everyone in the hobby industry that no one was buying anything related to slot cars. "No other product died so quickly," recalled Bob Reder. Like everyone else in the hobby industry, Monogram found itself with a whole product line—a motor and parts inventory purchased from outside vendors—and no customers. However, Bob Reder felt that Monogram weathered the crash reasonably well because it had been careful not to invest too much in a stock of products that had to be written off at a loss. "We never got hung out too far on a product."

In retrospect, the lasting impact of turning off on the slot car side road was that it slowed the introduction of new model kits, but that's something that became evident only in hindsight. Slot cars looked like a promising field at the time, so something had to be ventured in that game. Besides, the slot car hobby did survive the crash of 1967, and they are still humming today, but on a much reduced level of participation and sales.

Monogram's 1/32 scale figures (RS3103, RS3104) populated slot car track layouts in the 1960s. *Courtesy of Craig Clements and Ron Hanke.*

The Scarab (PC124 $35-45) and Ferrari 275P (PC102 $35-45) grand prix racers. *Courtesy of Dean Sills.*

The only significant new domain of plastic model kits that Monogram entered in the later 1960s was 1/72 scale aircraft. By this time aircraft models in that scale had been brought into the domestic market by Airfix, and America's industry leader Revell had also been selling them for several years. Thus a considerable market for 1/72 scale kits had been established among American kids. Monogram's first four kits appeared in the late winter of 1967. They included a P-51B Mustang, F8F Bearcat, Curtiss P-36A, and A-1E Skyraider (PA143, PA144, PA145, PA146). The hobby industry received these little models very well because they were new subjects in this scale and because they maintained Monogram's high standards of quality.

This trio of World War II era fighters launched Monogram's entry into 1/72 scale models. The P-51B (PA143 $6-8), F8F Bearcat (PC144 $6-8), and P-36 (PC145 $6-8). *Courtesy of Dean Sills.*

The A-1E Skyraider (PA146 $6-8) and F7F Tigercat (PC146 $10-12) in 1/72 scale. *Courtesy of Dean Sills.*

Ken Merker and Roger Harney came up with an innovative proposal to extend the 1/72 scale line. They asked Bob Reder if they could "bid the job" of developing more models, just as if they were outside contractors, and they would do the work on their own time in the evenings. Reder said OK, just as long as it did not interfere with their regular labors. So Merker drew up design plans for three 1930s biplanes on a card table at home, while Harney and two other model makers carved the patterns.

The molds for the Curtiss P-6E (PA208) and F11C-2 Goshawk (PA210) were tooled by the Portuguese company Abrantes, while the Boeing F4B-4 (PA209) was tooled by Peter Hoppner in Germany. The models came out just fine. Merker's plans incorporated the revolutionary idea of molding the interior struts and landing gear struts right into the fuselage. This made building these tiny biplanes much easier because the smallest struts, which usually caused the most headaches, were firmly anchored in place and provided a stable platform for assembling the upper and lower wings.

3 Fighting Planes of the Thirties (PC216 $25-35) is one gift set that you can buy at a modest price. *Author's Collection.*

Monograms model builders did these three biplanes as a home project in their off hours. The F11C Goshawk (PA209 $8-10), Hawk P-6E (PA208 $8-10), and Boeing F4B-4 (PA210 $8-10). *Courtesy of Dean Sills.*

As the year 1968 opened, Jack Besser penned a message to the Monogram family in the house bulletin *News & Views* (February 1968): "It is a gross understatement to merely say that Monogram makes a *good* product. In reality, we make the BEST, of the highest quality. ... To a certain extent this emanates from management's philosophy and recognizes that there are model companies that are bigger, that produce more kits, but there is *no* company that can produce a finer product, with such loving attention as those made by Monogram Co-workers." This was the testimony of a conservative Heartland American who took genuine pride in what he and his company had achieved. "We were conservative by nature," explained Bob Reder. "Pay the bills on time, don't speculate, don't borrow too much." However, Monogram was about to enter a new era in its history that would challenge the bedrock traditions that had long guided the company.

In the spring of 1968 Mattel, Inc., the world's largest toy company, contacted Monogram and asked to buy the company. "We were surprised. We had no thought of selling," recalled Bob Reder. Nevertheless, Besser and Reder agreed to a series of meetings with Mattel's representatives to consider the pluses and minuses of merging Monogram into the Mattel empire. Mattel had come courting because it was looking for ways of diversifying its product line. During the 1960s Mattel had done very well with Barbie Dolls and Hot Wheels die cast cars, but Ruth Handler and her husband Elliot, the founders of Mattel, knew full well that success in the toy business could be erratic and unpredictable. Thus they began searching for companies that had some relationship to the toy industry, but could also broaden the base of Mattel outside the toy field. In their search, the first company they hit upon was Monogram Models, which at the time was the fourth or fifth largest model kit company in America, following Revell, Aurora, AMT, and possibly MPC.

The Bell P-39 (PA227 $20-25) makes a very appealing subject for a model. *Courtesy of Dean Sills.*

Tom Morgan's P-40B (PA96 $20-25) box art is reminiscent of a scene from the 1942 John Wayne movie *Flying Tigers*.

Up to this time, Jack Besser and Bob Reder had always followed cautious business practices at Monogram, but they saw union with Mattel as a way of allying Monogram with a larger company that had much deeper financial pockets. Growth in the sales of model kits throughout the hobby industry had leveled off after more than a decade of rapid growth, so Monogram might be in a better position to diversify its product line in the future if another opportunity to extend its reach—such as slot cars had been—came along. The purchase was paid for by giving Mattel stock to Besser and Reder in exchange for their Monogram stock. The Handlers assured Besser and Reder that they would continue to manage Monogram's operations, and none of the staff would be replaced. The purchase would become official on October 1, 1968.

The box design for Hurst's 442 Olds changed when the kit's number went from PC175 to 6734 (PC175 $20-30, 6734 $20-25). *Courtesy of Dean Sills.*

About six weeks before that date, Monogram's employees learned of the sale. Folding chairs were set up in the plant, and the staff assembled for an announcement. Jack Besser stood up before the crowd and explained what had been done and assured everyone that operations at Monogram would go on just as before. Roger Harney did not take it that way. "I almost got sick," he recalled. "We were all family." When Besser realized that many in the gathering were taking the news badly, he declared: "I'm seeing some long faces. We should be happy. Mattel is a great company. This will help."

At first there was little apparent change at Morton Grove as projects already in the development pipeline continued through to completion. Then in 1969 Mattel reorganized its corporate structure in an attempt to rationalize its growing empire, which now included a movie studio, publishing company, playground equipment company, and Ringling Brothers Circus. Under this new regime, Monogram model kits were lumped into a sales division with Hot Wheels cars, crafts, and games. Marketing was taken over by this new Mattel department, and Monogram's existing force of salesmen was brusquely dismissed. An experienced sales staff that had been carefully nurtured over the years by Jack Besser and that knew the hobby industry thoroughly was suddenly replaced by men who understood only the toy marketplace.

The change hit Monogram pretty hard, especially at the top. Besser and Reder would travel to California on a regular basis to meet with the executives of Mattel and talk over business and financial matters. These meetings were particularly hard on Jack Besser. As Reder remembered it, "Besser was not used to taking orders, so there was a bit of tension there." Ruth Handler was a strong-willed business woman who was accustomed to giving orders. Her husband Elliot was a more easy-going engineer, and Reder enjoyed talking shop with him and the Mattel design employees.

Under Mattel's ownership, product selection was supposed to remain primarily with Monogram, although Reder understood that Mattel would have the final say. However, Mattel's toy orientation inevitably invaded operations at Morton Grove. From Mattel's point of view this only made good sense because the marketplace for toys was vastly larger than the market for hobby products. Thus, boys in the engineering and model shops at Monogram began to receive suggestions from Mattel for new products. Inevitably these were for simple models that could be played with like toys. In Harney's opinion, "goofy stuff." Development of "serious" scale models almost ceased.

When Mattel purchased Monogram, the Mattel trademark was incorporated into the Monogram logo. The P-51B Mustang (PA136 $10-15). *Author's collection.*

The first toy-like model to appear, Snoopy and his Sopwith Camel (6779), actually originated with Bob Reder and the staff at Monogram. Reder contacted Charles Schultz by telephone and arranged to fly out to California for an interview. Although Schultz did not easily grant licenses for his cartoon characters, he felt a model of Snoopy would be nice—if it were done well and in the spirit of Schultz's cartoons. Reder found that Schultz was indifferent to royalty money, but wanted to make sure that nothing in Monogram's product would portray Snoopy in a negative way. Thus Schultz had to OK the preliminary sketches, model prototypes, and packaging design to ensure quality before anything went into production. Monogram figure sculptor Chrisendo "Scotty" Forte, a Scotsman from an Italian family, carved the Snoopy figure. The result was, in Harney's words, "a real neat looking kit." It had an ingenious, simple snap-in motor that would spin the propeller when you gave the prop a bump and then could be stopped just by putting a finger in the blade's arc.

Snoopy and his Sopwith doghouse (6779 $60-75) flew very high for Monogram for several years. Courtesy *Courtesy of Tim Nolan.*

Even though Snoopy had been Monogram's idea, Mattel embraced it enthusiastically. In the fall of 1970 Mattel ran a national TV advertising campaign, just like it did for Mattel toys. This had never been attempted before with a model kit. Monogram also sponsored a cross country "Snoopy vs. the Red Baron" air race from Santa Rosa, California, to La Guardia Airport in New York. Red Baron, Jim Appleby, flew a replica Fokker triplane, while Snoopy, John Bagley, flew a Nieuport 28—which sort of looks like a Camel. After their arrival in New York, Appleby and Bagley went on the popular Gary Moore TV show "To Tell the Truth" and stumped the panel, which had no idea what a guy dressed up like a World War I pilot and another man in a dog outfit had been up to. The result of Mattel's promotions was phenomenal. Demand was so great that Monogram had to take the unprecedented step of cutting two production molds for the kit.

After a year on the market, one Mattel representative asserted: "It was the biggest selling plastic model kit ever created." Of course, Snoopy was not really a scale model, and most of the sales went to ordinary folks who just loved Snoopy. The simplicity of the model and its snap-together construction didn't deter anyone from purchasing the kit. The spectacular success of Snoopy and his Sopwith led to the production of five more Snoopy-themed models. Monogram artist, Dick Locher, who knew Charles Schultz as a fellow cartoonist, came up with the idea of Snoopy as Joe Cool on a surfboard (7502), but Locher's suggestion of a skin diver Snoopy with a spear gun was deep sixed as too risky for bathtub play. None of the follow-on Snoopy kits enjoyed the popularity of the original.

So far as sales went, Snoopy easily downed the Red Baron (5903 $60-75). *Courtesy of Revell-Monogram.*

Monogram extended the Snoopy line about as far as name recognition would carry it. Snoopy High Wire (6661 $75-100), Joe Cool (7502 $60-75), Snoopy & His Bugatti (6894 $60-75), and Snoopy & His Motorcycle (5902 $60-75). *Courtesy of Revell-Monogram.*

Mattel's interest in models with "play value" led Monogram to produce its first model boats in more than a decade and its first modern warships ever. In 1970 Monogram released the aircraft carrier USS *John F. Kennedy*, destroyer USS *Brooke*, and frigate *Halsey* (PB234, PB235, PB236). Each of these models was sixteen inches long, and thus they were not in scale with each other. This was a tip-off that the models were not intended for serious modelers. Each ship had a system of gears that turned all its missile launchers when you twisted the range finder. However, the models were reasonably well detailed, and in coming years Monogram would enter the realm of model ships in a substantial way.

Monogram's simple sixteen-inch ship models (3000-3007 $8-30) came out under a variety of ships' names. The John Steel art on the boxes was better than the models inside. *Courtesy of Revell-Monogram.*

Mattel's toy salesmen felt that the existing scale models in Monogram's catalog could be edged over into the toy market if a way could be found to make the finished models playable. Every builder of model airplanes has at one time or another held a completed model in one hand and given it a couple of zooms through the air, accompanied by appropriate engine and machine gun noises. Mattel wanted to exploit this primal urge by creating a mechanical flight simulator that a boy could operate with a pilot's joy stick. Thus the order came down that Monogram would produce Skystick.

It turned out to be a disaster. "It was Pearl Harbor on Waukegan Road," said Ken Merker. The plan was to have a base console unit with a pylon at one end to hold any Monogram airplane model and a control stick at the other end that would direct the movement of the model. You could climb, dive, and bank the model, while gages on the base console indicated the flight attitude. The fundamental problem was that styrene plastic was simply not robust enough to withstand the stresses of the working features. When the first Skystick units were assembled, they simply would not work. In Merker's judgment, "We had about $50,000 worth of junk. It didn't work. Period."

However, Monogram had announced release of the product in time for the Christmas season, and it had to be produced—quickly. Bob Reder told Merker that he would just have to make it work, and sent Merker and the design staff scurrying back to work. "So we redesigned that sucker." Merker went to outside suppliers and called up every favor he had coming to get half the mold rebuilt in about three weeks time. Production went ahead, even though the mechanisms still functioned poorly. Fortunately, not many shoppers bought Skystick, so not many people were disappointed.

Serious aircraft modelers were certainly disappointed during the 1970 through 1972 period when Mattel marketed Monogram's model kits. Essentially Monogram stood still, selling the same aircraft kits that had been in its catalog in 1969, without even changing the box art. The lone exception was a 1/72 scale model of the F-14 Tomcat Navy fighter, and it more closely resembled a toy than a scale model. *Scale Modeler* (July 1972) judged it "not up to the usual quality known to Monogram kits." It was easy to assemble, and the operating swing-wings were fun, but the little Tomcat lacked the fine detail of an authentic model.

The 1/72 scale F-14 Tomcat (5992 $4-6) box includes a plug for the ill-fated Sky Stick (5901 $35-45). *Author's Collection.*

The same thing happened in cars—at least so far as serious car modelers were concerned. Roger Harney could only gnash his teeth as he watched new MPC and AMT car kits appear on hobby shop shelves. One significant exception was the Snake vs. Mongoose series of dragster car kits. The rivalry between The Snake, Don Prudhomme, and The Mongoose, Tim McEwen, had been ginned-up by Mattel as a way of promoting sales of Hot Wheels cars. (Monogram had trademarked "The Snake" name for its Bill Koster-designed slot car, but Besser and Reder were happy to surrender the name to Mattel.) Mattel arranged for Roger Harney to come out to California to photograph and measure Prudhomme's car. The first models to come out, a pair of funny cars (6762, 6763), turned out well and looked really sharp with their elaborate decal treatments. Pruhomme's Barracuda and McEwen's Duster had body shells that looked like the fiberglass ones used on real funny cars, without door handles or panel lines. They shared a common, accurate chassis. This first pair was followed the next year with a set of Snake vs. Mongoose front-engine rail dragsters (5694, 5695), and the succeeding year by a set of rear-engine dragsters (7528, 7529). These models helped Monogram establish a foothold in the modern car category, but nothing more would be done so long as Mattel deflected Monogram's product selection away from accurate scale models.

The Snake vs. Mongoose series included a front engine rail (5694 $60-70) and a rear engine rail (7529 $25-30).

The big 1/16 scale Goin' Buggy (5990 $60-70) gave builders the option of two snap-on body styles—custom bug or dune buggy.

Symptomatic of Monogram's alienation from the hobby industry and its values was Monogram's decision to separate itself from the 1971 Hobby Industry Association annual meeting in the Sherman House Hotel and set up a separate exhibit in a nearby hall to show both models and Mattel toys. At the same time Monogram stopped advertising in the hobby industry trade journals and in hobby magazines. This went on for almost three long years, then in the fall of 1973, zooming to the rescue, came a big, black F-82 Twin Mustang with all the correctness and detail that had been hallmarks of Monogram's earlier models. *Scale Modeler* (April 1974) called it a "pretty darn good model" that could be built either as a F-82G night fighter or F-82E escort fighter. "Signaled by a collective sigh of relief from modelers everywhere, Monogram is back," announced *Scale Modeler*. "Like the Phoenix, Monogram has risen from the ashes," wrote Richard Marmo in another issue of *Scale Modeler* (October 1974).

What had happened? "A most unusual thing," according to Bob Reder. He and Jack Besser had been summoned to California for a meeting with Mattel CEO Ruth Handler, and she explained: "You fellows won't believe what I'm going to say. We thought we knew more about marketing hobby kits than you did. We were wrong." It turned out that Mattel's team of salesmen, quite understandably, had primarily pushed Mattel's large line of toys, with Monogram's smaller range of hobby kits trailing behind, almost as an afterthought. There was no instinctive enthusiasm among the Mattel sales staff for models. Naturally, the experiment in joint toy/hobby marketing failed. So Handler asked, "Would you like to take back control of marketing and new product selections?" They certainly would.

Jack Besser got busy rebuilding a sales force. He also wanted to bring the company back within the fold of the hobby industry—"to reintroduce Monogram to the distributors and dealers with whom we have lost contact." He added, "One of the most important facets in this building process is re-establishing the quality aspect of the Monogram name." Advertising again became a responsibility of the staff at Morton Grove. Bob Reder gathered the engineers, model makers, and tool men together and announced: "We are going back into the model business again."

Symbolic of a break with the recent past was a drastic change in the look of Monogram's packaging. In 1972 kits began to appear in clean, modern white boxes with photographs of the built kits on them rather than painted illustrations. Actually, the revolution in packaging was partly dictated by Mattel, which ordered Monogram to use photos on kit boxes just as Mattel did on toy packaging. Graphics director John Cather and his staff came up with the idea of placing the photos on all-white boxes. Cather knew that Monogram's in-store displays of built models were a tremendous selling tool, and he felt that the photo boxes with nicely-built models would also present the models to potential customers attractively. Both the displays and the boxes showed buyers what a well built model would look like. (Cather recalled that the "truth in packaging" law was not a factor in the decision to go to photos on the boxes.) However, Cather realized that photos of built models lacked the dynamics of a painted illustration. There was no action—the models just sat there. This was particularly noticeable with aircraft and ship models.

To harmonize with the new white photo boxes, Cather's department designed a contemporary Monogram logo. The old original Four Star Monogram trademark had evolved during the 1960s into a slightly cleaner company emblem. Each series of models had its own symbol: a boy holding a built model of a car, aircraft, ship, tank, or rocket. Yet the logo still had a distinctly 1950s flavor. The new trademark featured three bold red-white-and-blue bars with the "Monogram" name imprinted across them in black. It was a fine banner for Monogram Models, Inc. to carry into the 1970s.

The F-82G Twin Mustang (7501 $6-8) announced Monogram's return to serious scale modeling.

In the 1970s the Stuka's (6840 $8-10) box photo and decal sheet included the swastika, but in 1979 Mattel ordered Monogram to erase swastikas from all box art and decals—even the kill marks on Allied planes. Lou Drendel's box art Stuka from 1983 (6840 $8-10) flies without Nazi markings.

## Chapter 6

# The Tom Daniel Years

One day in 1967 a "to whom it may concern" letter came across the desk of Bob Reder from a man in California who wrote to say that he had some terrific ideas for new Monogram models. Monogram was bombarded with hundreds of such letters every year, but Reder was intrigued enough by this one to walk the letter over to Roger Harney for his opinion. Harney immediately recognized the writer of the letter, Tom Daniel, as the artist for *Rod & Custom* magazine's "Off the Sketchpad" concept car feature. "This guy is good," Harney told Reder. Harney knew that nobody on Monogram's staff had the time or the creative flair to produce car designs like those Daniel was turning out for *Rod & Custom*. Harney suggested to Reder that perhaps Monogram could profit handsomely by contracting to exploit the design skills of a professional like Daniel.

A short time later Reder flew from Chicago to California and arranged to rendezvous with Daniel at an auto show in the Los Angeles Coliseum. For a couple of days the two men wandered through the exhibits looking at exotic cars and conversing about the requirements of model making. Then Reder gave Daniel an assignment: submit detailed design plans to Monogram for a new model kit. It was a modest proposal that launched a stunning new era in Monogram history.

Tom Daniel had been born and raised in the sprawling environs of Los Angeles during the hard times of the Great Depression. His family were just working folks; so life taught him some tough lessons about hard labor. But the Southern California hot rodders and car customizers in his neighborhood also taught him about fun and excitement. From the time he was a little kid, he loved to make pencil drawings of cars, and he soon realized that he possessed a genuine talent for drawing. By the time he was in high school, he was winning prizes for his artistic sketches. He dreamed that maybe some day he could earn a living doing something exhilarating like designing cars. Then during his junior year in high school a "really hep art teacher" took his class on a tour of the Art Center School of Design in Los Angeles where Dick Locher had studied. Young Tom gazed at the pictures of futuristic car designs that lined the walls and said to himself: "Boy, that's what I want to do!" Suddenly his dreams for the future came sharply into focus. He spent every spare minute of his senior year in high school assembling a portfolio of automobile sketches to present to the Art Center. Normally the Art Center required its entering students to have two years of college under their belt before admission, but Daniel's portfolio impressed them, and they let the precocious youngster in directly from high school.

It turned out that Daniel's four years at Art Center became a demanding grind. He majored in transportation, learning the basic elements of industrial design. He didn't take as many courses in art as he might have, but he did master drawing, perspective, color theory, and the tools necessary for commercial illustration. One bright spot was the "side work" he did for Petersen Publishing, a company that produced car magazines. A friend who had worked for Petersen introduced him to the editorial staff, and Petersen paid him a generous $50 for every page of work they could use. During the summer breaks he, like most college kids, earned money by taking whatever jobs he could find. One summer he operated a skipshovel working construction.

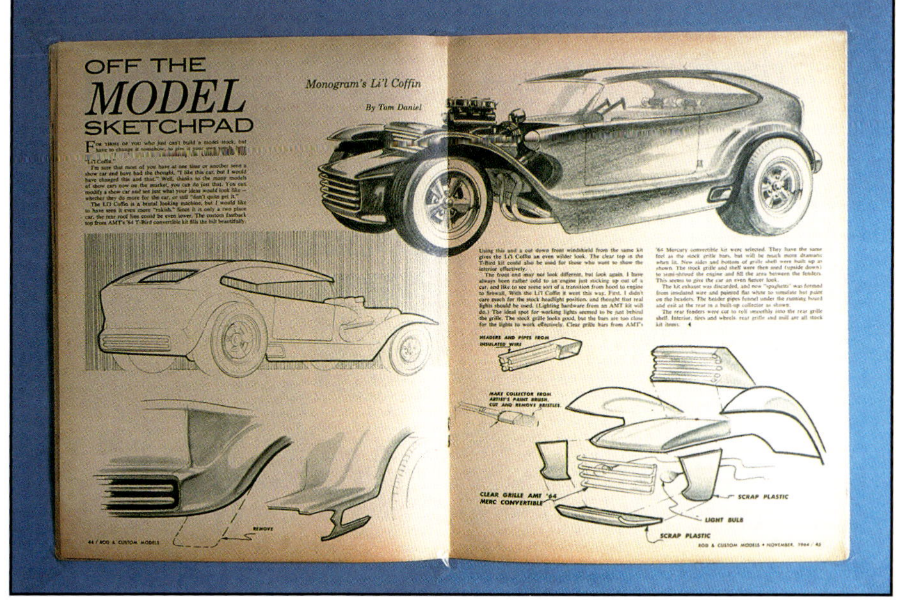


In the 1950s and 1960s Tom Daniel composed the "Off the Sketchpad" series for *Rod & Custom* magazine, and he did this modification of Monogram's Li'l Coffin for *Rod & Custom Models* (November 1964).

In 1955 Daniel's childhood dream became reality when General Motors' director of design Charles Jordan visited the Art Center and invited Daniel to join the GM team in Detroit. There he was put to work in the advance truck design studio where he conceived the hood that went on Chevy and GMC trucks for the '61-'66 model years—and that later showed up on the Monogram S'Cool Bus (6781).

Tom Daniel ponders one of his most famous creations, the S'Cool Bus (6781 $125-130).

Though Tom loved the exciting and highly stimulating work atmosphere at GM Styling, after barely a year and a half, family problems compelled him to return to the West Coast, ending his promising career as a General Motors stylist. Shortly after his return to the West Coast, Daniel, a U. S. Naval Reservist, was called to active duty during the Cuban Missile Crisis, serving with anti-submarine Squadron VS-772. After serving an eleven month tour of duty, Tom was honorably discharged and quickly took a position as design engineer with North American Aviation's Space and Information Systems Division plant in Downey, California, to begin working on the Apollo moon project. Then one day GM's Charles Jordan drove up in a red Pontiac convertible and asked Daniel if he would like to return to Detroit, but by then he had three children, and in one of those singular life-altering decisions Daniel decided to remain in California.

During this time Tom renewed his contacts with Petersen Publications and resumed his "Off the Sketchpad" design work and made other contributions to such magazines as *Rod & Custom*, *Rod & Custom Models*, *Car Craft*, *Hot Rod*, *Sports Car Illustrated*, *Power Boat*, and even *Guns & Ammo*. From time to time Daniel would write and illustrate a feature article on plastic model car kits or slot cars, sometimes showing how a stock model could be customized into something really special. Once he even did a box illustration for Revell—their '57 Chevy hot rod kit (H-1284) issued in 1963. Eventually he got to thinking about designing his own models right from scratch. One idea he began kicking around was taking a big version of those German military helmets that were popular with surfers and grafting it onto a T-bucket hot rod. This led him to "dash off" a letter to Monogram Models saying that he had ideas for some car models, although actually the only specific model he had in mind was the German helmet T-bucket rod. Daniel's letter led to the fateful meeting with Bob Reder at the Los Angeles auto show, and the Daniel-Monogram partnership was launched.

Back in Morton Grove, the men at Monogram had been watching all the "goofy stuff" appearing on the show car circuit as the decade of the 1960s careened into its

Monogram's store displays were always first rate. The Beer Wagon (PC189 $65-75). *Courtesy of Mark Mattei.*

psychedelic phase. Roger Harney wanted Monogram to do something wild, but at the same time somehow "neater." Harney and Reder had been pondering what a customized Mack truck might look like; so as Daniel's first assignment, Reder instructed him to try his hand at redesigning a classic Mack Bulldog. Daniel went straight to work on the project, but it quickly became apparent that the model he was creating would turn out to be a behemoth thing. Too big for a standard car model. Reder and Harney put their heads together and told Daniel: "Make it pickup truck size." That did the trick, and in December 1967 the Beer Wagon (PC189) rolled into hobby shops. It was an easy kit for boys to assemble and looked really nifty when completed. Monogram started selling lots of them.

Tom Daniel came along just at the right time for Monogram. With the collapse of the slot car bubble, the company needed a new product that would sell in large quantities. A new generation of eight to twelve-year-old boys had come on the scene, and kits that were fun, kind of wacky—but not childish—might really grab their attention. With just one professional designer producing the concepts, a whole unified line of kits with a consistent "look" could be marketed. Let a boy fall in love with one "Tom Daniel" car, and he would want to buy each new one as it showed up on the store shelf.

But before you had a series, you had to have a second model car to follow after the Beer Wagon. Daniel explained his original inspiration of a German helmet hot rod, and Harney thought it seemed like something Ed "Big Daddy" Roth might do—and Roth's model car kits were putting up big sales numbers for Revell. So Monogram gave Daniel the go-ahead for what became the Red Baron (PC205). When it came out in January of 1968, the response from the kids was astounding. "It sold like crazy," declared Harney, "and reached one million in sales very, very quickly." No Monogram kit had ever done as well in the marketplace. Sales hit two million kits within two years. To celebrate, the men at Monogram held a little ceremony and presented Daniel with a gold plated Red Baron mounted on a polished wood plaque.

The Big Red Baron (PC219 $175-200) was twice the size of the original model and the kit included a skull in a German spiked helmet. *Courtesy of Tim Nolan.*

The second release of the Red Baron (PC212 $75-95) included a small model triplane. *Courtesy of Tim Nolan.*

The only trouble was that many young modelers wrote in to Monogram saying that there was a picture of a Fokker Triplane on the box top, but no model airplane inside. It was not really a complaint, but more of a request for something extra. So Ken Merker drew up the design for a little HO scale model airplane, Harney carved the pattern in lemon wood, and the tool makers copied Harney's parts into a beryllium-copper alloy mold. It was all quick and neat. By summertime Monogram had the Red Baron out with its companion triplane (PC212).

Syl Wisneiwski, Tom Daniel (holding his gold-plated Red Baron), Ken Merker, and Roger Harney.

Meanwhile Bob Reder had sponsored another of Monogram's morale-boosting in-house contests among the employees. This competition asked workers to come up with an original design for a new model kit. Master pattern modeler Joe Sojka captured first prize with his concept of a customized hot rod garbage truck. Reder then turned Sojka's notion over to Daniel to be transformed into a finished design. First Daniel altered the shape of the cab, then he added surfboards, a rock 'n roll band in the back, and a toothy chomp-chomp decal. When the Hobby Industry Association show rolled around in January 1968, Monogram's model shop boys created a big 1/6 scale display model for Monogram's parlor. Industry representatives who stopped by the booth were treated to music coming from the back of the Garbage Truck (PC206) ostensibly produced by a rock band fashioned for the show from Barbie Dolls.

The Garbage Truck (PC206 $75-95) was originally dreamed up by pattern carver Joe Sojka. *Courtesy of Craig Clements and Gib Grayless.*

Following the initial three models came the T'rantula, Pie Wagon, and Paddy Wagon (PC190, PC192, PC217) on through the rest of 1968. The Tom Daniel line began to flow. Ken Merker warmly endorsed Daniel's designs: "He had some real fresh products. Things tend to go in cycles. Scale product [realistic models] was dying off and novelty product was picking up. His items were good. They were creative."

Daniel produced all these marvelous new car inventions from his modest home in the Southern California town of Walnut where he had turned a spare bedroom into a studio. Natural light entered only through one window, and even that light got cut down when he stuck a window air-conditioning unit into it. Daniel had constructed a large work table for himself from a hollow-core door, with drawers added to hold paints and sundry supplies. All his design drawings and illustrations were done on the same old ink stained eighteen by twenty-four inch portable drawing board that he had once carried to classes at the Art Center. The only drafting aid it possessed were metal strips running along the sides on which to position a t-square. At the start of each new project Daniel would tape on a fresh piece of railroad poster board to give himself a smooth surface on which to operate.

Work went on in the little bedroom/studio just about round the clock. Daniel later described himself as "young and eager," with a tremendous appetite for hard effort. "Work had been hard to come by, and I was glad to have a steady income."

The T'rantula (PC190 $100-125) included a small model of a spider. *Courtesy of Mark Mattei.*

The Pie Wagon (PC192 $100-125). *Courtesy of Mark Mattei.*

The decal on the store display of the Paddy Wagon (6741 $65-75) names the kit, while the actual decal in the kit reads "Police 3." *Courtesy of Mark Mattei.*

After the Beer Wagon and Garbage Truck designs, Monogram mostly left Daniel alone to come up with his own concepts for new model cars. The original inspiration for a new car design might come from anywhere. The Red Baron and Rommel's Rod (PC225) matured out of Daniel's long-standing "doodling" with German military hardware. Tijuana Taxi (PC222) was inspired by the taxis Daniel encountered on his trips south of the border. Sometimes a song might conjure up a mental image of a car, or sometimes Daniel would think of a really neat name for a car and then design a car to fit the name. Or the image of the car might come first and a name would have to be found for it later. Monogram gave Daniel freedom to let his creative imagination soar, and the results were a dazzling array of distinctive and clever auto models. Daniel enjoyed doing the work because nobody was imposing limits on his creative impulses. "I was just free to roam generally."

Rommel's Rod (PC225 $250-325) is a highly desirable kit because it has not been issued since the mid-1970s. *Courtesy of Revell-Monogram.*

The Tijuana Taxi (PC222 $250-300) is just plain fun. *Courtesy of Tim Nolan.*

The first step in the development of a new model would be for Daniel to freehand a three-quarter view color sketch—like the "Sketchpad" styling concepts—and send that off to Monogram to get approval to go ahead. Once Monogram gave the OK, the hard work began. The actual design process was long and arduous. "It was more agony than ecstasy," Daniel admitted. "There is no formula for the creative process," he said. "I don't think of the process. It is an abstract term." He would begin by laying down some perspective drawings: three-quarters from the front, three-quarters from the rear. If these didn't look right, he'd start over or perhaps just alter some lines. When the look was right, he would begin to make some scale design drawings, working in 1/12 scale, twice the size planned for the final model. Now things got serious because these drawings were intended to go to Monogram, and you were dealing with hard realities, not fanciful sketches. Geometry determined changes to the design. How far could a windshield wrap? How high should a fender rise? Often he would overlay his drawing with tissue paper to sketch-out possible changes and see how they worked. "The third time was usually the charm," he found. When the preliminary drawings were completed, Daniel would draft a hard-line final copy on quality vellum paper.

The Sand Crab (PC231 $125-150) came mounted on a sand dune base. *Courtesy of Mark Mattei.*

The Dragon Wagon (PC228 $250-325) can never be reissued since the production mold was reworked to create the Hangman (2208). *Courtesy of Mark Mattei.*

Just how long this process took varied widely. "Some things are just serendipity," explained Daniel. "Some things just fell together." Other times it was harder to force it all together. Usually it took about a month to complete a design. However, most of the time Daniel had several car model projects in various stages of the development pipeline simultaneously, and he had to switch gears from one to another depending on which one was most crucial at the moment. Then sometimes, to meet a deadline, Daniel explained, "I had to drive all the way to the Los Angeles international airport at two o'clock in the morning with a bundle of stuff so they'd get them the next day."

What the Monogram staff picked up at O'Hare airport was a package containing a couple of "color styling concept" drawings like Daniel's "Sketchpad" renderings, four drawings showing views from the front, back, side, and top, and cross sections of the car's side profile. If there was an unusual detail part, Daniel would include a close-up drawing of it. These were turned over to Monogram's design team.

Bad Medicine (6055 $100-125) looks real bad! *Courtesy of Tim Nolan.*

Fast Buck (7533 $50-75) was the Jinx Express (6899) in blue plastic. *Courtesy of Tim Nolan.*

Bob Reder was Daniel's main contact with Monogram, but the nitty gritty details were handled by veteran engineer Syl Wisniewski ("Daniel was a pretty good designer."), model shop supervisor Roger Harney ("Daniel was an incredibly talented designer."), and kit engineer Ken Merker ("He wasn't giving you something that was impossible to tool-up and manufacture."). As things went along, Harney and Merker would place long distance telephone calls to Daniel ironing out details of kit development. For example, when working on the Tijuana Taxi, Harney told Daniel that Monogram already had a Pontiac engine in its mold inventory; so Daniel agreed that the Pontiac mill was fine for the model.

Merker had the task of transforming Daniel's drawings into the engineering blueprints that the model makers would use to carve the parts of the model kit. Merker found that Daniel was easy to work with. If some part of a Daniel design was going to prove difficult to pull from a production mold, Merker would phone Daniel and ask for an alteration. Pretty quickly Daniel picked up on what was doable from the industrial standpoint. Merker was required to complete design details such as the underside of the chassis, suspension, and engine. He also came up with the parts breakdown and assembly—something that he just had a talent for. Monogram's car models were renowned for easy, logical construction and for snug part fit.

Ice T (6757 $50-75). *Courtesy of Mark Mattei.*

Major Tom Daniel fan Tim Nolan gave his Smug Bug (6659 $125-150) a custom paint job. *Courtesy of Tim Nolan.*

When Merker completed his work, Harney would walk the engineering drawings to the model shop and turn them over to the model makers. He also let them have Daniel's color styling drawings so the model makers could visualize the final product they were supposed to come up with at the end of the process. Joe Sojka was the primary model maker, and he worked in 1/12 scale to carve the wood pattern. When all the parts had been patterned and approved, epoxy tooling casts were made for each wood pattern. Then these casts, along with engineering drawings, were turned over to the mold engineering department. There a pantograph machine would reduce the scale down to 1/24 as the engraving machine copied the tooling casts into the steel production mold. The final touch was a thorough polishing with a special diamond powder polish that gave the mold cavities a mirror gloss.

Tom Morgan considered the Devil Chopper (5989 $225-250) box cover one of his least favorite painting assignments. *Courtesy of Revell-Monogram.*

Daniel approved of what Monogram ultimately produced from his handiwork. "The engineers and model makers at Monogram are the best in the business," Daniel said in a 1996 interview. "They always were. ... They took special care with detailing parts and pieces so they looked like what they were supposed to be, and they fit right." (Davis 1996)

The King Chopper (PC224 $275-350). *Courtesy of Tim Nolan.*

However, Daniel's work was not finished when the plastic model kit itself was complete. He also volunteered to do the illustrations and graphics that would go on the model box. The painting for the box lid usually was one of the last elements of the kit to be produced, and as a result Daniel often found himself jammed up against the deadline to mail it off to Chicago. Painting was hard, slow work—but it had to be compressed into about a week's time.

Tom Daniel painted the box illustrations for most of his kits. The Cherry Bomb (6761 $100-125) *Courtesy of Revell-Monogram.*

Like most commercial illustrators, he painted on art board. The board would be about twice the size of the kit box. First he would paint the background using acrylics. Often the background would be just wet slashes of color. Then Daniel would use his own sketches and mechanical drawings as references for the image of the car. Sometimes he would trace the outlines on tissue paper and transfer the image to the art board. The car would be painted in gouache, the opaque watercolor most often used by commercial illustrators. Gouache flowed onto the board easily, and, if you wanted to change something, you could rub it out with a wet cloth. Daniel described his painting style as "free ... loose."

For most of his kits, Daniel designed the decals and sometimes contributed elements of the instruction sheets. He even did the lettering and graphics for the box. He would go to a commercial shop in Los Angles that stocked a variety of type faces and pick out a style that suited the car. Modernistic, old fashion, exotic. Once the side panels were laid out, it was time to send the box art off to Monogram. For all this art work Daniel received less than $600 per kit.

The Cherry Bomb (6761 $100-125) has a cycle on a surfboard-shaped trailer. *Courtesy of Tim Nolan.*

It took almost a year for a model car to go from a gleam in Daniel's eye to a plastic-wrapped model kit on a store shelf. Remarkably, despite the many opportunities for flare-ups over creative decisions, Daniel and the men at Monogram never had a serious argument over any of the Daniel cars.

The Horn Toad (5987 $175-200) was redesigned as the Rattler (2210 $125-150) *Courtesy of Tim Nolan.*

Twice a year Monogram flew Daniel to Morton Grove to meet with the staff and review what was going on. He had a chance to interact with the designers and model makers face to face. These were pleasant occasions because everyone spoke the same language and played a part in working toward the same goal. Monogram appreciated Daniel's creativity, and Daniel was pleased that Monogram had given him a chance to show off his talents.

Bob Reder and Daniel became fairly good acquaintances. Reder discovered that the muscular Daniel, like Jack Besser, was a physical fitness buff who enjoyed lifting weights. Daniel even tried out the exercise room in the Morton Grove plant.

Monogram's advertising department turned Daniel into a celebrity personality. His name and face went on the kit boxes. Company president Jack Besser told hobby industry leaders that Daniel's "fun cars" were the top selling kits in the Monogram catalog. The first run of a Daniel model would be a healthy 60,000 units. Daniel's reimbursement came from the modest royalty paid on each kit sold. He didn't get rich, but his expectations were modest. He never quibbled over the financial aspects of his partnership with Monogram. The greater payoff came from seeing his creations go out to millions of boys across America. Bob Reder was surprised to find that Daniel even had a following in Canada and Europe as well.

The Red Baron emerged as the signature model of the Tom Daniel line. It was so popular that Monogram cut a new mold directly from the original wooden pattern, this time maintaining 1/12 scale. The result was the Big Red Baron (PC219). Monogram even gave permission for a full-size Red Baron car to be built for publicity purposes. Bob Larivee of Promotins, Inc. had Chuck Miller of Styline Custom in Michigan build the car at a cost of $10,000. It won a prize at the Oakland Roadster Sweepstakes. Tom Daniel even got to drive it once.

The Horn Toad (5987 $175-200) was redesigned as the Rattler (2210 $125-150) *Courtesy of Tim Nolan.*

The small, snap-assembly Li'l Red Baron (6650 $100-125) was the final incarnation of the Red Baron concept.

The Red Baron theme was taken to one more extreme. On a visit to California, Bob Reder asked Daniel how Monogram might capitalize on the success of the Red Baron trademark. While discussing this at a Mexican restaurant, Daniel explained, "I thought we could do something fun with the chrome helmet and sketched out the skeleton 'ghost' design on a place mat." Daniel's ultimate design featured a grinning skull wearing a chrome-plated German spiked helmet mounted on an Iron Cross base. It stood about seven inches high. The designers at Monogram tried supporting it on springs to give it a bobblehead effect, but it was Ken Merker who came up with a rubber band mount that worked. Merker liked the little skull figure and thought Monogram missed a trick by not putting it up for sale in automotive shops and truck stops. He thought the Ghost of the Red Baron (6742) would look nifty bouncing in the back window of a car.

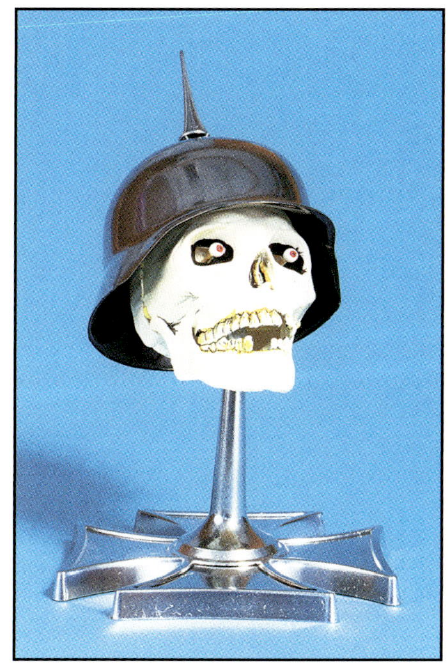

This example of the Ghost of the Red Baron (PC220 $350-450) has lost his tinted glasses. *Courtesy of Tim Nolan.*

Monogram sometimes sent Daniel out on promotional appearances where he could mingle with youngsters and listen to their excited talk about model building. He enjoyed reading the fan mail kids sent Monogram, but actually interacting with the boys who built his models was even more gratifying. They loved his cars, but many of the younger model builders expressed frustration at their inability to complete a model they could be proud of. Tube glue got smeared over everything. Chrome-plated parts wouldn't stick. The result was often a disappointing "glue bomb."

The Mojave Mule (2213 $30-40) was Tom Daniel's last design for Monogram. *Courtesy of Dean Milano.*

The first release of Tom Daniel's Badman (PC229 $75-100) came with a tinted windshield. *Courtesy of Tim Nolan.*

Daniel talked with Reder and conveyed the kids' frustrations. In response, the Monogram team came up with simple "entry level" kits that snapped together without any need for plastic cement. By the late 1960s several companies were already bringing out "snap together" models, so this was not a completely new innovation. Monogram felt that if first time modelers enjoyed success in their initial attempt at building a kit, they would try again and maybe catch the modeling bug.

It was Daniel's job to come up with a comprehensive vision for this new series of snap kits. He was long familiar with the idea of drawing a car in a distorted, lunging pose to give it an active, speedy look. This device had been used for years in comic strips and showed up in current advertisements for cars and tires. He also knew that caricatures of popular cars were being done by other model companies. So he put these two elements together and came up with Snap-Draggin's. His subjects were four popular cars: a Volkswagen, Dune Buggy, Corvette, and Mustang (6783, 6784, 6785, 6786). Each was reared-up in an "extreme pose" and mounted on a base shaped like the car's shadow. They snapped together easily (but not as snugly as Monogram's later snap kits). All four models came from the same production mold. Monogram would first produce an injection-molded run in red plastic, then switch to yellow, green, and blue for the following runs. Thus each car ended up being produced in all four colors.

Monogram's 1970 catalog highlighted Tom Daniel's designs in the Li'l Red Baron (6650 $100-125) and the base of the First Lunar Landing (6872 $25-35). *Courtesy of Dean Milano.*

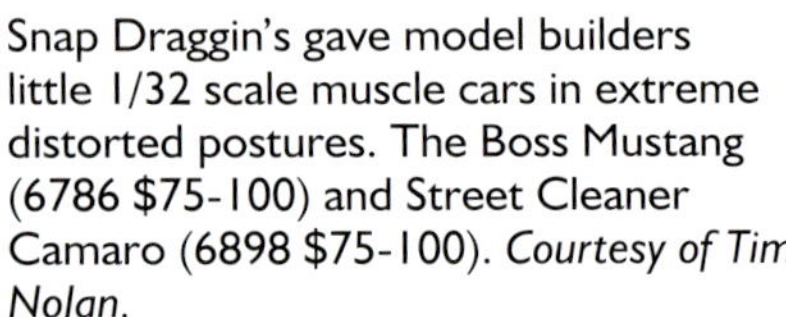

Snap Draggin's gave model builders little 1/32 scale muscle cars in extreme distorted postures. The Boss Mustang (6786 $75-100) and Street Cleaner Camaro (6898 $75-100). *Courtesy of Tim Nolan.*

The Snap Draggin's Super Nova (6896 $75-100) and Screamin' Vette (6785 $75-100). *Courtesy of Tim Nolan.*

By this time Monogram had been purchased by Mattel, and the giant toy company had entered its ill-fated three year attempt to sell model kits the same way they sold toys. Mattel loved Snap-Draggin's because they were an easy crossover product from hobbies to the realm of toys. With lots of push from Mattel, the Snap-Draggin's sold very well.

To build upon the success of the first set of Snap-Draggin's, Monogram issued another set of four in 1971. These were the Roarin' Rail dragster, Hemi Semi truck, Super Taxi Chevy Nova, and Street Cleaner Z-28 (6892, 6895, 6896, 6898). Daniel actually liked the first set a little more than the newcomers. Then the following year the Snap-Draggin's added another foursome set that included two cute little versions of his classic Red Baron and T'Rantula (6650, 6651). These were accompanied by the Leap Hog ATV and Roar 'n Peace cycle (6652, 6653). Only these last two came with driver figures, and the mustached rider of the Peace cycle waved the two-finger V peace sign. It was that time in American history.

The Leap Hog ATV (6652 $75-100). *Courtesy of Tim Nolan.*

In the history of Monogram this was the Tom Daniel era. By 1972 Daniel's models occupied six of the twelve pages in Monogram's section of the Mattel catalog. Partly this was due to Mattel's high comfort level with the Daniel models, which appealed to younger kids, and partly it was due to Mattel's inability to connect with the traditional universe of the hobbyist. In 1969, the final year in the '60s that Monogram printed a catalog separately from Mattel, there were 129 models listed, and only four of them were by Daniel. By the time of the 1972 catalog, the last done as a part of the larger Mattel catalog, the ratio had changed dramatically. The Daniel kits had risen to 54, while the other kit offerings dropped to just 97. Daniel later recalled Bob Reder once telling him that his cars produced 42% of Monogram's sales revenue at one point in time. If Daniel's recollection is correct, this must have been the time.

Harney and Merker agreed that Daniel's contribution to Monogram had a major impact on the company's financial success—although neither man was privy to Monogram's account books. Harney felt that Daniel's cars bailed Monogram out of a financial slump after the collapse of the slot car boom. "The Daniel items came at just the right time for Monogram," Harney explained. Merker's judgment was even stronger: Daniel "may have saved Monogram after the debacle of the slot car crash."

Draggin' Fly (6658 $150-175) came in response to Mattel's request for models with play potential. Monogram's serious model staff hated it. *Courtesy of Tim Nolan.*

Mini-bikes were popular in the 1970s; thus Popper Chopper (7534 $50-75). *Courtesy of Revell-Monogram.*

But there was still more to come from Daniel. In 1973 the Snap Draggin's series gained yet another set of four kits. This time they were caricatures of construction equipment in a thrust-forward action pose. Mattel had suggested the theme, and Daniel grabbed a hold and ran with it. Daniel later confessed that as a young boy he was possessed by "a fascination for construction things." He scraped play roads in the dirt of his back yard with a scratchbuilt grader, and then graduated to a full-size skipshovel during his art school days. He turned his interest and experience into the Boss Bulldozer, Extreme Shovel, Mountain Mover, and Screamin' Skipshovel (5690, 5691, 5692, 5693).

These little snap kits were cute, but two other pieces of construction machinery, the Groovy Grader and Unreal Roller (5697, 5698), permitted Daniel to do a bit more by moving up to Monogram's standard 1/24 scale size. The Groovy Grader earth scraper was a real laugh-out-loud model because Daniel didn't have to change the basic shape of the grader to turn it into a rail dragster. Anybody looking at it for the first time would have to think something like: "That's absurd—but why didn't I see the resemblance before?" The Unreal Roller, with its metal driver's seat sticking out in back and chromed rollers, had its own charming incongruity. Yet, still, one had to think, "I wonder just how fast a steam roller could turn a quarter mile?" The Daniel models *were* just fun.

Another suggestion coming from Mattel requested something in the way of a railroad locomotive. Daniel loved the chance to do a model along this line because he was a tremendous railroad enthusiast and HO model railroading hobbyist. When he submitted his preliminary sketches of the Honest Engine (6656) to Roger Harney, Monogram's model shop supervisor exclaimed, "What are you doing?" When the model came out, serious car modelers—who were accustomed to cutting Daniel some slack—thought this item was just plain silly—with no redeeming values whatsoever. Daniel's responded to the criticism by saying that this was one model he designed to please himself. "I did it for me," he explained, and if the little dragster-locomotive didn't suit other folks' fancies, that was just tough.

Some Snap Draggin's were hard working construction equipment. Mountain Mover (5692 $75-100), Screamin' Skipshovel (5693 $75-100), and Extreme Shovel (5691 $75-100). *Courtesy of Tim Nolan.*

Unreal Roller (5698 $150-175) was built to about 1/24 scale. *Courtesy of Tim Nolan.*

Tim Nolan gave his Honest Engine (6656 $125-150) unique Tom Daniel decals. *Courtesy of Tim Nolan.*

Daniel's next project once again tested modelers' tolerance for the aberrant. Mattel had brought an undeveloped idea to Monogram for a toy-like model airplane with wings that flapped like a bird's wings. Syl Wisniewski went to work putting together the electric motor and nylon gears that would comprise the innards of the model, but nobody had any idea what kind of plane to put the motor inside. When Daniel came by the plant, Wisniewski showed him the guts of the project and asked, "Can you do something with this?" Reder turned the design over to Daniel with the instructions: "It is a spoof. Do anything that will make it more spoofy." Back home in California Daniel got to thinking of an old comic strip called "The Heap" about a World War I German pilot who crashed into a swamp and eventually emerged as a monster who flew a swampy aircraft with birdlike wings. What ultimately emerged from Daniel's drafting table was a totally preposterous airplane with an oval fuselage, swept-back wings trailing feathered edges, a jet vent pipe in back, and a hot rod V-8 engine in front—complete with blower and eight exhaust stacks—to power the four-blade prop. Joe Sojka turned Daniel's ideas into a model pattern. The model was mounted on a black silhouette base shaped like a supersonic pigeon.

The boys back at Monogram figured out how to gear the model's single motor to move the plane's two machine guns in recoil action. As they were working on it, they discovered that the wire armature on which Daniel had mounted it worked fine as a stand because you got a nice weird bouncing movement from the action of the motor. Merker thought it was all very clever, but he warned, "It was one of those things you had to be very careful building. It was very unforgiving of mistakes." When the "Air Farce" Flapjack hit the market, aviation buffs loved it. It became a big seller for Monogram over a number of years. "It was so much fun," summed-up Bob Reder. Daniel's only regret was that Monogram never saw fit to release a Navy version of the plane.

Only once did Monogram reject a Daniel concept. One time he sent them prospective sketches of a heavyset police patrolman on a motorcycle styled like a kid's tricycle. Daniel dubbed him "Top Cop." The decision makers at Morton Grove showed it to some policemen to solicit their reaction, and when they didn't appreciate the humor, Monogram nixed the idea.

In spite of Daniel's association with such wonderful nonsense, he had been doing "serious" car designs for Monogram nearly from the start. Sometimes Daniel approached a new model project with the attitude, " What if we did a real car?" In these cases he worked just as he had been taught at the Art Center and GM, as if he were designing a car that might someday ride on the highway. The Chevy panel van Street Fighter (6752) of 1970 could have been built into a full size car, and the Chevy El Camino funny car Troublemaker (8283) of a few years later would also have been possible to make in the world of full scale vehicles.

Flapjack (7503 $75-100) looked great and really worked great too. *Courtesy of Tim Nolan.*

Tom Daniel gave Street Fighter (6752 $125-250) a red-tinted clear roof so you could see inside. *Courtesy of Mark Mattei.*

Street Fighter (6752 $125-250) evolved into Quicksilver (2202 $100-125) and then into Bad Actor (2267 $25-35). *Courtesy of Revell-Monogram.*

One Tom Daniel model did depict a real full size car: Daniel's own Corvette. He had applied and reapplied some custom styling tweaks to personalize it—first calling it "Piranha" and then "Puma." To produce the model, Roger Harney used some photos of the Daniel car, but made use of his own '70 Corvette for the photo shoot and measurements. The finished model went into the catalog as the California Street Vette (7504). The next time Daniel visited the Morton Grove plant, Bob Reder and the staff surprised him with a diorama done by Shepard Paine showing a little 1/24 scale Tom Daniel washing his car. It was a great diorama.

Monogram also employed Daniel to revamp some of their existing scale model cars, using him as a styling consultant, much as Starbird had done in years before. Daniel found it was much quicker to modify an existing car than to start one from scratch. For these projects Monogram would send him an example of the kit and some photos of the built kit. His first redesigns were a trio of the company's best beloved Ford models, the Little "T," Blue Beetle pickup, and Little Deuce (PC92, PC93, PC132). These were reissued in 1970 as Sweet "T"EE, Boss 'A' Bone, and Son of Ford (6756, 6755, 6754). These cars had originally been made during the Darryl Starbird era. Mainly Daniel added new engines, as well as finish parts such as exhaust pipes, wheels, and such to bring them up to current hot rod standards. It was a way for Monogram to extend and refresh the life of some old favorite sets of tooling.

During the decade of the 1970s the modeling world plunged into dragsters in a big way. Both funny cars and rail dragsters entered the lines of several model companies, with Revell enjoying the greatest success. However, Monogram actually beat Revell to the punch with a couple of large 1/12 scale drag models that had the added feature of battery powered gismos. The Mean Maverick (6775) came first in 1970. It used a little foot pedal to activate a motor that tilted the body up and reved the engine. Monogram president Jack Besser mandated the Maverick body. Besser was not a car guy, and he was not normally in the model development loop, but his daughter drove a Maverick—so he wanted a Maverick model.

Tom Daniel's own car was the California Street Vette (7504 $100-125). *Courtesy of Tom Daniel.*

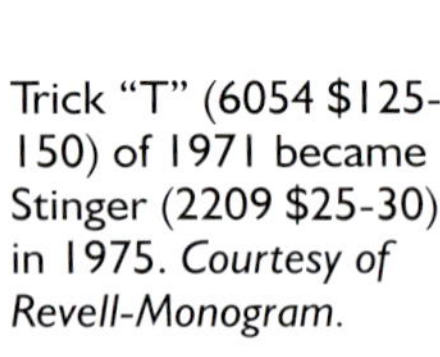

Trick "T" (6054 $125-150) of 1971 became Stinger (2209 $25-30) in 1975. *Courtesy of Revell-Monogram.*

Mean Maverick (6775 $325-375) had an electric motor to lift the body when you pushed the foot pedal. *Courtesy of Dean Sills.*

The next year Monogram showed Daniel a miniature drag chute that popped open and asked him to design a car to put it in. The Super Digger (5991) was even more elaborate than the Maverick. It sat atop a large base that held the electric batteries and motor that lifted the rail to wheelie angle, spin the rear wheels, and send the four-panel chute springing out from the rear end. These may have had some appeal as novelties, and Mattel no doubt thought they could sell them in toy stores, but serious modelers weren't interested in the power gimmicks.

Along the way, Monogram put Daniel to work on a few unusual design projects that seemed suited to his aptitudes. Snoopy and His Bugatti (6894) and Snoopy's nemesis The Red Baron and his Fokker Triplane (5903) seemed natural enough applications of Daniel's talents. However, using Daniel to design the base for the car-in-a-bottle kits (7547, 7548) might seem strange until you realize that such a task would be a bread-and-butter assignment for an industrial designer. Daniel also devised the lunar landscape diorama for the Tranquility Base (6872) Apollo lander model. One day while he was visiting the design shop at Morton Grove, the boys showed him photographs of the lander on the moon, and he noted the stark shadows. He knew that normal indoor lighting would not create that kind of otherworldly effect; so he included "shadow" indentations in the moon base that could be painted black to represent the shadows of the lunar lander and its equipment. "Daniel had a knack for that kind of stuff," noted Bob Reder. Thus when Reder built a new home, he asked Daniel to formulate the landscaping for it too.

Super Digger (5991 $350-400) was an attempt to interest 1970s youngsters with electronic gadgetry. *Courtesy of Dean Sills.*

Snoopy & His Bugatti (6894 $60-75) was designed by Tom Daniel. *Author's Collection.*

Tom Daniel's run as a major player at Monogram lasted about a decade. By the mid-1970s sales of Daniel-label model kits started to fall off, and rather than bringing out new cars, Monogram asked Daniel to redesign some of his original models. It was an opportunity to give them new life. For example, the old Sand Crab (PC231) from 1969 became the Li'l Van (7532) in 1973. In a radical makeover, the Dragon Wagon (PC228) of 1969 became the Hangman tow truck (2208) of 1975. So it went. "The Daniel cars were starting to cycle out a little," explained Harney. Public tastes were changing, and on the nation's highways such things as flower power vans were seldom seen. Merker agreed with Harney that the Daniel craze had simply run its course. "You can only do so many. You can only be so original after a while." By the early 1980s a typical Monogram catalog might list only two or three Daniel cars, and these would be the more serious ones like the classic '55 Chevy Badman.

Then in the mid-1980s Monogram began to cycle some of the Tom Daniel creations back in again. By 1987 seven of Daniel's old now-classic designs were back on the sales lists—along with those old custom car standards the L'il Coffin and Boot Hill Express. A decade later, the 1990s saw another wave of Tom Daniel nostalgia. Daniel received fan mail from aging men declaring, "My kids love these as much as I did when I was seven." In the future, Revell-Monogram can be expected to continue reissuing some old Tom Daniel blasts from the past.

Firecracker (5985 $125-150) was reissued as Fire Iron (7530 $50-75) with less extreme wheels and tires. *Courtesy of Revell-Monogram.*

Baja Beast (7527 $25-35) was a reworking of Baja Bandito (6759), Hangman (2208 $75-95) radically changed the Dragon Wagon (PC228), but Vandal (6657 $75-100) was a new design. *Courtesy of Revell-Monogram.*

## Chapter 7
# Things Get Serious

Tumultuous times hit America in the 1970s—Vietnam, Watergate, high inflation, high unemployment—and Monogram did not escape the turbulence. The Arab oil embargo of the early 1970s led not only to long lines of cars at gas stations but also to a scramble among toy and hobby companies for supplies of plastic. For a while it was difficult for anyone to find quantities of top quality styrene. Roger Harney remembered, "We had to take what we could. We had no other choice. It drove Bob Reder nuts." Monogram, which had prided itself on using only top quality plastics, had to make do with whatever plastic was available. Reder set up a program to recycle used plastic—of all colors and quality—but this was hardly a satisfactory answer to the problem. The most visible result to outsiders was that some kits appeared in oddball colors. Fortunately, the oil/plastics shortage turned out to be short lived, although it did lead to a permanent increase in the cost of plastic.

A more profound, longer term worry for model companies was the leveling off of growth in model kit sales. Dick Mayer, Mattel's marketing director, told hobby leaders that model kits just didn't appeal to the vast majority of modern boys and that fewer than half the boys who received models as gifts finished building them. Some parents were afraid to give models to children because of the glue sniffing scare. Moreover, the average boy, even the older ones, lacked the dexterity to build models. To overcome these drawbacks, Mayer explained, Monogram would be increasing its line of Snap-Tite kits pioneered with the Tom Daniel Snap-Draggins. Mayer declared that follow-up surveys showed kids liked the simplicity of snap kits and enjoyed playing with them after they were finished. "Monogram is convinced," concluded Mayer, "it has successfully lowered by two to three years the age at which kids first begin modeling." (*Craft, Model, Hobby* March 1971)

The B-52 (8292 $20-25) emerged in the 1970s cleansed of its Vietnam War camouflage, with inspirational new art by Dick Locher. *Courtesy of Revell-Monogram.*

Some hobby veterans scoffed at the snap kits. Nat Polk, the godfather of the hobby industry, declared that simple snap assembly models belonged in toy stores. Geoffrey Wheeler figured, "A kid may build a model, but if he thinks it looks lousy, he's not going to be proud of it just because he made it. He's going to throw it in the wastebasket. So its not just the kids who don't finish kits that should worry us. We should be concerned about the people who do finish them but are unhappy with the results."

Nevertheless, Monogram pushed ahead vigorously with its Snap-Tites and found that by the end of the decade the growth of snap kit sales actually outpaced the expansion of regular glue kit sales. Of course, snap kits always occupied only a secondary position in Monogram's business, but they did appeal to customers who otherwise might not have purchased a model kit at all. Some of the snap kits were pitched at a play toy level for youngsters, but a second generation of snap assembly models incorporated a high degree of detail and were aimed at older boys and men who wanted a nice model of, for example, a sports car, but didn't have the time or inclination to assemble a traditional kit. Staff designer Bob Johnson judged the '84 Corvette (1405) as "without question the zenith of this series." In the model aircraft category, Monogram's snap B-25B (1100) and B-26B (1101) were actually more accurate than the "serious" models that other companies had issued earlier.

By the 1980s Snap-Tite models were a major category of Monogram's product line. The Forest Ranger Chopper (1025 $4-6) and Fire Fighter Helicopter (1026 $4-6). *Courtesy of Revell-Monogram.*

The Patton Tank (7578 $8-10) and Tiger Tank (7579 $8-10) in 1/48 scale. *Courtesy of Revell-Monogram.*

Roger Harney holds up the '84 Corvette kit (1405 $8-10) while sitting in the real thing at a hobby show. *Courtesy of Roger Harney.*

At the same time that Monogram advanced on the snap assembly front, it continued to bring out innovative new scale models for serious hobbyists. In 1975 it took a major gamble on a big 1/48 scale kit of a B-17G that would build out to a model nineteen inches long, with a wingspan of twenty-six inches. The cost of tooling such a kit would be tremendous. Was it possible to sell enough of these kits to justify the investment? Monogram had already gambled on big kits before, the 1/8 scale cars and the B-52 from a few years earlier, which was actually a little larger in size than the B-17. The sales department figured that the kit could pay for itself if the big retail stores would carry it as a big ticket item. Engineering said that the cost could be held down by keeping the part count low. So the B-17 got the go-ahead for development.

In search of reference material, Roger Harney made a blind phone call to Boeing in Seattle and reached their archivist. He laughed and said that, sure, he'd be happy to loan Monogram some materials. When it arrived, Harney was staggered. It included the company's illustrated parts breakdown book, the erection and maintenance manual, and the pilot's manual. Plus a four-inch thick stack of photos. Plus a huge one-quarter scale drawing of the interior of the B-17! This drawing went up on the wall of the design shop, partly as reference and partly as inspiration. Thanks to this detailed information, the model would be one of the most accurate ever produced. However, not much of the interior detail from the drawing went into the interior of the fuselage. There was not even a detailed bomb bay interior because its doors were molded solidly into the fuselage halves. "We got shot down on the tooling costs," lamented Harney. The model kit ended up with just seventy-four parts—compared to the B-52's 207 parts. Any ten to fifteen year old ought to be able to build it. To make Monogram's sales force happy, the Flying Fortress was released in August 1975 so that it would available in stores just in time for the post-Thanksgiving Christmas sales rush. And it cost only $8.50.

That fall the response from the general public was excellent, and the serious modeling community loved the big B-17 just as well. "The Monogram B-17G Flying Fortress in 1/48th scale is a modeler's dream," exclaimed *Scale Modeler* (December 1975). "This is an outstanding work of modeling art." Of course, serious builders noted that the flight surfaces were molded in place and could not be positioned in just the right attitudes to suit them, but nobody was going to quibble very much with the merits of this highly desirable kit.

Revell admired the model so much that it copied the parts for its own 1/48th scale B-17F "Memphis Belle" (H-197). Monogram drew up a point-by-point indictment of Revell's model, noting, among other things, that the Revell model was smaller than the Monogram original by precisely the amount of plastic shrinkage that occurs when a new mold is made by copying the parts of an existing model. However, Monogram never made an issue of the case, other than Bob Reder making a phone call to let Revell know that they should not do that again.

The B-17G (5600 $25-30).

Four years later somebody at Monogram came up with the bright idea of giving the B-17 a clear fuselage half so the interior could be seen. The Visible B-17 (5620) did not prove to be a good seller but got a brief issue in 2007 (5614). However, the original issue B-17G Flying Fortress demonstrated year after year that it could go the distance. It has remained in the Monogram and Revell-Monogram catalogs continuously since 1975, always under its original kit number 5600. In 2005 it passed the vintage B-25 (PA7) for honors as the Monogram kit with the longest continuous string of years on the market.

The 1/48 scale B-25J (5502 $15-20) built into an impressive-size model.

The release of the big B-17G in 1975 marked the return of painted illustrations to Monogram's kit boxes. Appropriately, Dick Locher provided the art. He was pleased that Monogram had restored painted art because it provided more "pizzazz" than a photo. However, John Cather retained photographs on the side panels to show what the built kit would look like and to serve as references for the model builder. Locher wrote some proposed side panel text for the B-17, sneaking in the line "Stuttgart not included." (However, that didn't make it into the final version!) Locker enjoyed working with Besser and Cather. "It was so much fun talking with the draftsmen and model makers. They were really good people."

By this time Locher was working as the editorial page cartoonist for the *Chicago Tribune*. He had been doing cartooning all his life, thinking that making people laugh is a worthy ambition. From a technical point of view, he didn't encounter any artistic difficulties switching gears from cartooning to illustration and back again. In fact, he felt that both required a lot of research and attention to detail. When he portrayed the mayor of Chicago as a Kamikaze pilot, he had to make sure the pilot's equipment was correct and the Zero accurate—although the plane had be a plumped a little to accommodate the mayor.

The year 1983 turned out to be an important one for Locher. First he was awarded the Pulitzer Prize for editorial cartooning, and then he took over production of the *Dick Tracy* comic strip. About this time the assignments to do new illustrations for Monogram stopped coming in. Locher could recall no particular reason for this, but model companies do like to rotate their artists in order to present a fresh look to consumers. Besides, Locher stayed busy with *Tracy* until 2011 and still draws *Tribune* cartoons today.

When Monogram returned to painted box art, Tom Morgan also returned. One of his memorable covers is the F-16s Thunderbirds Team (5504) from 1983. At an air show Morgan got the members of the Thunderbirds to autograph his copy of the kit. The pilots appreciated the art, but chuckled that the maneuver depicted wasn't in their repertoire. Morgan, of course, had been more interested in displaying the plane from different angles than in portraying an authentic maneuver. The Air Force took the original painting and placed it in their permanent collection in the Pentagon.

This was about the last box cover Morgan did for Monogram. He quit working for commissions and accepted a less hectic position as senior art director with a Chicago corporation. "Freelance art is OK when you're young," explained Morgan. However, he still contributed to the Air Force Art Program over the succeeding years. He recently recalled, "Even though my days of model box top art are long past ... today collectors still identify my early kits by the bullet holes in the aircraft! I get calls and letters about my box top art and what it meant to them when they were a lot younger."

Dick Locher's F-105 Wild Weasel (5806 $12-15) box art. *Courtesy of Revell-Monogram.*

Locher's box art for the V/STOL Harrier (5420 $8-10) kicks up dust and excitement. *Author's collection.*

Tom Morgan captures the drama of the Thunderbirds (5504 $12-16) in his cover painting. *Author's collection.*

## New Management

A few months before the B-17's release, Monogram underwent a momentous shakeup at the top: Jack Besser was let go as president of Monogram. The origins of this action can be traced, at least partly, back to developments at Mattel. Earlier in 1970 and 1971 Mattel had suffered a sharp decline in sales of its Hot Wheels cars, as well as an assortment of other financial setbacks. However, these significant decreases in profits did not show up on Mattel's public financial reports for many months due to some questionable bookkeeping procedures. When Mattel was finally forced to admit the losses, the Securities and Exchange Commission filed suit against the executives of Mattel, and this ultimately led to the dismissal of the Handlers from Mattel and their replacement by new management. The accounting irregularities at Mattel headquarters in California had absolutely nothing to do with Monogram in Illinois, but there was an indirect spillover that had a major impact on Monogram.

Arthur Spear became the new CEO of Mattel, and under his administration the independent-minded Besser was seen as no longer fitting in. One day in the late spring of 1975, Spear arrived at the Morton Grove plant in a Checker cab, stayed fifteen minutes, and left. He had come to personally inform Besser of his release. Shortly thereafter Besser called the department heads into a conference room and announced his immediate departure. There would be no ceremony to mark his leaving. Monogram's graphics director, John Cather, later recalled that he was working late in the evening at the plant, and Besser stopped by to say that he had just finished cleaning out his office and would not be back. "It was extremely sad," felt Cather. "Monogram was like one of his children." It had been almost three decades since Besser stomped sawdust into waste barrels in the tiny loft plant on South Michigan Avenue.

Many years later Besser expressed the opinion that the hobby industry had undergone vast changes by the 1970s. He recalled that in the old days the hobby business had been composed of many mom and pop companies run by people who deeply loved their craft. They maintained a friendly competition and managed to make a living doing something they enjoyed. Then hobby companies were taken over by larger corporations. Aurora was purchased by Nabisco; Revell was bought by a large French toy company. As the big companies moved in, the company founders were replaced: Abe Shikes and Joe Giammarino at Aurora, Royle Glaser at Revell, and so on.

Mattel cross-marketed its Hot Wheels toy cars with Monogram's model cars in quartet of 1981 Snap-Tite kits. The Turbo Mustang (1038 $10-15). *Courtesy of Revell-Monogram.*

In later years Besser kept up friendly social relationships with a few men he had known at Monogram, and he purchased Bob Reder's half ownership of the building at Morton Grove, thus becoming Monogram's landlord. Then on October 19, 2004, nearly thirty years after his departure from Monogram, he passed away at the age of eighty-nine.

The man who followed Besser as president of Monogram was Thomas A. Gannon, Jr. In several respects he represented a clean break with Jack Besser. Gannon took pride in declaring that he had never built a model kit in his life. He explained that he was a businessman, not a hobbyist, and he felt that too many hobby companies were run by men who were hobbyists first and businessmen second. His job, he avowed, was to make profits for the company, and he did not care about the company's products, except in so far as product selection impacted the company's financial bottom line. (In fact, he knew Monogram's model kit line very well, but he felt the product end of the company should mainly be left to Bob Reder and his lieutenants.) The first order of business, he announced, was to increase Monogram's production capacity, sales, and profits.

Tom Morgan painted the backdrop for the Classic Cars series of the 1970s. The Mercedes 540K Coupe (2304 $15-20). *Courtesy of Mark Mattei.*

The Classic Cars came in clean, white 1970s era boxes. The '31 Rolls Royce Phaeton (2303 $15-20) and Mercedes 540K Coupe (2304 $15-20). *Courtesy of Revell-Monogram.*

The Mack Truck appeared in four different guises. The Dump Truck (2400 $20-25), Log Hauler (2401 $20-25), Mack Bulldog (7537 $20-25), and Mack Tank Truck (7539 $20-25). *Courtesy of Revell-Monogram.*

Tom Gannon had an interesting life story. He learned to fly an airplane before he learned to drive a car. He grew up in Depression-era Chicago, and when his father wrecked the family car, he didn't think it was worth the money to buy another one because you could get around the city on public transport. After graduating from high school, Gannon went on to study business at Fordham University, working at Macy's Department Store in the summers where he enrolled in their executive training program. When World War II came along, he enlisted in the Army Air Corps and stuck around long enough to learn to fly before being washed out. For the rest of the war he served as an armaments officer in North Africa, Sicily, Italy, and France. After the war he became a toy buyer for Montgomery Ward, and by 1969 he was president of AMT, the model car specialists.

When Gannon came to Monogram, Mattel gave him a free hand to fire anyone he wished, but Gannon realized that Monogram had a core of excellent men in all phases of the model making and marketing business, so everyone stayed. Bob Reder discovered that Gannon knew more about hobbies than he let on. As Reder put it, "His experience with AMT reduced the time we needed to indoctrinate him." Gannon's main emphasis was on expanding the company. Investing the capital was a gamble, but Gannon was confident that it would pay off, and he persuaded Mattel to pour investment money into Monogram's operations. The executives at Mattel generally left Gannon alone to manage Monogram, and for his part Gannon was careful to attend monthly meetings at the home office in California to assure Mattel its Monogram subsidiary was producing healthy profits.

The British Grant Tank (7535 $20-25) is so ugly its almost loveable. *Author's collection.*

When Gannon arrived in 1975, Monogram stood fourth in sales among American model companies, trailing Revell, AMT, and MPC. Revell had always chased sales volume, not bottom line profitability, and it enjoyed almost twice the total sales of Monogram in 1978—$42 million compared to $24 million. Partly this was due to Revell's aggressive overseas marketing, while Monogram sold mainly within the United States. (*Business Week*, February 13, 1978) Gannon wanted to move Monogram up in the sales ranking and at the same time maintain Monogram's unbroken tradition of profitability. He announced that Monogram was going to bring out fifty new models a year. That meant increased spending for new molds, which Gannon knew would be an expensive proposition. "That's what made Monogram. They had the best reputation for quality in the industry," explained Gannon. The kits produced from new tooling would be augmented by refurbishing old models for reintroduction into the line. Some of Monogram's old hands doubted that this ambitious program could be achieved, but Gannon established strict production schedules and demanded that they be adhered to. Weekly production meetings kept tabs on progress and focused attention on the schedule.

The Armored Car came as both an M-8 (4100 $10-15) with a turret and an M-20 (4101 $10-15) with a machine gun on a ring mount.

During the decade before Gannon, 1966 to 1975, Monogram had issued or reissued an average of twenty-seven kits a year, with sixteen of them coming from new tooling. Through Gannon's final ten years at Monogram, 1976 to 1985, the company issued an average of fifty-two kits a year, with twenty-one of them coming from new molds. Gannon later estimated that when he arrived at Monogram its gross sales were in the eight to nine million dollar range and that by 1985 the figure had increased to thirty-two million dollars.

To handle this increased volume of sales, Monogram had to make innovations in the way it acquired production tooling. From the beginning some molds had been produced by outside shops, but now outside sources of molds became more important. Ken Merker, who had left Monogram for several years in the '70s, returned to take the position of Vice President of Tool Engineering, which gave him responsibility for mold design, procurement, follow-up, and mold maintenance. Sometimes that meant being chief "mold chaser." He worked for years to build relationships with several precision tool companies that could cut molds that met Monogram's exacting standards. "Making tooling for plastic model kits is altogether different from normal tooling," Merker explained. "There's a lot of black magic. There's art there. A lot of companies just can't do it."

As Gannon put it, one of the big problems was that tool making was a declining industry in the United States. Too many of the men in the business were over the age of forty. The number of shops was declining, and the cost of tooling was rising. To cope with this difficulty, back in his days at AMT, Tom Gannon had begun using a tool company in Hong Kong to make molds. Now Monogram started doing its mold building in the Orient, where production costs were one-half to one-third lower than in the United States. At first just the basic milling of the tool was done in Hong Kong, and then the mold would be brought to Chicago for the finishing touches. However, eventually Monogram turned the whole job of making aircraft molds over to the Hong Kong tool shop. Molds for car models were done in Canada by Modern Mold and Bernald, Ltd.

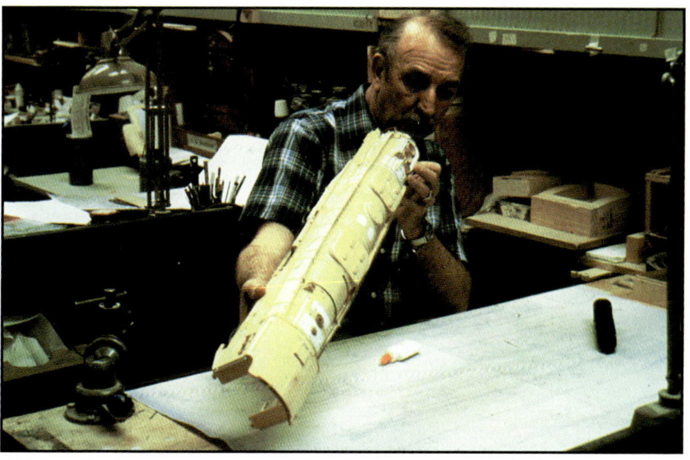
Ted Hobson carved the wooden pattern of the Hudson Locomotive (1107 $10-15) in twice the size intended for the model kit. *Courtesy of Revell-Monogram.*

The Hudson Locomotive (1107) was a simple snap-together kit, so that meant all the elaborate details of the locomotive engine had to be built into the production mold. *Courtesy of Revell-Monogram.*

When the first test shot of the Hudson (1107) came out of the injection molding machine, Monogram's craftsmen got to see how their labors turned out. *Courtesy of Revell-Monogram.*

The Hudson Steam Locomotive (1107) builds into a very respectable display model. *Author's collection.*

Once the molds were complete, Gannon wanted to put them to good use by accelerating the pace of production. He purchased new molding machines to replace the old, worn machines that had handled in-house molding for years and add to the total number of presses. By 1979 Monogram had forty-four injection molding machines pumping out trees of plastic parts. This was three times the former number of presses. They did their work in the molding room at the back of the plant, which was hot and noisy and smelled like molten plastic. Reder approved of the increased molding capacity at the plant because it allowed for greater control of production; however, Monogram still continued to use about a half dozen outside vendors to handle some of its molding needs.

After he became president of Monogram, Gannon changed the way the company purchased and used plastic. From its earliest days Monogram had bought pre-colored plastic that came in the form of pellets packed in bags. Workers had to fill the injection molding machines by climbing a ladder to the top of each individual machine and pouring in a fresh bag of pellets. Gannon wanted a more efficient way to feed the presses. Again, thanks to its Mattel connection, Gannon could negotiate a better deal on purchase of uncolored plastic in large quantities. Tall silos were erected at the side of the Morton Grove plant to store raw plastic in the form of milky white or crystal clear beads. From these silos the beads would be ducted through an elaborate system of pipes to "color blenders" where the raw plastic would be mixed with color pigments, and then this blend would be automatically fed into the injection molding machines.

Monogram imported one batch of motorcycle models from the small Japanese company Union. When that lot was sold, the cycle kits disappeared from Monogram's sales sheets. The Honda CBX (2410 $20-25), Kawasaki Z1R (2411 $20-25), and Kawasaki 2400 FX (2412 $20-25). *Courtesy of Revell-Monogram.*

In order to create space for the increased number of molding machines, the area formerly occupied by the packaging department was incorporated into the molding department. This could be done because Monogram opened a new facility in Des Plaines, six miles away from the Morton Grove plant, to handle packaging. The new building, christened Plant 2, opened late in 1978. It was actually larger than Morton Grove—a "gigantic warehouse" with offices located at one end. One manager used a bicycle to get from one end to the other. Kits would be packaged and warehoused at Des Plaines before being shopped out to customers. This ruthless mass merchandising approach had some downsides. Tom Daniel was upset that the front end of his beloved S'Cool Bus was cut off so that the kit would fit into a standard size box.

The Go Bots were popular Tonka toys, but no eight year old kid would have the skills or patience to build the model versions Tonka furnished to Monogram. Turbo (6069 $3-5) transforms from robot into Ferrari. *Author's collection.*

The Radio Controlled Tank (6970 $25-35) is an example both of a one-shot import from Japan and Monogram's consistent failure to find profitable products outside the realm of plastic assembly model kits. *Author's collection.*

Monogram took out this creative advertisement in a trade journal to announce the opening of its Des Plaines facility. *Model Retailer* (May 1979).

## Super Models

The makeup of the staffs in the engineering and model departments evolved over time. (By this time there was one female designer and one female model maker—both darn good.) One of the new guys in the engineering department was Bob Johnson. He was hired just before Christmas 1973 as a draftsman, but over the years he would come to play ever larger roles in the company. Like so many others, Johnson first arrived at Monogram in response to an advertisement in the newspaper. He had grown up in Western Massachusetts. In school he was the proverbial underachieving student who sat in the back of the room drawing cars and airplanes. However, this inclination led him to the Illinois Institute of Technology where he earned a degree in industrial design. From there he was off to a tour in the Air Force, serving as a maintenance officer for B-52s that flew missions out of Guam on bombing runs over Vietnam. After the Air Force it was a short step to Monogram.

Johnson liked working for Roger Harney and learning the ropes of model design. Harney was a Chevy guy who drove a Corvette, while Johnson leaned toward Fords. He recalled that the design and model area was a fun place to work, where a certain amount of good natured fun happened. Staffers had to be constantly on the alert for practical jokes. The squeaky door to the shop served as an early warning signal that someone was coming and everyone should be found in his place at his assigned task. However, it didn't take long for Johnson to feel restricted in the design studio. He knew he could do more than just draw, and he sought more responsibilities. Thus Harney assigned him the task of gathering the data needed for planned kits. Johnson was gifted with a hyperactive, outgoing personality that helped him gain access to people in the Air Force and executives with the car companies in Detroit who could furnish information needed to develop new model kits. By 1982 Johnson was product manager for the company.

Sometimes Johnson found himself working directly with Tom Gannon, who had a bluff, decisive manner that could be intimidating. "Gannon was a difficult man to work for," Johnson later recalled, "but he sure taught you a lot." Once after a heated discussion in the new products committee, Johnson was nominated by the committee members to visit Gannon's office and ask him to rescind a decision. When he presented his petition, Johnson remembered, Gannon slammed his palm on the desk and declared: "What do you think I'm running, a democracy?" But Johnson learned to appreciate Gannon's up-front, no nonsense approach to managing the company. It was all strictly business. Actually, Gannon welcomed fresh ideas and wanted the rough and tumble of open dissent. One of his sayings was, "Resistance makes the kite fly higher." But ultimately he made the decisions.

Because Gannon came to Monogram from AMT, some people assumed that he directed Monogram into the field of modern car models, but actually Gannon was not a car enthusiast and did not take the lead in product selection. The impulse for Monogram to begin making serious models of contemporary cars came more from Harney and Johnson—and from the brute fact that these were the kits that sold the most in stores. Gannon, of course, knew all this, and he felt that he had a good sense of what products would sell, so he fully supported the move toward serious modern cars.

Don Greer, noted for his illustrations for Squadron/Signal books, was one of the new artists who began to produce box art for Monogram in the 1980s. The Douglas AD-6 Skyraider (5429 $15-20). *Author's collection.*

Monogram launched what Johnson called an "exploratory effort" in 1976 with a dazzling array of a half dozen 1/24 scale modern-day foreign sports cars: a Porsche 911, Mercedes 450SL, Capri II, Datsun 280Z, Triumph TR7, and Porsche 924 (2101-2106). Monogram advertised them as "simplified" models that anyone with a casual interest in car models could build. They required cement, but had the attributes of large snap-together kits. Model car expert Phil Jensen was taken aback when he first got a look at one of these new cars. "Our initial reaction on opening the box was that plastic model car kitting had retrogressed by some twenty years. The parts were reminiscent of those early kits derived from factory 'promotionals.'" (*Model Retailer* November 1976) There were no opening hoods and no engines. The seats and interiors were molded into one large part.

In spite of their limitations, these "curbside" models looked great when assembled. Sales results confirmed the series was a success. Now Monogram was ready to go after AMT and MPC. The next generation of car kits would have opening hoods, detailed engines, and complete interiors—as well as options to build stock or street rod versions. Rather than trying to guess which contemporary 1970s cars might have staying power on hobby shop shelves, Monogram reached back into the 1960s to model two established muscle car classics: the '66 Chevrolet Malibu SS and '69 Camaro Z/28 (2219, 2220). The Malibu proved to be a breakthrough model, but to Roger Harney's dismay the Camaro "unfortunately, didn't come out so great." Nevertheless, these were quickly followed by a '57 Chevy and '57 Corvette (2225, 2227). To please the growing legions of truck modelers, there were a '55 Ford Panel and a '75 Chevy Stepside Pickup (2226, 2228). It amounted to an impressive entry into the serious car modeler realm.

Whenever Monogram brought out a new car model, it had a second version of the kit already planned for release a year of two later. The Porsche 911 (2101 $15-25) came out in 1976, and the Porsche RSR (2107 $15-25) followed in 1978. The Porsche 924 (2106 $15-25) was issued in 1977, and the Porsche 924 Group 4 (2112 $15-25) was released in 1978. *Courtesy of Revell-Monogram.*

The Capri in three guises. Capri II S (2103 $15-25), Capri Group II (2108 $15-25), and Capri II Rally (2120 $15-20). *Courtesy of Revell-Monogram.*

Monogram issued its popular Jeep CJ-7 in a variety of ways, but only briefly as the Mork & Mindy Jeep (2261 $20-25). *Author's Collection.*

On the model airplane side of the business, Monogram continued its program of bringing out a big 1/48 scale World War II bomber each fall. The follow-on to the B-17G was a B-24J (5601). Searching for reference material, Bob Johnson found a B-24 that had served in the Indian Air Force preserved at the Pima Air Museum in Tucson, Arizona. Continuing an old Monogram tradition, the mold was designed so that it could be converted to produce a B-24D (5604) in subsequent years.

The next two big bombers rolled out were a B-25H (5500) and a B-26 (5501). These two were designed by a newcomer, Clark Macomber, who had been hired in 1976 to help cope with the increased demand for new model output. Macomber was another local Chicagoan who, like Johnson, had graduated from the Illinois Institute of Technology. His previous work experience included package design for American Can Company and tenure as a design professor at North Carolina State. Macomber embodied the higher standards of design in model making that had come in by the mid-1970s. He made it a point never to rely on drawings that had been done by someone else, such as those appearing in secondary sources like magazines. Instead he started each new model assignment from scratch. However, research for reference material was, in Macomber's words, "catch as catch can." When he was not satisfied with the completeness of the reference material that had been gathered on the B-25, he and a pattern maker drove out into the countryside to Mundelein, Illinois, where a local man had made it his mission in life to save old aircraft slated for scrapping. There in his rustic part-boneyard, part-museum Macomber found a weathered B-25 to photograph and measure.

When Macomber was given the assignment of producing the razorback version of the P-47, he went back into Monogram's archives to examine the reference materials that had been gathered all the way back to Speedee-Bilt days. Included in the file was a letter of reply from Fairchild-Republic dating from the 1960s telling Monogram that World War II was a long time ago and data on the P-47 was unavailable. Undeterred by this response, Bob Johnson wrote another letter to Republic, and this time he "hit the jackpot." Fairchild sent Monogram tables of data that gave coordinates on the shape of the plane almost inch-by-inch. Using this "killer material," Macomber went to work. He discovered that the wings on Monogram's P-47D (PA187) model were one-eighth of an inch too far back. This had resulted from the earlier design team's reliance on an impressive, but slightly inaccurate, three view drawing in a British model magazine. Macomber's design put the wings in the right place, and then pattern carver Joe Sojka dug out the old epoxy molds for the P-47D and resculpted the wing position.

Shep Paine's final diorama for Monogram was this scene on the B-26 assembly line. (5501 $15-20). *Courtesy of Revell-Monogram.*

By this time Monogram had just about exhausted the possibilities for World War II subjects, so it began to explore classic fighters of the 1950s. An obvious place to start was a pair of dogfighters from the Korean Conflict, the F-86 Sabre Jet and the Mig-15 (5402, 5403). Bob Johnson went to the Air Force Museum in Dayton, Ohio, to gather data on the two planes—and made sure to get the dimensions of the Mig right since models of the plane by other companies, supposedly in 1/48 scale, sometimes turned out to be too small in size. These models continued Monogram's practice of limited part count, combined with accuracy and fine detail molded into the parts. Both planes had service panels that removed to show the gun bays. Monogram's last new offering for the Bicentennial Year of 1976 was a 1/48 scale F-16 Fighting Falcon (5401) with decals for either a standard Air Force plane or the patriotic red-white-and-blue prototype version.

Stars of the Korean War, the Mig-15 (5403 $8-10) and F-86 Sabre Jet (5402 $8-10). *Courtesy of Dean Sills.*

The F-80 Shooting Star (5404 $10-15) has a removable panel to show interior details, which Monogram molded into the fuselage part. *Courtesy of Dean Sills.*

The A-4E Skyhawk (5406 $15-20) was one of the modern aircraft that joined the Monogram lineup in the 1970s and 1980s. *Courtesy of Gil Hodges.*

In the midst of its forward-looking expansion and modernization program, Monogram introduced a product that brought back a name from the 1940s: Speedee-Bilt. Veteran designer Syl Wisniewski came up with the bright idea of using the new space age material expanded polystyrene plastic to make some old time rubber band powered flying model airplanes. This polystyrofoam was actually lighter and stronger than balsa wood. To demonstrate how well this material could work in a flying model airplane, Wisniewski took a prototype out in the parking lot, wound it up, and turned it loose. It promptly spiraled up and landed on the roof of the plant—proving Wisniewski's point that the planes were excellent fliers. In 1976 Monogram released three timeless standards from civil aviation, the Cessna 180, Citabria, and Piper Cub (6000, 6001, 6002). These planes were easy to assemble and used just common household white glue to hold them together. Wisniewski gave the wings lots of dihedral so that they had great stability. The next year Monogram brought out a trio of exciting fighters, the Spitfire, Me-109, and P-51 Mustang. These low-wing planes were not as stable, but still flew well. Unfortunately, the public just didn't take to the revived Speedee-Bilts, and they disappeared.

The first set of new Speedee Bilt flying models were high wing civilian aircraft. The Cessna, Citabria, and Piper Cub (6000-6002 $8-10). *Courtesy of Revell-Monogram.*

The second set of new Speedee Bilts were low wing fighters. The Spitfire, Messerschmitt, and Mustang (6003-6005 $8-10). *Courtesy of Revell-Monogram.*

## The Sun Sets on Aurora

By the 1970s the big box retail chain stores represented sixty to seventy percent of the model kit market. The most popular kits in the big stores were model cars, while model airplanes did better in the hobby shops. K Mart, Target, and Toys R Us led the way (Wal-Mart would not become a factor until the late 1980s). As Bob Johnson explained it, the head buyer for K Mart "had a big pen. His orders could make or break you." Depending on the size of the store, K Mart had shelf space devoted to models that was either twelve feet, sixteen feet, or twenty feet long. Model kits presented a stock clerk's nightmare because there were so many different models and so many model companies. Each company had an assigned allotment of shelf space, but jockeying for "flex space" was a constant struggle. One of Monogram's strategies to enlarge its exposure was simply to increase the number of kits it had on the market. As Harney put it, "to push the competition off the shelves." Another tactic was to offer special deals, most notably big, expensive kits, such as the B-17, that would appear in stores on the Friday after Thanksgiving at the start of the Christmas shopping season.

In 1977 an opportunity to eliminate one of the players in the competition presented itself. Nabisco decided to break up its subsidiary Aurora Products Corporation of West Hempstead, New York, and sell its component parts: slot cars, games, toys, and model kits. Interestingly, three years earlier Nabisco had approached Tom Gannon when he was president of AMT with an offer to take over the leadership of Aurora, but Gannon declined because he suspected that Nabisco just wanted someone to liquidate Aurora. Now Gannon decided to buy Aurora's large inventory of model kit tooling. Gannon explained that this was primarily just a way of eliminating a rival. As Bob Johnson put it: "We were fighting for shelf space in the stores. The fear was that someone else would buy the molds and keep Aurora's kits on the market. Their kits were cheaper, and the average buyer didn't know that Aurora's kits were lower in quality." However, Gannon did feel that some of Aurora's kits were good enough to be incorporated into the Monogram line.

Gannon and Reder traveled to West Hempstead to inspect Aurora's molds. Reder thought that many of Aurora's aged molds had no use "except as anchors," but he felt that some could be reworked and brought up to Monogram standards. So the purchase was made. Late in the year the molds were packed in containers, loaded on flatcars, and shipped by train to Monogram, but on the way the train derailed, scattering molds across the frozen landscape. When they arrived in Morton Grove the molds were stored in a warehouse, many of them caked in mud and ice; many of them obviously damaged. When Monogram's staff went through them, there was, in Bob Johnson's words, a "feeding frenzy" of mold destruction as they were sold for their scrap metal content.

Monogram reissued four of Aurora's airliners (5412-5415) almost immediately in the late spring of 1978. Ken Merker, the former airline employee, had looked over the airliner molds and found them to be made of very hard steel—"kryptonite" he called it. So Monogram resorted to acid etching to add surface detail to the kits before reissuing them. The airliner models were welcomed by hobbyists who fancied civilian airliner kits, but the number of such hobbyists is limited, so the airliners went out of the catalog after a run of only three years.

Monogram paired its old P-51B with Aurora's 1/48 scale Panther Tank on a plastic base to create the Tank Hunter (6035 $15-25) diorama. *Author's collection.*

The Fokker D-7 (5203 $8-10) had been a great seller for Aurora over many years, but it did not take hold with hobbyists in the 1970s. *Author's collection.*

At the end of 1978 Monogram brought back four of Aurora's very nice 1/25 scale European sports cars, with their opening doors, detailed engines, and incredibly nice spoked wheels. The Jaguar XK-E, Ferrari GTO, Maserati 3500, and Aston Martin DB-4 (2243-2246) made only a brief two-year appearance, but they would reappear again in later years. Of Aurora's fine assembly of World War I aircraft, only the Fokker D-VII, Sopwith Camel, and SE-5A (5203-5205) were reworked and reissued. Monogram just didn't have a tradition in World War I planes. Aurora's excellent line of modern warships provided a selection of worthy models to augment Monogram's hitherto meager offerings in the ship category. John Cather, Monogram's art director, had already been using John Steel, the great marine artist who had created most of Aurora and Revell's outstanding warship box art. Steel had stopped painting model box art in the mid-1960s to go and serve five years in the Vietnam War; then returned to Northern California to specialize in nature art. However, he returned to his old trade to originate a whole line of model art for Monogram's ships. The most impressive of the ex-Aurora ships were the Forrestal class carriers (3503-3505) and the three-foot long model of the nuclear-powered supercarrier USS *Enterprise* (3700). These popular kits found a home in the Monogram kit lineup for many years.

Aurora's Ferrari GTO (2244 $15-20) made a nice addition to Monogram's exotic foreign car lineup. *Author's collection.*

Aircraft carriers had sold well for Aurora, and the kits also attracted customers under the Monogram label. The USS *Independence* (3503 $20-30). *Author's collection.*

Aurora had been most famous for its figure kits, particularly its movie monsters and comic book superheroes. This was foreign territory to Monogram. One problem was that the molds for the figures were beryllium copper alloy, a soft metal that required careful treatment. Ken Merker recalled that Monogram's mold shop found the molds a problem. "They had to work at it just to get them to run. They were pretty beat up." Monogram's first submission to the marketplace from Aurora's figure mold inventory was an odd couple: Godzilla and Superman (6300, 6301). Then came a nice collection of some of Aurora's best selling models, the snap-together prehistoric dinosaurs. These first appeared in 1979-1980 and have been reissued several times since then.

Surprisingly, Monogram waited until 1983 to bring back Aurora's most famous figure model: Frankenstein's monster (6007), along with his sidekicks Dracula, the Wolf Man, and the Mummy (6008-6010). Monogram gave test shots of the monsters to its diorama specialist Shep Paine, who built them and placed them in spooky settings for the photographer to shoot for the box art. The monsters didn't capture the public's fancy at the time, but by the 1990s Aurora's old figure kits had acquired legendary status, and Monogram resurrected the old time monsters once again.

Monogram found that Aurora's dinosaurs continued to attract customers in large numbers. The Armored Dinosaur (6045 $25-35). *Author's collection.*

The Mummy (6010 $15-25) had sold millions of copies back in the 1960s under the Aurora trademark, but enjoyed only spotty success for Monogram. *Author's collection.*

Although eventually about three dozen Aurora models made it into the Monogram catalog, the purchase of Aurora's molds did not have a major impact on Monogram's product line. However, the absorption of Aurora did have its intended result—a major competitor had been eliminated. The triumph of Monogram and the demise of Aurora was all the more striking since only a dozen years earlier Monogram had trailed a great distance behind Aurora in kit sales. Frank Carver, an Aurora executive, had once dismissed Monogram as "a great company, but no factor" in the competition for market dominance. Now Aurora was gone, and Monogram had risen perhaps as high as the number two spot in kit sales in the United States.

Aurora's F-111 tooling was extensively retooled to produce Monogram's F-111 (5804 $8-10). *Author's collection.*

For Corvette fans—and Roger Harney was a huge one—1978 marked a significant landmark: the silver anniversary of the introduction of the Corvette. Monogram decided to celebrate the milestone by bringing out its first new 1/8 scale car in more than a decade. From a business perspective, this would be even more of a gamble than the big scale B-17 because it would cost even more to tool. Something in the range of $150,000. But management decided that the practice of offering an expensive new model for the Christmas season was working, so the '78 Corvette project went ahead. To save some development money, the new Vette borrowed the chassis and engine block from the old '65 Corvette. Monogram was fortunate in that Harney and Johnson had developed a good working relationship with Charles M. Jordan, General Motors' director of design and Tom Daniel's old boss. Jordan described himself in a letter to Johnson as "an enthusiastic model car nut. ... You make small cars. We make big ones. In both cases, I think enthusiasm and a love for cars is important." Jordan saw to it that Monogram's model car designers received all the data they needed to produce an accurate model of the Corvette. "We are always proud to have the Monogram name on a model of one of our cars," wrote Jordan.

The big 1/8 scale '82 Corvette (2606 $90-100) included wax to polish the finished model. For the sake of safety, Turtle Wax had to provide Monogram with a wax so mild that you could almost eat it. *Courtesy of Revell-Monogram.*

Actually, Monogram produced two versions of the Silver Anniversary Corvette in 1978: the 1/8 scale model in orange plastic and a 1/24 scale version in black plastic (2603, 2253). Both kits came with decals to produce a model of the Indianapolis 500 pace car, although the 1/8 scale model would have to be painted black and silver to match the color of the real pace car.

In an effort to attract the attention of adult modelers, in 1977-78 Monogram released a series classic cars with die-cast metal bodies. These metal-body models had a certain heft that demanded more respect than a lightweight plastic model. Their metal bodies could be painted with real automobile lacquers, waxed, and polished to a mirror shine. The chassis, motor, interior, and detail parts were plastic. It was this mix of metal and plastic that turned out to be the fatal flaw of the kits. They were high quality kits, but mainstream plastic modelers didn't know how to handle the metal bodies, and the men who specialized in metal cars, such as Hubley die-casts, didn't think the plastic parts integrated well with the metal bodies. The cars selected for the models were fine. Hobbyists loved the '53 Corvette, '56 Thunderbird, MG-TC, Jaguar XK-120, Duesenberg, and '31 Packard (6100-6103, 6200, 6201), but the kits didn't find a market. To salvage something from the series, the molds for the Corvette, T-Bird, and MG were retooled to receive hot plastic instead of molten zinc, and re-emerged as very popular all-plastic kits (2289-2291).

The failure of the Jaguar XK-120 was considered a great tragedy because it ranked among the best models ever to come out of the design department. It had been designed by Clark Macomber, who explained that the Jaguar was one of those undertakings that just progressed smoothly from beginning to end. "Maybe it's putting on airs," Macomber later reflected, "but model making can be an art form. ... Some projects come together and you get exactly what you want." Macomber's perfectionist attitude resulted in a time consuming design period, during which he attempted to achieve both perfect accuracy and a logical part breakdown that would offer the model shop men something easy to carve, give the mold engravers parts that could be readily cut into a mold, and ultimately hand the injection molding crew a production tool suited for trouble-free mass production. At the end of the progression, the goal was to have a model kit that a hobbyist could open, shake the box, and the parts would just fall together into a model.

Everything worked right for the Jaguar—except for the next to last step where customers were supposed to buy the kit. (Actually, the Jaguar XK-120 did gain a new lease on life in the 1990s when it was retooled for all-plastic and released by Revell of Germany.)

The MG-TC (6102 $15-20) first appeared as this metal-body model, and then later in an all plastic version. *Courtesy of Revell-Monogram.*

The box art for the die-cast metal cars captured the look of a metal body. The Packard (6201 $15-20) and the Jaguar XK-120 (6203 $15-20). *Courtesy of Revell-Monogram.*

The '56 Thunderbird was a welcome model subject, whether in metal body (6101 $15-20) or all plastic (2289 $10-15). *Courtesy of Revell-Monogram.*

The year 1980 emerged as what Ken Merker called "the year of the monster tooling program." At the hobby industry trade show in February, Monogram announced "by far the largest investment in new tooling that we have ever made." It amounted to almost two million dollars. This commitment meant that the model development team was very busy. "It was a very interesting year," recalled Merker. "We didn't have the drawing board time available. So you took shortcuts and hoped for the best. It worked out pretty good." The centerpieces of the extravaganza were three really big new models: the largest plastic model airplane ever produced, a Convair B-36 bomber (5703), a two-foot long Pontiac Turbo Trans Am (2605), and the largest model truck kit ever created, a twenty-inch long Peterbuilt (2500).

The real B-36 Peacemaker was a mammoth aircraft, built in the early days of the Cold War, with six big piston engines that shook the ground when the plane flew overhead. Model airplane fanatics had been begging for this model for a long time, so Monogram decided to oblige them. Bob Johnson traveled to the SAC Museum in Omaha in January to photograph the B-36. "It was so cold, my trusty Nikon froze!" The model followed the tradition of Monogram's earlier big bombers: lots of detail, but few parts and no working parts. The wingspan came out to just short of three feet. When the kit appeared in stores, the sales results were disappointing. Aircraft model aficionados loved it, and no IPMS show is complete without a beautifully finished one, but sales in the stores to typical customers were disappointing. Nevertheless, the behemoth B-36 became a Monogram standard over the years.

The F-4C Phantom (5439 $6-8) was an awesome addition to Monogram's catalog. *Courtesy of Ken Belisle.*

The great Jack Leynnwood painted hundreds of box illustrations for Revell and Aurora, but only one of his paintings appears on a Monogram box. The image for the Final Countdown (6032 $20-30) was taken from a poster Leynnwood painted for the movie. *Author's Collection.*

The Rambo Attack Set (6039 $30-35) attempted to capitalize on the publicity generated by the Rambo movies. *Courtesy of Revell-Monogram.*

Among car modelers of the 1970s, the brawny Pontiac Firebird attracted a mob of enthusiastic followers. Monogram already had released several Firebirds in 1/32 and 1/24 scale when it brought out its Super Scale '80 Pontiac Trans Am. Behind the use of the "Trans Am" name lay a story. The name "Trans Am" belonged to the Sports Car Club of America and was licensed by Pontiac for use on the Firebird. Monogram's Bob Johnson and Roger Harney thought Monogram ought to license the name too, but Monogram's sales manger pointed out that nobody had ever raised the question of using the Trans Am tag on model kits, and it was best to not to raise an issue where one did not exist. But Johnson went ahead and negotiated a contract with SCCA to license exclusive rights to the Trans Am name on model kits for a three percent royalty on wholesale sales. Monogram's sales manager hit the ceiling when he learned of the deal, but thereafter other model companies had to think up alternate names for their Trans Ams. MPC's became Blackbirds.

Roger Harney liked developing the Trans Am because it was a totally new product. "We started with a clean sheet of paper." Nifty touches such as textured three-part bucket seats could be designed, as well as a detailed multi-piece dashboard. When the kit came out, the big Trans Am won rave reviews from the car modeling community. Denis Doty pronounced it "probably the most impressive kit in the Monogram 1/8 scale series." (*Craft, Model, Hobby Industry*, November 1980). Its high gloss black exterior, with its Firebird decal, achieved just the right over-the-top quality that a Trans Am was supposed to flaunt. The tan plastic interior looked like leather. The only working parts were removable T-top panels, posable front wheels, and an opening hood. So far as Bob Johnson was concerned, it had only one defect. "We should have modeled the 6.6 litre V-8 rather than the anemic Turbo engine."

Monogram made simple sixteen-inch models of the *Cutty Sark*, *Constitution*, and *United States* (3500-3502 $8-10). When hobbyists asked why make additional models of these already much-kitted subjects, Monogram replied, "Because we know those ships sell." *Courtesy of Revell-Monogram.*

The *Susquehanna* (3702 $30-40) was one of a set of sailing ships molded by Monogram from tooling leased from Imai of Japan. The steel in the molds was so soft that Monogram damaged the molds producing the kits and had to repair them before returning the molds to Japan. *Courtesy of Revell-Monogram.*

When John Steel painted the USS *Wisconsin* (3006 $8-10) he left the top strip white where the box text and Monogram logo would be placed. *Courtesy of Revell-Monogram.*

Burt Reynolds drove a Trans Am in that classic 1970s chase picture *Smokey and the Bandit*, but the other outlaw vehicle in the movie was a big highway hauler tractor-trailer truck. By the 1970s big-rig trucks, along with their CB radios, were cultural icons. Also by that time AMT, MPC, and ERTL were selling lots of 1/25 scale truck model kits. Monogram carved out a niche in this market by issuing an extensive line of smaller 1/32 scale Snap-Tite trucks, beginning in 1978 with a GMC General, Chevy Bison, Freightliner Conventional, and Freightliner Cabover (1200-1203). These snap kits were aimed at young modelers, but their detail and quality gave them appeal for adults, too.

1980's big 1/16 scale Peterbilt 359 aimed to hit the other side of the 1/25 scale truck market. It was a big project for Monogram's model making team, and Roger Harney's designers had to simplify the model a bit to bring it in under budget, but the kit that emerged from the process was outstanding. As usual with these breakout models, there was fear that a big truck would not sell, but the Peterbilt did just fine in the stores. Thus it was followed during the next two years by a big Kenworth Conventional and Kenworth Aerodyne (2501, 2502).

The 1/25 scale version of the Peterbilt Conventional (1500 $15-20) and its companion Kenworth (1502) were the only 1/25 scale trucks or cars Monogram ever designed. *Courtesy of Revell-Monogram.*

Monogram sold trucks and trailers separately, allowing model builders to customize their rigs. The Fruehauf Reefer (1206 $15-20), Fruehauf Van (1207 $15-20), Union Tanker (1211 $15-20), and Texaco Tanker (1212 $15-20). *Courtesy of Revell-Monogram.*

The Metal Glow plastic of the big 1/16 scale Kenworth (5202 $75-85) was created by mixing tiny mica flakes—like that used in ladies' eye shadow—into the molten plastic. *Courtesy of Revell-Monogram.*

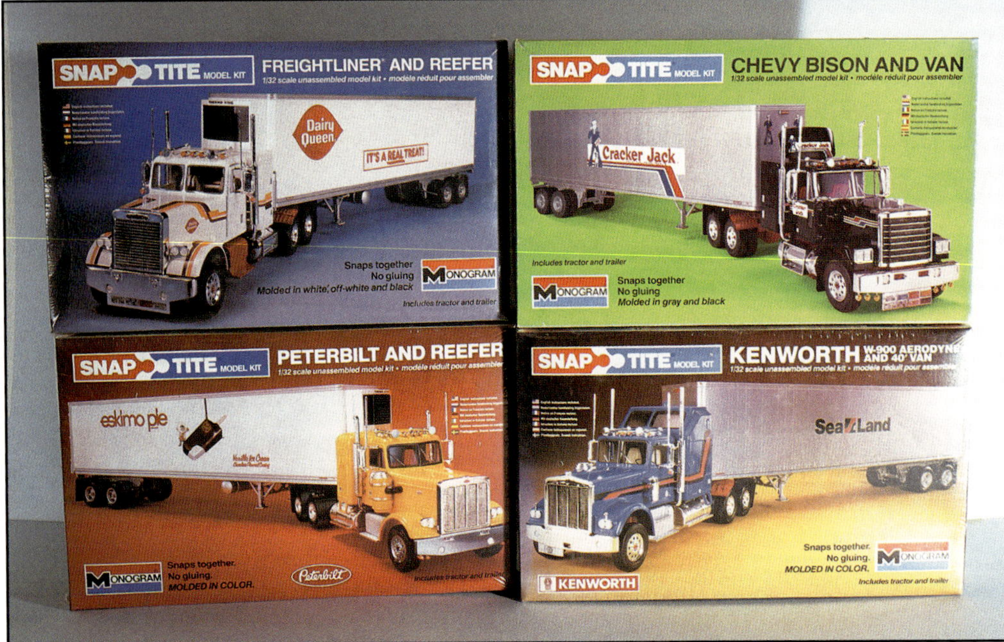


Monogram's extensive line of 1/32 Snap-Tite trucks were very popular kits (1300-1303 $25-30). *Courtesy of Revell-Monogram.*

In 1981 the Daytona 500, for the first time, had television cameras mounted inside the cars so that race fans watching on TV could get a drivers' eye view of the competition. The day after the race Bob Johnson and senior designer Clark Macomber had the same reaction to the race: "Wow! We gotta do a Grand National car!" They had watched the 500 in their homes on TV, and so had millions of other Americans. Maybe this was the wave of the future, and Monogram should try to catch it. Models of stock cars had been around for a long time, but nobody had made a new stock car model in years, and the popularity of NASCAR still mostly centered in the South. But Johnson and Macomber thought that situation might be changing as television gave this racing genre national exposure. So they made a presentation to the new products committee and received the go-ahead to develop some kits.

Johnson already had a race car of the sort he wanted in the development pipeline. He had developed a good relationship with the men in Ford's merchandising and public relations divisions, and he knew that Ford was interested in getting back into auto racing after dropping out in the early 1970s. One of Ford's first projects was an IMSA racer with a fiberglass Mustang body over a tubular racing chassis. Monogram turned it into a 1/24 scale model released as the Miller Mustang and Motorsport Mustang (2296, 2297) in 1982. While the Mustang was under development, Johnson got busy learning the arcane technical requirements of NASCAR vehicles. He knew that Ford was planning to replace its boxy 1981 Thunderbird with a sleek new model for 1983. Clark Macomber developed preliminary three-view design drawings for the new T-Bird model based on just three 8 x 10 photos of the prototype bodies supplied by Ford. The new Ford had a 104 inch wheelbase, and NASCAR required 110, so Macomber moved the rear wheel back six inches on the chassis and adjusted the body to fit.

Next Johnson went to Arden, North Carolina, to pay a visit to the garage of Banjo Matthews, the legendary designer of stock cars. Johnson recalled that Matthews was at first a bit unsure what to make of this fast-talking Yankee until Johnson pulled out his three-view design drawings of the still-secret 1983 Thunderbird body. After that Matthews was only too happy to let the Monogram boys measure and photograph the chassis he was building for use under the new T-Bird. Meanwhile, Matthews tweaked Monogram's designs a little to improve their aerodynamics. After this, Monogram sent the revised designs to Ford for their approval. Ford adjusted them a little, and then Matthews built the first two T-Bird racing bodies based on the designs that had originated in Monogram's engineering shop. The model was ready for production before the race cars made their public debut. Macomber and Johnson were delighted with how closely the models matched the real cars. "It was fantastic how close we'd come."

Monogram caught the tidal wave of growing NASCAR popularity with its colorful Grand National models. The first four were the Mountain Dew Buick (2204 $20-25), Uno Buick (2205 $20-25), Wrangler Thunderbird (2206 $20-25), and Melling Thunderbird (2207 $20-25). *Courtesy of Revell-Monogram.*

Monogram's Thunderbird model debut in 1983 with decal treatments for both the Dale Earnhardt Wrangler car and the Bill Elliott Melling car (2206, 2207). This T-Bird was paired with a Buick Regal that ran on a Mike Laughlin-designed chassis for speedway cars. This was the Darrell Waltrip Mountain Dew car and the Buddy Baker Uno car (2204, 2205). To show off the accurate chassis, as well as the racing interior (and even the tiny TV cameras), Monogram designed the cars so that the bodies could be removed. This meant that the interior and roll cage of the cars had to be designed to stand alone as complete models separate from the bodies. The public's response to these cars was astounding! They virtually launched a whole new category of model cars. In Bob Johnson's words, "These kits were wildly successful in hobby shops and mass merchants. They attracted builders of all ages." To satisfy race fans' desires for models of their favorite drivers, aftermarket companies sprang up to supply decals for every driver and sponsor.

David Lord painted the box art for the first generation of NASCAR racers, including the Valvoline Buick (2707 $10-15). *Courtesy of Revell-Monogram.*

The ex-Aurora Wolf Pack U-Boat (3102 $10-15) incorporates lots of fine detail into an inexpensive model.

Of course, Monogram began to expand its lineup of NASCAR models and offer new versions of the cars every year. Sometimes just the decal scheme changed, but in 1984 a Chevrolet Monte Carlo body was put on the Laughlin chassis and offered in two versions: the Terry Labonte Piedmont Airlines car and the Waltrip-Bonnet Budweiser car (2299, 2245). In 1986 a Richard Petty #43 Pontiac Grand Prix (2722) body was mated with the Laughlin chassis. In later years a variety of Ford and General Motors car body styles and new chassis versions would be added. By the year 2000 about three million NASCAR kits had been sold—perhaps the best selling model car collection of all time by any company.

By the time of Tom Gannon's fifth year at the helm of Monogram, it was obvious that his initiative in growing the company was paying huge dividends. Bob Reder thought it was high time to celebrate, and he invited the company's executives to a party at his home. As a surprise for Gannon, Reder asked the model shop to build a fully detailed F-16 model with the top fuselage part kept separate from the lower part. This top piece had a hole drilled in the middle of its center. Through the lower half of the model a large steel bolt protruded. The F-16 model was presented to confirmed non-model builder Gannon in a box that bore the inscription: "For company presidents or children under five years of age." Gannon opened the box, examined the parts, inserted the upper fuselage part over the bolt, and then threaded a hex nut on the bolt. So, finally, it could be said that he had built a model!

A couple of years after this party, Bob Reder reached the age of sixty-five, and under Mattel's strict rules, he was obliged to retire. However, he maintained a desk in the plant at Morton Grove and dropped by from time to time to see how things were getting along. Reder left the company on an upbeat note. In his book *A Brief History of Monogram Models, Inc.* (2000), he wrote "Aside from my family, my hobby has been one of the main sources of happiness and satisfaction to me." Actually, he was not quite through with Monogram yet. Within a few more years he would become again a part owner of the company.

The Pro-Stock Dragsters made great models, but when the real cars stopped being competitive on the track, the models went off Monogram's sales list. The 7-Eleven Thunderbird (2210 $10-15), Iaconio Camaro (2217 $20-25), and Smith Thunderbird ($10-15). *Courtesy of Revell-Monogram.*

The Piedmont Airlines Monte Carlo (2299 $10-15) by David Lord. *Courtesy of Revell-Monogram.*

It happened this way. In the early 1980s trouble at Mattel headquarters in California once more impacted the affairs of Monogram. Recently Mattel had ventured into the video game business and lost huge sums of money. This, combined with the unprofitability of several of its earlier acquisitions, led to a retrenchment aimed at taking Mattel back to its core toy business. Mattel began looking for a buyer for Monogram.

Tom Gannon had stepped down as president of Monogram in December 1983, and was replaced by John Stoneman. However, Mattel president Arthur Spear informed Gannon that all potential buyers he had approached wanted Gannon to come back as chief executive at Monogram. Then one day Spear asked Gannon if he would like to buy Monogram himself. Spear said Gannon could have thirty days to come up with an offer.

Monogram made a model of the experimental F-16XL (5206 $10-15). Aircraft models usually have a longer life expectancy in the catalog than modern cars, but the F-16XL never went into production and thus the model didn't stick around long either. *Courtesy of Harry Swett.*

Barbie's Corvette (1408 $15-20) was originally planned in pink plastic, but came out in silver. Monogram's model car staff knew the model would not sell, but it was issued anyway to please Mattel. *Author's Collection.*

Gannon began telephoning people he knew, saying that he must raise twelve million dollars cash. He also explained that he wanted to own the company for only another two to five years and then sell it at a profit. Gannon's credibility was so great and Monogram's reputation for profitability so good, that he was able to raise the money, and the sale was announced in April of 1984. Among the backers were some of the current executives at Monogram, Bob Reder, as well as investors in the Orient—although none of the silent partners were publicly disclosed. After the separation from Mattel, things didn't change much at Morton Grove, except that Mattel outsiders were no longer dropping in. Stoneman continued as president of Monogram, while Gannon served as chairman of the board.

By the mid-1980s, Monogram was a mature company, securely established as one of the top hobby companies in America, with developing relationships in both production and sales in the growing economies of the Orient. It had accumulated a tool bank of hundreds of top quality molds. Many of the models in its line were enduring classics that could be reintroduced to the public again and again over the years. Yet every year Monogram added a few more new subjects to its inventory with the idea that they too would become regular income producing products.

As the passage of time moved World War II from the forefront of public consciousness, Monogram's aircraft model offerings showed a definite shift away from the old World War II staples toward modern jet age warplanes. Some models that had been new in the 1960s, like the P-40B (5209) and Spitfire (5208) were still around, but the mix shifted to a preponderance of both newly-classic aircraft from the 1950s such as the F-101 (5811) and F-106 (5809) and up-to-the-minute planes such as the Tornado (5426), F-15 (5801), and A-18 (5807).

For Bob Johnson, finding new subjects for models had elements of intrigue and just plain fun. While researching the F-105G (5806) Johnson was at a National Guard base in Georgia photographing one of the planes when the officer shepherding him around said, "Gee, we could go for a ride if only you had an altitude card." Johnson replied that he certainly did have a card and would love to fly with him. So after being cleared by the public affairs officer (a knockout female major), Johnson got his joy ride. Back on the ground, the friendly pilot informed him that he could not take photos of the secret back seat displays—but then led him to a work stand where he could get a shot of the rear cockpit with a telephoto lens.

Monogram's salesmen reported that Revell enjoyed steady sales with its old SR-71 model and recommended that Monogram try to tap into that market. Thus Johnson, an Air National Guard officer with top secret clearance, prevailed upon some old friends to get him into Lockheed headquarters. Lockheed was willing to provide him with detailed drawings of the SR-71 so that Monogram could produce a more accurate model than Revell's—which had been based on photographs alone. Soon afterwards, while exploring around Davis-Monthan Air Force Base, Johnson spotted a black-painted, unmanned craft sitting on a trailer. He took measurements and photos of this mystery craft and only later was it discovered that this was the DS-21A drone designed to be carried by the SR-71. Thus, partly by accident, Monogram got a bonus with its SR-71A (5810).

Model builder Harry Swett put his 1/72 scale F-105G (5431 $4-6) in the Georgia Air Guard.

Modeler Ken Belisle gave his A-18 (5807 $6-8) Marine Corps markings.

Miami Vice was a trendy TV show, and the Daytona Spyder (2737 $10-15) was equally fashionable. *Author's collection.*

The '82 Camaro (2607 $90-100) in 1/8 scale had just about everything anyone could want in a model kit. *Courtesy of Revell-Monogram.*

The venerable Big T came back in 1985 in black plastic as the Golden "T" Street Rod (2609 $90-100) and returned again in 2005 as the original Big T in red plastic. *Courtesy of Revell-Monogram.*

By the mid-1980s America had left behind the turmoil of the '70s and entered into modern times. On television stylishly dressed "Miami Vice" detectives Crockett and Tubbs tooled around the streets of South Florida in a Daytona Spyder. Monogram decided to cash in on the popularity of the TV show by making a model of this car, but they had to act fast because the life of any television show is as uncertain as the life of a vice cop. So the Monogram guys butchered some molds to produce a model in just six months. The real car has a Ferrari body and interior riding on a Corvette chassis and motor. So Monogram salvaged the chassis and engine from Tom Daniel's California Vette (7504), while borrowing the nice two-piece wire wheels came from the old Ferrari 275P (PC102). Since the actual car used in the TV show was not an authentic Daytona Spyder, Monogram copied the body and interior of one they found in an exotic car dealership in Lake Forest. It all fit together nicely, and the kit sold fabulously.

In 1986 an opportunity for Tom Gannon and his partners to sell Monogram presented itself in the form of a buyout offer from Odyssey Partners of New York. Odyssey was an investment group just looking to make a profitable deal, and it had acquired an option to purchase Revell, Inc. However, Revell was not, and never had been, a very profitable company. It led the world in model kit sales by a wide margin, but the company's bottom line had seldom been good—and, in fact, had been nonexistent for seven straight years. Odyssey saw these losses as an opportunity. If Revell were merged with a profitable company, those losses could be carried forward to help offset the purchase price of the second company. The logic of uniting profitable Monogram with indebted Revell made financial sense, and in the summer of 1986 Odyssey Partners became the owner of the two leading model companies in the United States.

The marriage of the splashy West Coast company with the conservative Midwest company was actually pretty much a one way deal. None of the Revell staff or employees joined the new organization, and all of Revell's assets were moved to Monogram's facilities at Plant 2 in Des Plaines. Bob Johnson and a handful of other Monogram people ventured to California to assess what could be salvaged from the Revell plant in Venice. They found Aurora-Revell veteran Tom West presiding over a partly abandoned facility.

Production of Revell model kits continued to fill existing orders, but all of the inventory of molds not in use at the time was loaded on railcars and shipped to Des Plaines. It was difficult to account for all the molds because they were scattered among Revell's contract molding companies and overseas subsidiaries. Johnson discovered an engine mold insert for Revell's 22 Jr. dragster (H-1224) being used as an ash tray.

Monogram decided to keep Revell and Monogram products separate, so Des Plaines became Revell headquarters. At first just a small crew of Monogram executives rattled around in the empty offices at Plant 2. They didn't even have secretaries to answer the phone. Most company functions, from model design to kit production, were consolidated at the Morton Grove plant, meaning that the old Monogram team was now developing and producing products for two companies.

The ZZ Top '33 Ford (2702 $10-15) came from new production tooling. Even the ZZ Top connection seems to have attracted some buyers to the model. *Courtesy of Craig Clements and Gib Grayless.*

The unified company took the name Revell-Monogram, Inc., although some Monogram staffers groused that the names should be reversed. Gannon explained that for tax purposes the Revell name had to be paramount, and, besides, surveys showed that world-wide the Revell name was much better known than Monogram. Nevertheless, the old timers at Monogram could enjoy quiet satisfaction in knowing that its long-time rival had ultimately been absorbed by an American heartland company operated on a conservative philosophy of good products, dependable service, and sound business practices.

Shortly after the sale of Monogram, Tom Gannon retired and moved to St. Louis to be near his children. It was there in April 2005, shortly after being interviewed for this book, that he passed away.

Although Monogram and Revell maintained separate corporate identities so far as the public was concerned, as early as 1988 models made from Revell tooling began appearing in Monogram boxes and vice-versa. Then beginning in 1997 all kits were packaged in boxes with a new consolidated Revell-Monogram company logo. The exceptions were the Monogram Pro Modeler kits that included extra parts and decals to enhance the basic model. It was quite a tribute to the reputation of the Monogram name and the quality of Monogram's kits that they could still be viewed as elite level kits almost thirty years after their original introduction.

Although it was a snap-assembly kit, the Mack Fire Pumper (1213 $15-20) built into a good looking model. The art department gave it a decal with Morton Grove markings. *Author's collection.*

Some old kits reappeared in their original, or at least vintage, packaging to appeal to kit collectors and the nostalgia market. From 1992 through 1994 a number of Monogram (and Revell) kits appeared in the "Selected Subjects" series. Then in the year 2000 the Monogram Classics series brought back twenty-six old-time standard kits, with their original box art, under a retro Monogram label that harkened back to the early 1960s. In another tribute to the past, each kit included a collector trading card and an individualized cloth patch. Beginning in 2000 the old Monogram Tiger trademark reappeared on some old and new slot car racers and accessories.

From time to time the men at Revell-Monogram have considered dropping the Monogram name, but each time the decision has been to recognize the continuing magic of the Monogram trademark.

Meanwhile, the ownership of Revell-Monogram, Inc. (including Revell, Germany) went through several changes of hands. In 1994 the company was sold to Hallmark Cards and put into its subsidiary Binney & Smith, the makers of Crayola crayons. In 2001 Revell-Monogram was sold to Alpha International of Cedar Rapids, Iowa, which produced Gearbox Toys. Then, just over a year later, the company was sold again to the Revell Group, a corporation headed by Chicago businessman John Long. Veteran Monogram executive Jim Foster became president.

The new Revell-Monogram began operating out of a different facility in December of 2004 in Northbrook, just a few miles away from the old plant at Morton Grove. Then, in 2007, Revell-Monogram was sold once again, this time to the major hobby distribution company Hobbico. The business headquarters moved to Elk Grove Village, Illinois, where the development of new models remains in the hands of a group of dedicated modeling enthusiasts, although the manufacturing and packaging of products has been transferred to the Orient.

Hobbyists looking through the latest Revell catalog will find some of the old classic Monogram models being offered anew to the present-day generation of youngsters.

The sun may have been setting on Don Greer's F-4 Phantom (5440 $6-8), but Monogram's place in the American hobby industry was never higher than in the late 1980s. *Courtesy of Revell-Monogram.*

# Bibliography


Bergedick, Bob. "Early Monogram Plastic Car Kit History," *Kit Collector's Clearinghouse* (August, 1999).

Bergedick, Bob. "Monogram's Beloved Hot Rod," *Mobila* (January 1995).

Boyd, Tim. *Collecting Model Car and Truck Kits*. Osceola, Wisconsin: MBI Publishing, 2001.

Burns, John W. *Collectors Value Guide for Scale Model Plastic Kits, Seventh Edition*. John W. Burns, 1999.

Burns, John W. *PAK-20: Plastic Aircraft Kits of the Twentieth Century and Beyond*. John W. Burns, 2003.

Coulter, Bill and Bob Shelton. *The Directory of Model Car Kits*. Acworth, Georgia: Bob Shelton, 2000.

Coulter, Bill. *Stock Car Model Kit Encyclopedia*. Iola, Wisconsin: Krause Publications, 1999.

Daniel, Tom. His website is tomdaniel.com.

Davis, Phil and Mark Carey. *Tom Daniel: The Man Behind the Models*. Barefoot Ventures, 1996. This is a sixty minute videotape.

Gustavson, Mark. "The Predicta Project," thepredictaproject.org.

*Internet Modeler* on line hobby magazine at internetmodeler.com.

Irvine, Mat. *Creating Space: The Story of the Space Age Told Through Models*. Burlington, Ontario: Collector's Guide Publishing, 2002.

Irvine, Mat. "The Selected Subjects Program," *Scale Models International* (November 1994), 48-51.

Jesse, Terry. *Hot Rod Model Kits*. Osceola, Wisconsin: MBI Publishing, 2000.

Jesse, Terry. "Tom Daniel," *Scale Auto Enthusiast* (February 2000), 36-39.

Dave Rasmussen, *Dave's Show Rod Rally* at showrods.com.

Reder, Robert. *A Brief History of Monogram Models, Inc.* Robert Reder, 2000.

"The Tom Daniel Story," AE Classic at aeclassic.com.

# The Model Kits

Collecting Monogram model kits can be an engaging pleasure for anyone, regardless of their budget and level of knowledge. Many vintage Monogram kits can be purchased for modest amounts, while others are extremely rare and bring top dollar prices at auction. Regardless of a hobbyists goals and interests, this kit compendium will help to sort out the complexities of the Monogram model kit line from 1945 through 1986, the year in which Monogram and Revell merged.

Originally Monogram's kits came in heavy cardboard boxes with slick paper wraps, imprinted with the box graphics, pasted to the outsides. In 1965-66 Monogram converted its packaging to folding boxes made of thin cardboard with the box graphics printed directly on the cardboard. These new boxes were predominantly blue, and the art work on the lid was set apart in a box on the right side of the panel. These are known as Blue Border or Blue Background boxes. The exceptions to this rule were the armor kits, which appeared in olive boxes with a distinctive single white star logo and the label "Monogram Combat Series." Some car and rocket models came in white border boxes.

In 1973 Monogram switched to white boxes with photos of built models on the box top. However, by 1975 some models began appearing with painted illustrations on the top panel and photos on the side panels. Thereafter various kits came with either painted box art or photo box art.

The first all plastic kits issued in 1954 did not have any logo on them. The "Four Star Plastikit" logo appeared first in 1955 with the P4/P5 Cadillac models, and by 1956 all Monogram kits bore the Four Star logo. By 1957 the trademark still showed four stars, but the inscription varied from kit to kit, often describing the series of a kit, such as "Space Age Hobby Kits." In 1966, with the switch to blue border boxes, the logo became red and blue bars on the left side reading "Monogram, Quality Hobby Kits." On the right side was a black box with a picture of a boy holding a car, plane, rocket, or ship. In 1972-73 the logo switched to the familiar red-white-blue bars with the Monogram name. Beginning in 1991 the "M" in Monogram was no longer capitalized and the color of the blue bar became a shade lighter.

In 1969 Monogram began using a computer to keep track of its products, and this necessitated a switch from the letter-number system it had been using to a four-digit number system. Kits in production at the time were given new kit numbers, and thus are indicated as "renumbered" not "reissued" in this kit index. Some kits issued in 1969 were printed with both letter-number and four-digit kit numbers on the end panels, but this list does not attempt to identify those kits.

In the 1990s Revell-Monogram reissued many classic Monogram kits in facsimile boxes in the "Selected Subjects Program." These kits can be distinguished from original issues by the added 1990s copyright dates on their side panels.

Kits in this compendium are listed by the identification number printed on their end panels. All reissues of a particular kit are listed under the original kit issue only. Each reissue will refer back to the original issue only, not to other reissues of that kit. Each kit entry will show the years that the kit was listed in the Monogram catalog, the scale of the model, and the current collectors' value of the kit. Kit values assume mint-in-the-box condition. Of course, kit values are only approximate, as prices in any transaction will vary widely depending on market circumstances.

# Organization of Kit Compendium

## Wooden Models



## All-Plastic Models



# Wooden Models

## Control Line Models

**C1 Whirlwind** 1946-51 $200-225
30 inch wingspan. Took .45/.60 motor.
**C2 Whirlwind, Jr.** 1947-51 $150-175
19 inch wingspan. Took .15/.25 motor.
**C3 Piper Cub** 1948-52 $190-210
35 inch wingspan
**C3 Piper Cub** (Improved) 1953-55 $180-200
**C4 Aeronca Sedan** 1949-52 $190-210
35 inch wingspan.
**C4 Aeronca** (Improved) 1953-55 $180-200

## Free Flight Models

**F1 Pirate** 1947-55 $250-300
31 inch wingspan. Cabin model. Rubber powered. Wisniewski designer.
**F2 Prowler** 1947-55 $250-300
28 inch wingspan. Stick model. Rubber powered. Wisniewski designer.

## Speedee-Bilt Kits

All Speedee-Bilts have injection molded acetate plastic cowls, propellers, pilot figures, and other detail parts. Wire landing struts and rubber wheels. The canopies are vacuum-formed acetate. The balsa wood fuselages and wings are prefabricated to the proper shapes and most are pre-painted. Includes plans and tips for better flight. Decals.

**G1** **Piper Cub** 1949-64 $100-125
18 inch wing span.
**G2** **Aeronca Sedan** 1949-56 $100-125
18 inch wing span.
**G3** **Monocoupe** 1949-56 $100-125
18 inch wing span.
**G4** **Ercoupe** 1949-56 $100-125
18 inch wing span.
**G5** **Boeing Kaydet** 1949-64 $75-100
14 inch wing span.
**G6** **Long Midget** 1949-64 $100-125
12 inch wing span.
**G7** **Cessna Seaplane** 1950-56 $125-150
18 inch wing span.
**G7** **Spad 7** 1950-64 $125-150
13 inch wing span.
**G9** **F-51 Mustang** 1950-64 $100-125
13 inch wing span.
**G10** **F-84 Thunderjet** 1950-64 $100-125
12 inch wing span.
**G11** **Ryan Navion** 1950-56 $100-125
14 inch wing span.
**G12** **F6F Hellcat** 1950-64 $120-140
14 inch wing span.
**G13** **F-86 Sabre Jet** 1951-64 $125-150
11 inch wing span.
**G14** **F4U Corsair** 1951-64 $150-170
13 inch wing span.
**G15** **P-40 Warhawk** 1951-64 $150-170
14 inch wing span.
**G16** **F9F Panther** 1953-64 $125-150
12 inch wing span.
**G17** **P-47 Thunderbolt** 1953-64 $125-150
13 inch wing span.

The H1 and H2 De Luxe Speedee-Bilts were not designed to fly. Included decals, instructions, full-size drawings, sandpaper, paper set-up templates.

**H1** **B-25 Mitchell** 1953-60 $225-250
17 inch wing span. Thirty-four plastic and fifty-seven finished balsa parts.
**H2** **B-26 Invader** 1953-60 $225-250
19 inch wing span. Thirty-four plastic and fifty-one finished balsa parts.

The H3 and H4 Five Star Super De Luxe Speedee-Bilts also included a tube of Mono Glue and four jars of Mono Dope.

**H3** **B-17 Flying Fortress** 1954-60 $400-500
20 inch wing span. Fifty plastic and forty-nine finished balsa parts.
**H4** **B-24 Liberator** 1954-60 $450-600
22 inch wing span. Forty-six plastic and forty-nine finished balsa parts.

## Wood Solid Superkits

These were balsa and plastic display models. Each came with several plastic parts and a plastic display stand. Some balsa parts are pre-painted. Includes decals, instructions, full-size plans, sandpaper, and paper set-up templates.

**T1 P-51 Mustang** 1952-56 $50-75
8 inch wing span.
**T2 F4U Corsair** 1952-56 $50-75
8 inch wing span.
**T3 F-84 Thunderjet** 1952-56 $50-75
7 inch wing span.
**T4 Mig-15** 1954-58 $50-75
7 inch wing span.
**T5 F-86 Sabre Jet** 1954-58 $75-90
7 inch wing span
**T6 P-40 Warhawk** 1954-58 $75-90
8 inch wing span.

## Bild 'n Fly

These kits featured thin balsa wood parts (no tissue), laminated with markings, plastic detail parts, and wire landing gear.

**F1 Mr. Mulligan** 1960-63 $100-125
17 inch wing span. Thompson Trophy racer.

**F2 Beaver** 1960-63 $125-150
21 inch wing span. Air Force utility plane.

**F3 Cosmic Wind** 1960-63 $125-150
16 inch wing span. Goodyear midget racer.

## New Speedee-Bilt

**6000** **Cessna 180** 1976-77 $8-10
18 inch wing span.
**6001** **Citabria** 1976-77 $8-10
18 inch wing span.
**6002** **Piper Cub** 1976-77 $8-10
18 inch wing span.
**6004** **Spitfire** 1977 $8-10
15 inch wing span.
**6005** **Messerschmitt** 1977 $8-10
15 inch wing span.
**6006** **P-51 Mustang** 1977 $8-10
15 inch wing span.

## Wood Ship Models

These ship models are all balsa, with no plastic parts. They have detailed plans and decals.

**B1 LST 608** 1945-56 $75-100
**B2 USS *Hobby*** 1945-56 $75-100
**B3 USS *Chicago*** 1945-56 $75-100
**B4 USS *Missouri*** 1946-56 $75-100
**B5 USS *Shangri-La*** 1946-56 $100-125
**B6 Aqua Jet** 1947-60 $40-70
Futuristic jet boat with vacuum formed canopy.

**Three Historical Ship Models** c. 1950 $300-400
This regular heavy cardboard model box contains models of B2 *Hobby*, B4 *Missouri*, B5 *Shangri-La*. This gift set bears no kit number or copyright date.

## Wood Car Models

The balsa wood kits come with some plastic parts, metal axles, and rubber wheels. Each has a receptacle in the rear for a CO2 cartridge.

**R1 Hot Shot** 1946-60 $75-100
8 inches long. Futuristic speed car.
**R2 Terra Jet** 1947-56 $100-125
8 inches long.
**R3 Mono-Jet** 1948-60 $75-100
8 inches long. Indianapolis racer.
**R4 Mid-jet Racer** 1948-60 $75-100
7 inches long. Midget racer.

# All-Plastic Models

## PA Aircraft Models

## 1955-1969

**MGP-5** **TWA Airliner Set** 1956 $300-400
Gift set containing PA9 TWA DC-3 and PA19 TWA Super Constellation.
**MGP-7** **Air Force Patrol** late 1950s $400-500
Gift set containing PA10 B-66, PA11 C-47, and PA20 Albatross.
**P6/PA6** **B-26 Invader** 1955-67 1/67 $30-40
Silver, clear plastic. Decals. Reissued as PA195 (1968), 6818 (1970).
**P7/PA7** **B-25 Mitchell** 1955-67 1/68 $30-40
Silver, clear plastic. Decals. This model stayed in the Monogram catalog continuously for thirty years. Reissued as PA196 (1968), 6819 (1970).
**P8/PA8** **PBY Catalina** 1955-67 1/100 $35-45
Blue, clear plastic. Early releases in silver plastic. Rubber wheels. Decals. Reissued as PA197 (1968), 6820 (1970).
**P9/PA9** **Douglas DC-3** 1955-64 1/90 $50-70
Silver, clear plastic. Pilot, co-pilot, hostess, passenger figure. Door can be built open with passenger stairs. TWA decals. Reissued as PA11 (1955), PA147 (1966), PA203 (1968), 6826 (1970), 7590 (1975), 6059 (1983).
**P10/PA10** **Douglas B-66** 1955-67 1/82 $30-40
Silver, clear plastic. Air Force decals. Trigger on top of fuselage drops bomb. Reissued as PA176 (1967), PA204 (1968), 6827 (1970).
**P11/PA11** **C-47 Skytrain** 1955-66 1/90 $50-70
Olive, clear plastic. Cargo doors can be built open. Crew ladder. Two crew and four paratroopers figures. Decals. Reissue of PA9 (1955).
**P14/PA14** **T-28B Trainer** 1956-64 1/51 $35-45
Yellow, clear plastic. Student, instructor, mechanic with fire extinguisher figures. Retracting landing gear, arresting hook lowers, canopy slides open. Three-blade propeller. Navy decals. Reissued as PA28 (1958), PA121 (1965), 6805 (1970), 5100 (1975).
**P15/PA15** **Ford Tri-Motor** 1956-64 1/77 $30-40
Silver, clear plastic. Interchangeable wheels or skis landing gear. Dog sled, dog team, crew in parkas. Model of the plane that flew to the South Pole in 1929. Monogram copied it at the Ford Museum in Dearborn, Michigan. Antarctic Expedition decals. Reissued as PA122 (1965), PA161 (1967), 6811 (1970), 7592 (1975), 6056 (1983).
**P19/PA19** **Super-G Constellation** 1956-64 1/134 $40-60
Silver, white, clear plastic. Two hostess figures, boarding ramp, ground power unit truck. TWA decals. Reissued as 7591 (1975), 6058 (1983).
**P20/PA20** **Albatross Rescue** 1957-66 1/72 $30-40
Silver, clear plastic. Three crew, two survivor figures in life raft. Air Force decals. Reissued as PA160 (1967), 6837 (1970), 5400 (1975), 6065 (1984).
**PA25** **Piper Tri-Pacer** 1957-65 1/32 $30-40
Silver, clear plastic. Decals. Doors open, cowl removes to show engine. Pilot with camera, hunter with dead puma. Reissued as PA199 (1968), 6822 (1970).
**PA26** **Cessna 180 Amphibian** 1957-64 1/41 $50-70
Silver, clear plastic. Decals. Doors open, cowl removes to show engine. Pilot, girl in swim-suit figures. Reissued without floats as PA123 (1965).
**PA28** **T-28A Trainer** 1958-64 1/51 $30-40
Silver, clear plastic. Two-blade propeller. Landing gear retracts. Air Force decals. Reissue of PA14 (1956).
**PA29** **Blue Angels** 1958-67 1/101 $50-70
Blue, clear plastic. Navy decals. Four F11F-1 Tigers on a clear stand. Reissued as PA200 (1968), 6823 (1970).
**PA30** **Kitty Hawk** 1958-67 1/39 $25-35
Off-white, brown plastic. Figures of Wright brothers. Monorail launching track, carrier dolly, display stand. Also bench, toolbox, oilcan, clamp, and shovel that appear in a 1903 photo. Rigging string. Based on the Wright Flier in the Smithsonian. Reissued as PA201 (1968), 6824 (1970), 5300 (1976), 6057 (1983).
**PA31** **TBF Avenger** 1958-70 1/48 $25-35
Blue, clear plastic. Canopy slides open, wings fold, landing gear retracts, weapons bay door opens to drop torpedo. Navy decals. Four figures. Reissued as 6829 (1970).
**PA32** **B-58 Hustler** 1958-67 1/121 $30-40
Silver, clear plastic. Three crew, two ground support figures. Cockpit canopies open, button on top releases weapons pod. Air Force decals. Reissued as PA198 (1968), 6821 (1970).
**PA33** **F-105 Thunderchief** 1958-66 1/72 $35-45
Silver, clear plastic. Metal spring. Trigger on side of fuselage ejects spring-loaded pilot, bomb bay door rotates to drop bomb. Reissued as PA149 (1966), 6808 (1970). This model was copied by IMC, which issued it with "battle damaged" decals.
**PA50** **Jet Helicopter Iroquois** 1959-66 1/48 $30-40
Olive brown, clear plastic. Pilot, two stretcher bearers, two wounded on stretchers. Army decals. Reissued as PA151 (1966), PA152 (1966), 6810 (1970).
**PE52** **Wright Cyclone Engine** 1959-63 1/12 $120-130
Black, gray plastic. Flexible vinyl brass-colored ignition harness. Mounted on red plastic service dolly. Removable cylinder side shows working piston inside. Booklet on the engine. Can be electrified. Reissued as PE252M (1959), 6052 (1983).
**PA53** **A3J Vigilante** 1959-67 1/72 $30-40
Gray, clear plastic. Metal spring. Navy decals. Trigger on underside of fuselage ejects spring-loaded bomb from rear end of model. Box art by Tom Kowal. Reissued as PA177 (1967), 6814 (1970).
**PA54** **SBD Dauntless** 1960-70 1/48 $30-40
Blue, black, clear plastic. Pilot, gunner, armorer, signal officer figures. Navy decals. Bomb on bomb cart. Landing gear retracts, tab opens/closes dive breaks, bomb drops. Reissued as 6830 (1970).
**PA56** **Air Power Set** 1959-60 1/240 $225-275
Silver, blue plastic base. Wire stands. 24 page booklet. Eighteen planes mounted on a 12 by 15 inch base. Scale of individual planes varies. Select groups of planes reissued as P407, P408, P409 (1960).
**PA58** **Gulfhawk II** 1960-64 1/32 $40-50
Orange, silver, clear plastic. Fabric texture on wings. Standing pilot figure. Decals. Rigging thread. Canopy slides open, control surfaces move, turning the prop retracts the wheels. Based on the Gulfhawk in the Smithsonian. Reissued as military version F3F-3 PA70 (1962). Reissued as PA 184 (1967), 6850 (1970).

**PA66 F4F Wildcat** 1961-70 1/48 $25-35
Blue, clear plastic. Pilot, ground crew figures. Wings fold. Navy decals. Reissued as 6798 (1970).

**PA67 Phantom Mustang** 1961-70 1/32 $100-140
Clear, red, green, silver, black plastic. Decals. 144 parts. Display pylon holds one motor and two D batteries. Second motor inside model's engine. One button spins prop. Second button retracts all three landing gear. Two levers release bombs. Reissued as PA77 (1962), 6866 (1970), 5701 (1979), 6054 (1983).

**PA69 SB2C Helldiver** 1961-70 1/48 $25-35
Blue, black, clear plastic. Navy decals. Both canopies slide open, wings fold, landing gear retract, bomb bay doors open to drop bomb. Box art by Locher. Reissued as 6831 (1970).

**PA70 F3F-3** 1962-66 1/32 $40-50
Silver, red, yellow, clear plastic. Navy decals. Canopy slides open, movable control surfaces, turning prop retracts landing gear. Military version of Gulfhawk PA58 (1960). Most visible difference is cowl with machine gun ports. Box art by Locher. Reissued as PA186 (1967), 6851 (1970).

**PA73 Zero A6M5** 1962-70 1/48 $25-35
Silver, black, clear plastic. Decals. Landing gear retracts. Box art by Locher. Reissued as 6799 (1970).

**PA74 Messerschmitt Me109E** 1962-70 1/48 $20-25
Green, black, clear plastic. Decals. Landing gear retracts. Box art by Locher. Reissued as 6800 (1970).

**PA77 F-51D** 1962-70 1/32 $45-55
Silver, black, clear plastic. Air Force decals. Landing gear retracts, canopy slides open, bombs drop. Reissue of PA67 (1961) without the "visible" feature. Box art by Locher. Reissued as 6847 (1970).

**PA79 Spitfire** 1962-70 1/48 $20-25
Gray, clear plastic. Decals. Landing gear retracts. Box art by Locher. Reissued as 6801 (1970), 5208 (1985).

**PA80 F6F Hellcat** 1963-70 1/48 $20-25
Blue, black, clear plastic. Navy and Marines decals. Two figures. Drop tank, two bombs, six rockets. Wings fold, landing gear retracts. Box art by Locher. Reissued as 6832 (1970).

**PA82 F4U Corsair** 1963-70 1/48 $20-25
Blue, black, clear plastic. Navy and Marines decals. Wings fold, landing gear retracts. Three drop tanks, 2 bombs, 8 rockets, wing radome. Box art by Locher. Reissued as 6833 (1970).

**PA90 Hawker Hurricane** 1964-70 1/48 $10-15
Gray, black, clear plastic. Decals for several variants. Landing gear retracts. Optional parts for five variants. Box art by Morgan. Reissued as 6802 (1970).

**PA96 P-40B Tiger Shark** 1964-70 1/48 $20-25
Olive brown, black, clear plastic. Decals for Flying Tigers, USAAF, RAF. Box art by Morgan. Reissued as 6803 (1970), 5209 (1985).

**PA97 P-38L Lightning** 1964-70 1/48 $40-65
Silver, black, clear plastic. Decals. Two figures. Panel in nose removes to show gun bay. Builds four versions, including the two-seat P-38M nightfighter variant. Box art by Locher. Renumbered 6848 (1970).

**PA107 Focke Wulf FW-190** 1965-70 1/48 $15-20
Dark green, black, clear plastic. Decals. Optional parts to build six variants. Box art by Bill Koster. Renumbered 6804 (1970), 6034 (1984).

**PA121 T-28D Trojan** 1965-70 1/48 $20-30
Dark gray, clear plastic. Underwing ordinance. US Air Force and Vietnamese air force decals. Ground attack variant of the T-28 used by the South Vietnamese air force. Box art by Morgan. Reissue of PA14 (1956).

**PA122 Ford Tri-Motor** 1965-66 1/77 $20-30
Silver, clear plastic. TWA decals. Reissue of P15 (1956) with wheels and without the Antarctic dog sled team. Box art by Locher.

**PA123 Cessna 180** 1965-67 1/41 $30-40
Silver, clear plastic. Decals. Reissue of PA26 (1957) with amphibian floats replaced by wheels. Box art by Locher. Reissued as PA202 (1968), 6825 (1970).

**PA129 DeHavilland Mosquito** 1966-70 1/48 $25-35
Gray, black, clear plastic. Decals. Optional parts to build four variants. Detailed cockpit interior and bomb bay. "Words fail us to describe it. Suffice to say, this is the best American kit ever to come down the pike in 1/4 inch." (*Scale Modeler*, July 1965) Morgan box art Reissued as 6849 (1970), 5408 (1978), 6061 (1984).

**PA135 OSU-3 Kingfisher** 1967-70 1/48 $15-25
Blue, clear plastic. US and British decals. "It is getting to be old hat now, but Monogram seems to outdo itself with every new offering. By any yardstick, the Kingfisher is the best plastic aircraft kit ever produced in this country and, for that matter, the world." (*Scale Modeler*, June 1967). Reissued as 6834 (1970), 5304 (1977). Box art by Morgan.

**PA136 P-51B Mustang** 1967-70 1/48 $10-15
Olive, clear plastic. Two canopies: standard, British Malcolm hood. "Ding Hao!" decals. Box art by Locher. Reissued as 6806 (1970), in 6035 (1984).

**PA143 P-51B** 1967-70 1/72 $6-8
Olive, clear plastic. Decals. Released at same time as 1/48 scale PA136 Mustang. Box art by Locher. Reissued in PA218 (1968), 6788 (1970).

**PA144 F8F-1 Bearcat** 1967-70 1/72 $6-8
Dark blue, clear plastic. Bombs, rockets, drop tanks. Navy decals. Box art by Morgan. Reissued in PA218 (1968), 6789 (1970).

**PA145 Curtiss P-36A** 1967-70 1/72 $6-8
Silver, clear plastic. Decals. Builds either A or C variant. Box art by Locher. Renumbered as 6790 (1970).

**PA146 A-1E Skyraider** 1967-70 1/72 $10-12
Gray, clear plastic. Air Force decals. This model was copied by IMC, which issued it with "battle damaged" decals. Renumbered 6807 (1970).

**PA147 AC-47 Puff the Magic Dragon** 1966-70 1/90 $15-20
Olive green, clear plastic. Air Force decals. Box art by Morgan. Reissue of PA9 (1955) with three Vulcan cannons pointing out the side door and two of the rear windows.

**PA148 AC-47 Puff the Magic Dragon** 1966-69 1/90 $20-25
Tan fuselage and wing parts with pre-painted dark green camouflage pattern sprayed on. Olive green small parts. Clear windows. Air Force decals. Box art by Morgan. Reissue of PA9 (1955).

**PA149 F-105 Thunderjet** 1966-70 1/72 $10-15
Olive, gray, clear plastic. Decals. Bomb bay with opening door is deleted. Two drop tanks and two 750 pound bombs are added. Reissue of PA33 (1958).

**PA150 F-105 Thunderjet** 1966-69 1/72 $20-25
Olive, gray, clear plastic. Pre-painted tan camouflage pattern sprayed on plastic parts. Air Force decals. Reissue of PA33 (1958).

**PA151 HU-1B Huey Chopper** 1966-70 1/48 $15-20
Olive brown plastic. Army decals. Reissue of PA50 (1959). Reissued as 6809 (1970).

**PA152 Huey Rescue Chopper** 1966-70 1/48 $15-20
Olive, clear plastic. Army decals. Rescue medics and stretcher figures included. Reissue of PA50 (1959). Reissued as 6810 (1970).

**PA160 SA-16B Albatross** 1967-70 1/72 $15-25
Silver, clear plastic. Air Force rescue decals. Reissue of PA20 (1957).

**PA161 TWA Ford Tri-Motor** 1967-70 1/77 $15-20
Silver, clear plastic. TWA decals. Box art by Locher. Reissue of P15 (1956).

**PA162 Messerschmitt Bf-110E-1** 1967-70 1/72 $10-12
Dark green clear plastic. Decals. Six bombs. Reissued as 6812 (1970). Box art by Lou Drendel.

**PA163 F7F Tigercat** 1967-70 1/72 $10-12
Blue, clear plastic. Decals. Box art by Locher. Reissued as 6813 (1970).

**PA164 F-101B Voodoo** 1967-70 1/109 $8-10
Silver, clear plastic. Air Force decals. Reissue of P401 (1960).

**PA165 P-40N Warhawk** 1967-70 1/72 $6-8
Olive, clear plastic. Decals. Reissue of P402 (1960).

**PA166 TU-16 Badger** 1967-70 1/96 $15-20
Silver, clear plastic. Decals. Reissue of P403 (1960).

**PA176 RB-66A Destroyer** 1967 1/82 $10-15
Silver, clear plastic. Air Force decals. Box art by Morgan. Reissue of PA10 (1955).

**PA177 A-5A Vigilante** 1967-70 1/72 $15-20
Gray, clear plastic. Navy decals. Reissue of PA53 (1959) with no spring-motivated bomb release. Box art by Locher.

**PA184 Gulfhawk II** 1967-70 1/32 $20-25
Orange, silver, clear plastic. Decals. Reissue of PA58 (1960).

**PA186 F3F-3 Grumman** 1967-70 1/32 $15-25
Silver, clear plastic. Pre-war Navy decals. Box art by Locher. Reissue of PA70 (1962).

**PA187 P-47D Thunderbolt** 1967-70 1/48 $10-15
Olive, clear plastic. Decals. Box art by Locher. Reissued as 6838 (1970), 5302 (1977), 6838 (1983).

**PA191 Huey Cobra Combat Team** 1968-70 1/72 $30-40
Olive, clear plastic. Decals. Clear stand holds two identical AH-1G models. Model based on early production versions with tail rotor on left side. Reissued as 6839 (1970), 5000 (1977).

**PA195 B-26 Invader** 1968-70 1/67 $10-15
Silver, clear plastic. Air Force decals. Reissue of PA6 (1955). BB Box art by Lou Drendel.

**PA196 B-25 Mitchell** 1968-70 1/68 $10-15
Silver, clear plastic. Air Force decals. Reissue of PA7 (1955). BB Box art by Drendel.

**PA197 PBY-5 Catalina** 1968-70 1/100 $15-20
Blue, clear plastic. Navy decals. Reissue of PA8 (1955). Box art by Drendel.

**PA198 B-58 Hustler** 1968-70 1/121 $10-15
Silver, clear plastic. Air Force decals. Reissue of PA32 (1958). BB Box art by Drendel.

**PA199 Piper Tri-Pacer** 1968-70 1/32 $20-25
Cream, clear plastic. Decals. Reissue of PA25 (1957).

**PA200 Blue Angels** 1968-70 1/100 $25-35
Blue, clear plastic. Decals. Reissue of PA29 (1958).

**PA201 Kitty Hawk** 1968-70 1/39 $10-15
Cream, brown plastic. Reissue of PA30 (1958).

**PA202 Cessna 180** 1968-70 1/41 $20-25
Silver, clear plastic. Decals. Box art by Locher. Reissue of PA26 (1957).

**PA203 AC-47 Puff the Magic Dragon** 1968-70 1/90 $20-35
Olive, clear plastic. Air Force decals. Box art by Morgan. Reissue of PA147 (1966). Renumbered 6826 (1970).

**PA204 RB-66 Destroyer** 1968-70 1/82 $10-15
Silver, clear plastic. Air Force decals. Box art by Morgan. Reissue of P10 (1955).

**PA207 Junkers Ju-87G-1 Stuka** 1968-70 1/48 $10-15
Dark green, clear plastic. Decals. Underwing cannon gondolas. Box art by Locher. Reissued as 6840 (1970).

**PA208 Hawk P-6E** 1968-70 1/72 $8-10
Yellow, clear plastic. Decals. Includes display stand. Box art by Locher. Reissued as PA216 (1968), 6794 (1970), 6852 (1970).

**PA209** **Boeing F4B-4** 1968-70 1/72 $8-10
Gray, clear plastic. Decals for USS *Lexington*. Includes display stand. Box art by Locher. Reissued as PA216 (1968), 6795 (1970), 6852 (1970).
**PA210** **F11C-2 Goshawk** 1968-70 1/72 $8-10
Silver, clear plastic. Decals from USS *Saratoga* "High Hat" squadron. Includes display stand. Box art by Locher. Reissued as PA216 (1968), 6796 (1970), 6852 (1970).
**PA211** **Boeing SST** 1968-70 1/400 $25-35
White, clear plastic. Decals. Wings move from landing position to sweptback. Mounted on stand. Renumbered 6815 (1970).
**PA213** **Typhoon IB** 1969-70 1/48 $10-12
Gray, clear plastic. Decals. Box art by Locher. Reissued as 6841 (1970), 5303 (1977).
**PA214** **Dornier Do 17Z** 1969-70 1/72 $10-12
Dark green, clear plastic. Decals for two versions. Box art by Morgan. Reissued as 6842 (1970), 5305 (1978).
**PA215** **B-52 Stratofortress** 1968-70 1/72 $55-65
Olive green, black, clear plastic. Operating bomb bay doors, engine panel removes. Battery-powered "jet engine" sound. Reissued as 6868 (1970), 8292 (1973). Photo box art on first release; Locher art on second.
**PA216** **3 Fighting Planes of 30s** 1968-70 1/72 $25-35
Includes PA208, PA209, PA210.
**PA218** **2 Pylon Racers!** 1968-70 1/72 $20-30
Red, blue, clear plastic. Includes P-51 (PA143) and Bearcat (PA144) mounted on a cardboard racing pylon. Civilian decals. Reissued as 6843 (1970).
**PA226** **Huey Phantom Chopper** 1969-70 1/24 $300-350
Clear, silver, light green, black plastic. Chrome plated engine. Pilot, co-pilot figures. Decals for medical evacuation copter. Two D batteries power "putt-putt" engine sound maker and motor to turn rotors. Reissued as 6867 (1970), 5602 (1976). Box art by Bill Koster.
**PA227** **P-39/400** 1969-70 1/48 $20-25
Olive green, clear plastic. Optional parts for four variants. Decals for four variants (including one Russian). Panels remove to show engine, gun compartment. Box art by Locher. Reissued as 6844 (1970).
**PE252M** **Wright Cyclone Engine** 1959-63 1/12 $65-80
Black, gray, red plastic. Motorized version of PE52 (1959).
**P401/PA401** **F-101 Voodoo** 1960-65 1/109 $10-12
Silver, clear plastic. Two crew figures. Two Genie missiles. A Forty-niner 49 cent kit. Box art by Kowal. Reissued as PA164 (1967), 6791 (1970).
**P402/PA402** **P-40N Warhawk** 1960-65 1/72 $10-12
Olive brown, clear plastic. Army Air Corps decals. A Forty-niner kit. Box art by Kowal. Reissued as PA165 (1967), 6792 (1970).
**P403/PA403** **TU-16 Badger** 1960-65 1/92 $20-25
Silver, clear plastic. Soviet decals. A Forty-niner kit. Box art by Kowal. Reissued as PA166 (1967), 6793 (1970).
**P407** **U. S. Fighters** 1960-65 1/240 $60-70
Silver, blue plastic. Decals. Select models from PA56 (1959): F-100, F-101, F-102, F-104, F-105.
**P408** **U. S. Bombers** 1960-65 1/240 $60-70
Silver, blue plastic. Decals. Select models from PA56 (1959): B-57, B-58, B-66.
**P409** **Refueling Group** 1960-65 1/240 $60-70
Silver, blue plastic. Decals. Select models from PA56 (1959): KC-135, B-47.

## 1970-1979 Aircraft Models

**1002** **Messerschmitt Me-109** (snap) 1975-86 1/64 $4-6
Olive, clear plastic. Decals.
**1003** **Spitfire** (snap) 1975-84 1/64 $4-6
Tan, clear plastic. Decals. Photo box art.
**1008** **Huey Chopper** (snap) 1976-83 $4-6
Also issued as 1009 (1976).
**1009** **Police Chopper** (snap) 1976-84 $4-6
White, clear plastic. Decals. Also issued as 1008 (1976).
**1015** **F-15 Eagle** (snap) 1978-86 1/72 $4-6
**1100** **B-25B Mitchell** (snap) 1978-86 1/72 $6-8
Olive, clear plastic. Decals.
**1101** **B-26 Marauder** (snap) 1978-86 1/72 $6-8
Olive brown, clear plastic. Decals. A model of an early short-wing B-26B.
**1102** **F-4 Phantom** (snap) 1979-86 1/72 $6-8
Olive brown, clear plastic. Decals.
**5000** **Huey Cobra AH-16** 1975-84 1/72 $10-15
Olive, clear plastic. Decals. Reissue of a single model from PA191 (1968).
**5100** **Trojan T-28B** 1975-78 1/51 $10-15
White, clear plastic. Decals. Reissue of PA14 (1956).
**5101** **P-51D Mustang** 1977-84 1/48 $6-8
Silver, clear plastic. Canopy slides open. Wing panel removes to show guns. Lower cowl removes to show engine. Two drop tanks. Photo box art. Reissued as 5207 (1985).
**5200** **F-16 Fighting Falcon** 1977-86 1/72 $6-8
Gray, clear plastic. Decals. Photo box art. Reissued as 5504 Thunderbirds (1983).
**5201** **Huey Hog** 1977-86 1/48 $6-8
Olive brown, clear plastic. Marines decals. This was a brand new mold to produce a modern version of the Huey. Photo box art. Reissued as 5202 (1978).
**5202** **Huey Chopper** 1978-83 1/48 $6-8
Gray, clear plastic. Box art by Locher. Reissue 5201 (1977).
**5203** **Fokker D-7** (Aurora) 1979-80 1/48 $8-10
Dark green plastic. Decals.
**5204** **Sopwith Camel** (Aurora) 1979-80 1/48 $8-10
Olive plastic. RFC decals.
**5205** **British SE-5A** (Aurora) 1979-80 1/48 $8-10
Olive plastic. RFC decals.
**5300** **Kitty Hawk** 1976-77 1/39 $8-10
Off white, tan plastic. Reissue of PA30 (1958).
**5302** **P-47 Razorback** 1977-83 1/48 $6-8
Olive brown, clear plastic. Two decal options. Modified reissue of PA187 (1967).
**5303** **Hawker Typhoon** 1977-79 1/48 $6-8
Gray, clear plastic. RAF decals. Reissue of PA213 (1969).
**5304** **OS2U Kingfisher** 1977-79 1/48 $10-15
Blue, clear plastic. US or British decals. Reissue of PA135 (1967).
**5305** **Dornier Do 17Z** 1978-79 1/72 $4-6
Green, clear plastic. Decals. Reissue of PA214 (1969).
**5306** **AT-6 Texan** 1979-85 1/48 $10-15
Silver, clear plastic. Air Force or Navy decals. Student and instructor figures. Photo box art. Reissued as 5307 (1983).
**5400** **HU-16E Albatross** 1975-78 1/72 $10-15
White, clear plastic. Coast Guard decals. Reissue of PA20 (1957).
**5401** **F-16** 1976-86 1/48 $4-6
White, clear plastic. Decals for red-white-blue prototype version or Air Force. Reissued as 5421 (1981).
**5402** **F-86F Sabre Jet** 1976-79 1/48 $8-10
Silver, clear plastic. Korean War decals. Canopy slides open. Panel removes to show guns. Reissued as 5417 (1979), 5427 (1983).
**5403** **MiG-15** 1976-79 1/48 $8-10
Silver, clear plastic. Decals for Soviets, Chinese, North Koreans. Service panel removes from fuselage.
**5404** **F-80 Shooting Star** 1977-80 1/48 $10-15
Silver, clear plastic. Optional parts for bomber or fighter variants. Decals from A, B, or C versions. Tail removes to show engine. Cradle for tail section. Panel removes to show gun bay. Photo box art. Reissued as 5428 (1983).
**5405** **Fairchild A-10** 1977-85 1/72 $4-6
Gray, clear plastic. Canopy hinged to open. Panel removes to show engine. Sixteen bombs and drop tanks. Box art by Morgan. Reissued as 5430 (1983).
**5406** **A-4E Skyhawk** 1977-86 1/48 $15-20
Gray, clear plastic. Navy or Marines decals. Separate leading edge slats and flaps. Reissued as 5411 (1979), 5422 (1981), 5436 (1985).
**5407** **F-5E Tiger II** 1978-83 1/48 $8-10
Gray, clear plastic. Air Force or Navy decals. Pilot figure and boarding ladder. Reissued as 5423 (1981), 5441 (1985).
**5408** **Mosquito Bomber** 1978-79 1/48 $8-10
Gray, black, clear plastic. RAF decals. Reissue of PA129 (1966).
**5409** **F-104 Starfighter** 1978-83 1/48 $8-10
Silver, clear plastic. US, Canada, German, Netherlands decals. Reissued as 5433 (1984).
**5410** **Me-262** 1978-81 1/48 $8-10
Green, clear plastic. Decals. Panels remove to show gun compartment, engine.
**5411** **A-4 Aggressor** 1979-81 1/48 $10-12
Beige, clear plastic. Air Force or Aggressor decals. Reissue of 5406 (1977).
**5412** **Boeing 747** (Aurora) 1978-79 1/156 $20-25
White, clear plastic. Pan American decals.
**5413** **Douglas DC-10** (Aurora) 1978-79 1/144 $20-25
White, clear plastic. American Airlines decals.
**5414** **Boeing 727** (Aurora) 1978-79 1/96 $25-30
White, clear plastic. TWA decals.
**5415** **Boeing 737** (Aurora) 1978-79 1/72 $25-30
White, clear plastic. United decals.
**5417** **Canadair Sabre 6** 1979-81 1/48 $8-10
Gray, clear plastic. Canadian or German decals. Canopy slides open, gun compartment panel removes. Reissue of 5402 (1976).
**5418** **A-7A Corsair II** (Aurora) 1979-86 1/48 $10-12
Light gray. Clear plastic. Aurora put recessed panel lines into this mold before Monogram reworked it.
**5500** **B-25H** 1977-83 1/48 $12-17
Olive, clear plastic. Two decal versions. Two crew, one ground crew figures. Solid nose version. Reissued as 5502 (1981).
**5501** **B-26 Marauder** 1978-83 1/48 $15-20
Olive, clear plastic. Two seated and one standing crew figures. Two AAF decal versions, including "Flak Bait." Two tail gun variants. Photo box art.
**5600** **Boeing B-17G** 1975-86 1/48 $25-30
Silver, black, clear plastic. Three crew and two ground crew figures. Four bombs and bomb cart—but no opening bomb bay doors or bomb racks inside bomb bay. Decals for two variants. Only 74 parts to this large model because flight surfaces are molded into wings and usually separate parts molded together. Box art by Locher. Reissued as 5620 (1979).

**5601** **B-24J Liberator** 1976-81 1/48 $25-35
Silver, black, clear plastic. Three crew, two ground crew figures. Tow tractor. Decals for two variants. Belly turret retracts. Turret in nose. Box art by Locher. Reissued as 5604 (1983) with glass nose.

**5602** **Huey UH-1B** 1976-79 1/24 $20-25
Olive, gray, black, clear plastic. Reissue of PA226 (1969).

**5603** **C-47 Skytrain** 1978-83 1/48 $30-35
Olive, clear plastic. Decals for RAF, Confederate Air Force, and "Buzz Buggy." versions. Three crew, nine paratrooper figures. Box art by Locher.

**5620** **Visible B-17** 1979-81 1/48 $130-160
Clear, olive, black plastic. Optional olive fuselage half. Two decal versions. Reissue of 5600 (1975).

**5700** **B-29 Superfortress** 1977-86 1/48 $40-45
Silver, black, clear plastic. Decals. Optional parts for atomic bombers Enola Gay, Box Car, and conventional bomber Thumper. Five crew figures. Little Boy and Fat Man atomic bombs. Twelve conventional bombs. At the time of its release, this was the largest plastic model airplane ever.

**5701** **Phantom Mustang** 1979-81 1/32 $50-60
Clear, red, green, silver, black plastic. Air Force decals. Reissue of PA67 (1961).

**5800** **F-4 Phantom II** 1979-84 1/48 $8-10
Olive, clear plastic. Air Force decals. Sparrow and Sidewinder missiles. Standing and seated crew. Reissued as 5805 (1981), 5813 (1985).

**5801** **F-15 Eagle** 1979-86 1/48 $4-6
Gray, clear plastic. Pilot, ground crew figures. Decals.

**5901** **Skystick with P-51B** 1971-72 1/48 $70-90
Red, off-white plastic. Table-top controller that operates as a flight simulator for any model attached to its top. Also came with a flat outline model of the P-51.

**5992** **F-14A Tomcat** 1971-86 1/72 $4-6
Gray, clear plastic. Nvay decals. Wings swing out or swept back. This was the first F-14 model kit issued and was based on preliminary information from Grumman. This was the only new aircraft model issued by Monogram from 1970 to 1972. Box art by Morgan.

**6788** **P-51B Mustang** 1970-84 1/72 $4-6
Olive brown, clear plastic. Renumber of PA143 (1967).

**6789** **F8F Bearcat** 1970-84 1/72 $4-6
Blue, clear plastic. Box art by Morgan. Renumber of PA144 (1967).

**6790** **Curtiss P-36A** 1970-83 1/72 $4-6
Silver, clear plastic. Renumber of PA145 (1967).

**6791** **F-101B Voodoo** 1970-83 1/72 $6-8
Silver, clear plastic. Renumber of P401 (1960).

**6792** **P-40N Warhawk** 1970-84 1/72 $4-6
Olive, clear plastic. Renumber of P402 (1960).

**6793** **TU-16 Badger** 1970-76 1/72 $10-15
Silver, clear plastic. Russian decals. Renumber of P403 (1960).

**6794** **P-6E Hawk** 1970-83 1/72 $6-8
Yellow plastic. Renumber of PA208 (1968).

**6795** **Boeing F-4B-4** 1970-84 1/72 $6-8
Gray plastic. Renumber of PA209 (1968).

**6796** **F11C-2 Goshawk** 1970-84 1/72 $6-8
Silver, clear plastic. Renumber of PA210 (1968).

**6798** **F4F Wildcat** 1970-83 1/48 $4-6
Blue, clear plastic. Renumber of PA66 (1961).

**6799** **Japanese Zero A6M5** 1970-84 1/48 $4-6
Dark green, clear plastic. Renumber of PA73 (1962).

**6800** **Messerschmitt Me109E** 1970-84 1/48 $4-6
Dark green, black, clear plastic. Renumber of PA74 (1962).

**6801** **British Spitfire** 1970-84 1/48 $10-15
Gray, clear plastic. Renumber of PA79 (1962).

**6802** **Hawker Hurricane** 1970-78 1/48 $4-6
Gray, clear plastic. RAF decals. Renumber of PA90 (1964).

**6803** **P-40B Tiger Shark** 1970-84 1/48 $4-6
Olive, clear plastic. Decals. Renumber of PA96 (1964).

**6804** **Focke Wulf FW 190** 1970-84 1/48 $8-10
Dark green, black, clear plastic. Renumber of PA107 (1965).

**6805** **T-28D Fighter Bomber** 1970-75 1/51 $10-15
Gray, clear plastic. Decals. Renumber of PA121 (1965).

**6806** **P-51B Mustang** 1970-83 1/48 $6-8
Olive green, clear plastic. "Ding Hao!" decals. Renumber of PA136 (1967). Box art by Locher.

**6807** **A-1E Skyraider** 1970-82 1/72 $4-6
Gray, clear plastic. Air Force decals. Renumber of PA146 (1967).

**6808** **F-105 Thunderchief** 1970-82 1/72 $6-8
Tan, clear plastic. Decals. Renumber of PA149 (1966). Box art by Morgan.

**6809** **Huey Armed Chopper** 1970-77 1/48 $6-8
Olive green, clear plastic. Box art by Bill Miller. Renumber of PA151 (1966).

**6810** **Huey Rescue Chopper** 1970-77 1/48 $6-8
Olive, clear plastic. Army decals. Box art by Bill Miller. Renumber of PA50 (1959).

**6811** **TWA Ford Tri-Motor** 1970-71 1/77 $8-10
Silver, clear plastic. TWA decals. Renumber of PA161 (1967).

**6812** **Messerschmitt Bf-110E-1** 1970-79 1/72 $4-6
Olive, clear plastic. Renumber of PA162 (1967). Box art by Drendel.

**6813** **F7F-3 Tigercat** 1970-79 1/72 $4-6
Blue, clear plastic. Navy decals. Renumber of PA163 (1967).

**6814** **A-5A Vigilante** 1970-76 1/72 $8-10
Gray, clear plastic. Navy decals. Renumber of PA53 (1959).

**6815** **Boeing SST** 1970-75 1/400 $30-35
White, clear plastic. Renumber of PA211 (1968).

**6818** **B-26 Invader** 1970-81 1/67 $10-12
Silver, clear plastic. Air Force decals. Renumber of P6 (1955).

**6819** **B-25 Mitchell** 1970-85 1/68 $8-10
Silver, clear plastic. Air Force decals. Renumber of P7 (1955).

**6820** **PBY-5A Catalina** 1970-75 1/100 $14-18
Blue, clear plastic. Black vinyl tires. Navy decals. Renumber of P8 (1955).

**6821** **B-58 Hustler** 1970-83 1/121 $8-10
Silver, clear plastic. Renumber of PA32 (1958).

**6822** **Piper Tri-Pacer** 1970-80 1/32 $15-20
White plastic. Decal. Renumber of PA25 (1957). Later releases in photo box art.

**6823** **Blue Angels F11F-1** 1970-75 1/100 $35-45
Blue, clear plastic. Decals. Renumber of PA29 (1958).

**6824** **Kitty Hawk** 1970-75 1/39 $8-10
Off white, tan plastic. Reissue of PA30 (1958).

**6825** **Cessna 180** 1970-80 1/41 $10-15
Silver, clear plastic. Decals. Renumber of PA202 (1968).

**6826** **AC-47 Puff the Magic Dragon** 1970-71 1/90 $8-10
Dark green, clear plastic. Decals. Renumber of PA203 (1968).

**6827** **B-66 Destroyer** 1970-75 1/82 $8-10
Silver, clear plastic. Renumber of P10 (1955).

**6829** **TBF Avenger** 1970-83 1/48 $8-10
Blue, clear plastic. Navy decals. Renumber of PA31 (1958).

**6830** **SBD Dauntless** 1970-83 1/48 $8-10
Blue, clear plastic. Navy decals. Renumber of PA54 (1960).

**6831** **SB2C-5 Helldiver** 1970-86 1/48 $12-15
Dark blue, black, clear plastic. Matthew Waki box art on 1983 issue. Renumber of PA69 (1961).

**6832** **F6F-5 Hellcat** 1970-83 1/48 $10-15
Blue, clear plastic. Renumber of PA80 (1963).

**6833** **F4U-4 Corsair** 1970-86 1/48 $10-15
Blue, clear plastic. Korean War decals. Renumber of PA82 (1963).

**6834** **OS2U-3 Kingfisher** 1970-75 1/48 $8-10
Blue, clear plastic. US and British decals. Renumber of PA135 (1967).

**6837** **HU-16B Albatross** 1970-75 1/48 $10-15
Silver, clear plastic. Renumber of PA20 (1957).

**6838** **P-47D Thunderbolt** 1970-86 1/48 $6-8
Silver, clear plastic. Decals. Renumber of PA187 (1967).

**6839** **Huey Cobra Team** 1970-75 1/72 $12-15
Olive, clear plastic. Renumber of PA191 (1968).

**6840** **Ju 87G1 Stuka** 1970-86 1/48 $8-10
Dark green, clear plastic. Renumber of PA207 (1968). 1983 release box art by Lou Drendel.

**6841** **Hawker Typhoon** 1970-75 1/48 $4-6
Gray, clear plastic. RAF decals. Renumber of PA213 (1969).

**6842** **Dornier Do 17z** 1970-75 1/72 $4-6
Dark green, clear plastic. Decals. Renumber of PA214 (1969).

**6843** **2 Pylon Racers!** 1970-75 1/72 $12-17
Red, blue, clear plastic. Decals. Renumber of PA218 (1970).

**6844** **P-39 Aircobra** 1970-86 1/48 $8-10
Olive green, clear plastic. US and Soviet decals. Renumber of PA227 (1969).

**6847** **F-51D Mustang** 1970-78 1/32 $20-25
Silver, black, clear plastic. Air Force decals. Renumber of PA77 (1962).

**6848** **P-38 Lightning** 1970-86 1/48 $8-10
Silver-gray, black, clear plastic. Decals. Renumber of PA97 (1964).

**6849** **DeHavilland Mosquito** 1970-76 1/48 $8-10
Gray, black, clear plastic. Decals. Photo box art in 1973. Renumber of PA129.

**6850** **Gulfhawk II** 1970-75 1/32 $15-20
Orange, silver, clear plastic. Decals. Includes standing figure of pilot Major Al Williams. Renumber of PA58 (1960).

**6851** **F3F-3 Grumman** 1970-75 1/32 $15-20
Silver, clear plastic. Navy decals. Renumber of PA70 (1962).

**6852** **Fighting Planes of the 30s** 1970 1/72 $15-20
Gift set includes: Hawk P-6E (6794), Boeing F4B-4 (6795), Goshawk F11C-2 (6796).

**6866** **Phantom Mustang** 1970-75 1/32 $50-60
Clear, red, green silver, black plastic. Decals. Renumber of PA67 (1961).

**6867** **Phantom Huey** 1970-75 1/24 $250-275
Renumber of PA226 (1969).

**6868** **B-52 Stratofortress** 1970 1/72 $30-35
Gray, black, clear plastic. Renumber of PA215 (1968) with new box art. Still has the sound feature.

**7501** **F-82 Twin Mustang** 1973-78 1/72 $6-8
Black, clear plastic. Decals. Optional parts for F-82G night fighter or F-82E escort fighter. Reissued as 6063 (1984).

**7538** **Dornier Do 335** 1974-78 1/48 $15-20
Dark green, clear plastic. Decals. Two ground crew. Builds single seat fighter or two seat night fighter. Panels remove to show engine, which is built into fuselage parts. Flaps separate. Photo box art.
**7546** **P-61 Black Widow** 1974-86 1/48 $10-15
Black, clear plastic. Builds A or B variants. Hatches remove to show interior, nose cone removes to show radar. Optional parts for open or closed cowl flaps.
**7575** **TBD Devastator** 1974-86 1/48 $10-15
Light gray, clear plastic. Decals for pre-war or wartime colors. Wings fold, removable engine and gun panels. Pilot and two deck figures.
**7576** **P-51D Mustang** (snap) 1974-86 1/64 $4-6
Silver, clear plastic. Peel-stick decals.
**7577** **P-40F Tiger Shark** (snap) 1974-86 1/64 $4-6
Olive, clear plastic. Peel-stick decals.
**7580** **F-15 Eagle** 1974-83 1/72 $3-5
Light blue, clear plastic. Canopy hinged to open. Pilot, crew chief figures. Air Force decals.
**7590** **Navy DC-3** 1975-78 1/90 $8-10
Silver, clear plastic. "United States Navy" decals. Reissue of PA9 (1955).
**7591** **Super G Constellation** 1975-78 1/134 $8-10
Silver, white, clear plastic. USAF decals. Reissue of PA19 (1956).
**7592** **Ford Tri-Motor** 1975-78 1/77 $10-12
White, clear plastic. Decals for "Island Airlines" which still used the Tri-Motor on flights to islands in Lake Erie. Reissue of PA122 (1965).
**8292** **Boeing B-52D** 1973-86 1/72 $20-25
Gray, black, clear plastic. Decals. Bomb bay doors open, flaps slide in and out, spoilers move up and down, engine panel removes to show engine. Reissue of PA215 (1968) without the sound feature. Box art by Locher.

## 1980-1986 Aircraft Models

**1025** **Forest Ranger Copter** (snap) 1980-83 $4-6
**1026** **Fire Helicopter** (snap) 1980-83 $4-6
Red, clear plastic. Fire fighter decals.
**1103** **F-18 Hornet** (snap) 1980-86 1/72 $3-5
**1104** **F-14 Tomcat** (snap) 1980-86 1/72 $3-5
Gray, clear plastic. Shark's mouth decal.
**1108** **B-1B** (snap) 1984-86 1/144 $3-5
White plastic. Red, white, and blue decals. Wings move. Mounted on display stand.
**1109** **SR-71A** (snap) 1985-86 1/110 $3-5
Black, clear plastic. Decals. Mounted on display stand.
**1111** **F-15** (snap) 1986 1/100 $3-5
Mounded on display stand.
**5206** **F-16XL Fighter** 1983-86 1/72 $10-15
Gray, tinted clear canopy. Decals. Experimental delta wing version of the F-16.
**5207** **P-51D** 1985-86 1/48 $4-6
Silver, clear plastic. Decals. Reissue of 5101 (1977).
**5208** **Spitfire** 1985-86 1/48 $4-6
Gray, clear plastic. RAF decals. Reissue of PA79 (1962).
**5209** **Tiger Shark P-40B** 1985-86 1/48 $6-8
Olive, clear plastic. Box art by Don Greer. Reissue of PA96 (1964).
**5306** **AT-6 Texan** 1983-85 1/48 $10-15
Silver, clear plastic. Air Force decals. Reissue of 5306 (1979). Box art by Lou Drendel.
**5307** **Miller Racer** 1983-85 1/48 $10-15
Gray, clear plastic. Red, white, blue color scheme decals. T-6/SNJ as Reno racer. Reissue of 5306 (1979). Box art by Drendel.
**5416** **F-100 Super Sabre** 1980-85 1/48 $10-15
Silver, clear plastic. Decals for two versions. Pilot and ground crew figures. Reissued as 5424 (1981).
**5419** **A-1H Skyraider** 1980-86 1/48 $8-10
Gray, clear plastic. Decals for US Navy or South Vietnamese air force. Reissued as 5429 (1983). Photo box art.
**5420** **V/STOL Harrier** 1981-86 1/48 $8-10
Dark gray, clear plastic. US Marines and RAF decals. Box art by Locher.
**5421** **F-16 Fighting Falcon** 1981-86 1/48 $4-6
Gray, clear plastic. Reissue of 5401 (1976).
**5422** **Blue Angels A-4** 1981-83 1/48 $10-15
Blue, clear plastic. Navy decals. Reissue of 5406 (1977).
**5423** **F-5E Tiger** 1981-85 1/48 $8-10
Silver, clear plastic. Air Force decals. Reissue of 5407 (1978).
**5424** **F-100D Fighter Bomber** 1981-84 1/48 $12-15
Olive brown, clear plastic. Reissue of 5416 (1980).
**5425** **Mirage 2000** 1982-86 1/48 $8-10
White, clear plastic. French Air Force decals.
**5426** **Tornado** 1982-86 1/72 $3-5
Dark gray, clear plastic. RAF and Luftwaffe decals. Wings pivot.
**5427** **F-86 Sabre Jet** 1983-86 1/48 $10-15
Silver, clear plastic. "The Huff" decals. Reissue of 5402 (1976).
**5428** **F-80 Shooting Star** 1983-86 1/48 $10-15
Silver, clear plastic. AF decals. Box art by Morgan. Reissue of 5404 (1977).
**5429** **AD-6 Skyraider** 1983-86 1/48 $15-20
Blue, clear plastic. Navy decals. Reissue of 5419 (1980).
**5430** **A-10 Warthog** 1983-86 1/72 $4-6
Olive green, clear plastic. Box art by Morgan. Reissue of 5405 (1977).
**5431** **F-105 Wild Weasel** 1984-86 1/72 $4-6
Olive, clear plastic. Air Force decals. Box art by Greer.
**5432** **F-84F Thunderstreak** 1984-86 1/48 $10-12
Gray, clear plastic.
**5433** **F-104C Starfighter** 1984-86 1/48 $8-10
Olive, clear plastic. Air Force decals. Reissue of 5409 (1978).
**5434** **F-15 Strike Eagle** 1984-86 1/72 $3-5
Olive, clear plastic. Air Force decals. Reissue of 7580 (1974).
**5435** **EF-111 Raven** (Aurora) 1984-86 1/72 $6-8
Gray, clear plastic. Reissue of 5804 (1981).
**5436** **OA-4M Skyhawk** 1985-86 1/48 $10-12
Gray, clear plastic. Reissue of 5406 (1977).
**5437** **F-84F Republic** 1985-86 1/48 $10-12
Silver, clear plastic. Don Greer box art. Reissue of 5432 (1984).
**5438** **F-105 Fighter Bomber** 1985-86 1/72 $8-10
Silver, clear plastic. Air Force decals. Reissue of 5431 (1984).
**5439** **F-4C/D Phantom II** 1985-86 1/72 $6-8
Olive, clear plastic. Air Force decals. Also issued as 5440 (1985).
**5440** **F-4J McDonnell Navy** 1985-86 1/72 $6-8
Gray, clear plastic. Navy decals. Also issued as 5439 (1985).
**5441** **F-5 Aggressor** 1985-86 1/48 $8-10
Beige, clear plastic. Navy war games "aggressor" decals. Two seat version. Reissue of 5407 (1978).
**5442** **Thunderbirds F-100** 1985-86 1/48 $12-15
Silver, clear plastic. Thunderbirds decals. Reissue of 5416 (1980).
**5443** **AH-64 Apache Helicopter** 1986 1/48 $8-10
Olive, clear plastic.
**5444** **AH-15 Cobra Chopper** 1986 1/48 $8-10
Olive, clear plastic.
**5445** **F-20 Tigershark** 1986 1/48 $8-10
Silver gray, clear plastic. Decals.
**5502** **B-25J Mitchell** 1981-86 1/48 $15-20
Silver, clear plastic. Air Force decals. Reissue of 5500 (1977) with glass nose. Box art by Locher.
**5504** **F-16 Thunderbirds Team** 1983-86 1/72 $12-16
White plastic. Smoked clear plastic canopies and clear base. Thunderbird decals. Box art by Morgan. Reissue of 5200 (1977).
**5505** **A-10 Thunderbolt II** 1986 1/48 $8-10
Olive, clear plastic. Decals. Canopy can be built open or closed; flaps can be positioned. Lots of underwing ordinance.
**5604** **B-24D Liberator** 1983-86 1/48 $20-25
Olive, black, clear plastic. AAF decals. Box art by Greer. Reissue of 5601 (1976) with glass nose.
**5605** **B-1B Bomber** 1983-86 1/72 $15-20
White, clear plastic. Red, white, blue color scheme decals. Four crew. Seventeen cruise missiles. Wings pivot to sweptback position. Reissued as 5606 (1986).
**5606** **Camouflaged B-1B** 1986 1/72 $12-17
"European green," clear plastic. Decals for "Spirit of Abilene," the first operational B-1B. Reissue of 5605 (1983).
**5703** **B-36 Peacemaker** 1980-86 1/72 $30-35
Silver, clear plastic. Four crew members. Two decal versions. Optional parts for B-36H or RB-36H reconnaissance variant with four radomes. 80 bombs in bomb bay. This is Monogram's largest model of all time, with a wing span of three feet. Only 120 parts. Box art by Locher.
**5704** **B-58 Hustler** 1985-86 1/48 $20-25
Silver, clear plastic. Air Force decals.
**5802** **F-18 Hornet** 1980-83 1/48 $6-8
White, clear plastic. Decals. This model is based on the Hornet prototype. Reissued as 5807 (1983).
**5803** **F-14 Tomcat** 1981-86 1/48 $6-8
Gray, clear plastic. Navy decals. Box art by Sonny Schug.
**5804** **F-111 Swing Wing** (Aurora) 1981-86 1/48 $8-10
Dark olive brown, clear plastic. This model is made from an extensive reworking of the Aurora mold. Don Greer box art. Reissued as 5435 (1984), 5815 (1985).
**5805** **U. S. Navy F-4J** 1981-86 1/48 $8-10
Black, clear plastic. Navy, bunny decals. Reissue of 5800 (1979).
**5806** **F-105G Wild Weasel** 1982-86 1/48 $12-15
Olive brown, clear plastic. Decals. Two seat electronic warfare version of F-105. Box art by Locher. Reissued as 5808 (1983), 5812 (1985), 5816 (1985).
**5807** **A-18 Attack Fighter** 1983-86 1/48 $6-8
Gray, clear plastic. Four bombs and Sidewinder missiles. Monogram updated 5802 (1980) to incorporate changes made in the production version of the F-18.
**5808** **F-105F Thud** 1983-84 1/48 $12-15
Silver, clear plastic. Air Force shark mouth decals. Reissue of 5806 (1982) as single-seat fighter-bomber. Box art by Greer.

**5809** **F-106 Delta Dart** 1983-86 1/48 $12-15
Gray, clear plastic. Air Force decals. Two canopy versions. Four Falcon, one Genie missiles. Box art by Sonny Schug.

**5810** **SR-71 Blackbird** 1984-86 1/72 $8-10
Black, clear plastic. Decals. With GTD-21 drone.

**5811** **F-101B Voodoo** 1985-86 1/48 $20-25
Gray, clear plastic. Two Falcon, two Genie missiles. Air Force decals. Nose section is separate part to permit reissues as different variants. Don Greer box art. Reissued as 5818 (1986).

**5812** **F-105D Thunderchief** 1985-86 1/48 $10-15
Olive, clear plastic. Decals. Reissue of 5806 (1982).

**5813** **F-4J Phantom II** 1985-86 1/48 $8-12
Gray, clear plastic. Navy decals. Reissue of 5800 (1979).

**5814** **F-4 Phantom II** 1985 1/48 $8-12
Olive, clear plastic. Air Force decals. Issued in connection with the TV series Call to Glory. Reissue of 5800 (1979).

**5815** **F-111A** (Aurora) 1985 1/48 $10-15
Olive green, clear plastic. Call to Glory. Reissue of 5804 (1981).

**5816** **F-105** 1985 1/48 $10-15
Silver, clear plastic. Sharksmouth decals. Call to Glory. Underwing tanks, 250 pound bombs, 750 pound bombs. Reissue of 5806 (1982).

**5817** **SR-71A Blackbird** 1985 1/72 $8-10
Black, clear plastic. Call to Glory. Reissue of 5810 (1984).

**5818** **RF-101B Recon Voodoo** 1986 1/48 $10-15
Olive brown, clear plastic. Reissue of 5811 (1985).

**6036** **Blue Thunder Helicopter** 1984-86 1/32 $20-25
Dark metallic blue, clear plastic. Model of the copter used in the TV series "Blue Thunder." Actual copter was a modified French-made Gazelle.

**6038** **Rambo Combat Chopper** 1986 1/24 $30-35
Olive, silver, clear plastic. Decals based on *First Blood, Part II* movie. Box art by Elmore. Reissue of 6867 (1970).

**6039** **Rambo Attack Set** 1986 1/48 $30-35
Contains Rambo Combat Chopper 6809 (1970) in olive plastic and RAG River Patrol Boat PB179 (1967) in gray plastic.

**6052** **Cyclone Engine** 1983 1/12 $50-60
Red, silver, black, gray plastic. Silver foil sticker name plate. Heritage Collection. Reissue of PE52 (1959).

**6053** **Grumman Gulfhawk II** 1983 1/32 $15-20
Orange, silver, clear plastic. Gulf decals. Heritage Collection. Reissue of PA58 (1960).

**6054** **P-51 Mustang** 1983 1/32 $20-25
Silver, black clear plastic. Decals. Heritage Collection. Reissue of PA67 (1961).

**6056** **Ford Tri-Motor** 1983 1/77 $8-10
Silver, clear plastic. Heritage Collection. With skis and dog sled team. "Antarctic Expedition" decals. Reissue of P15 (1956).

**6057** **Kitty Hawk** 1983 1/39 $6-8
Off white, tan plastic. Heritage Collection. Reissue of PA30 (1958).

**6058** **Super G Connie** 1983 1/134 $8-10
Silver, white, clear plastic. TWA decals. Heritage Collection. Reissue of PA19 (1956).

**6059** **C-47 Spooky** 1983 1/90 $8-10
Olive, clear plastic. Decals. Heritage Collection. Reissue of PA9 (1955) in Vietnam gunship version.

**6062** **F7F Tigercat** 1984-85 1/72 $6-8
Blue, clear plastic. Heritage Collection. Reissue of PA163 (1967).

**6063** **F-82 Twin Mustang** 1984-85 1/72 $4-6
Silver, clear plastic. Air Force decals. Heritage Collection. Gun compartment opens. Reissue of 7501 (1973).

**6064** **Mosquito Bomber** 1984 1/48 $6-8
Gray, black, clear plastic. RAF decals. Heritage Collection. Reissue of PA129 (1966).

**6065** **HU-16B Albatross** 1984 1/72 $12-15
Gray, clear plastic. Air Force decals. Heritage Collection. Reissue of PA20 (1957).

**6831** **SB2C Helldiver** 1983-86 1/48 $12-15
Blue, clear plastic. Navy decals. Reissue of PA69 (1961).

**6833** **F4U Vought Corsair** 1983-86 1/48 $6-8
Blue, clear plastic. Reissue of PA82 (1963).

**6838** **P-47D Thunderbolt** 1983-86 1/48 $6-8
Gray, clear plastic. Decals. Reissue of PA187 (1967).

**6844** **P-39 Aircobra** 1983-86 1/48 $8-10
Olive green, clear plastic. Decals.

## Missiles, Rockets, and Spacecraft

The following six kits were composed of individual missiles selected from the PD40 Missile Arsenal set and packaged in plastic bags with header cards.

**MP1** **Five Missiles** 1959 1/128 $45-55
Cream plastic. (Some are silver plastic.) Decals. Honest John, Jupiter, Rat, Talos, Thor.

**MP2** **Two Missiles** 1959 1/128 $45-55
Red plastic. Decals. Matador, Snark.

**MP3** **Ten Missiles** 1959 1/128 $45-55
Silver plastic. Decals. Bullpup, Dart, Falcon, Jupiter C, LaCrosse, Little John, Polaris, Sergeant, Sidewinder, Sparrow.

**MP4** **Eight Missiles** 1959 1/128 $45-55
Silver plastic. Decals. Atlas, Genie, Hawk, Nike Ajax, Petrel, Tartar, Terrier, Vanguard.

**MP5** **Three Missiles** 1959 1/128 $45-55
Blue, white plastic. Decals. Bomarc, Rascal, Regulus.

**MP6** **Three Missiles** 1959 1/128 $45-55
Cream plastic. Decals. Corporal, Nike Hercules, Redstone.

**PD27** **Snark SM-62** 1957-63 1/90 $125-150
Red, yellow plastic. Four figures. Tractor and elevating launching ramp.

**PD38** **Little John** 1958-60 1/35 $190-210
White, olive plastic. Decals. Three figures. Tow jeep (PM21), elevating mobile launcher.

**PD39** **Regulus II** 1958-60 1/68 $160-190
Blue, white, yellow, black plastic. Navy decals. Three figures. Tractor, elevating mobile launcher.

**PD40** **US Missile Arsenal** 1958-63 1/128 $190-240
White, red, blue, clear plastic. Decals. Thirty-one missiles. Two figures. Thirty-two page booklet with introduction by Willy Ley. Clear plastic base with cardboard insert printed with the names of the missiles. Reissued as PD43 (1959), PS221 (1969), 6871 (1970), 6055 (1983).

**PD41** **Earth Satellites** 1958-61 1/96 $190-240
Gray, white plastic. Decals. Vanguard and Jupiter C rocket with Explorer I satellite. Launch pads. Nameplates. Four figures.

**PD42** **Bell Rascal GAM-63** 1958-63 1/48 $190-220
Red, yellow, black, white plastic. Transporter with elevating launcher. Three figures. Fins on missile are hinged to fold.

**PD43** **Missile Mobile** 1959-63 1/128 $120-140
White, red, blue plastic. Selected models from PD40 Missile Arsenal can be hung from ceiling with mobile hangers. Includes Bomarc, Matador, Rascal, Regulus II, Snark. Also includes an Atlas model from a new mold.

**PS44** **T.V. Orbiter** 1959-60 1/96 $130-150
Mustard, gray, clear plastic. Launch pad, service tower. Three ground crew figures. Willy Ley designed. Box art by R. Price.

**PS45** **Space Taxi** 1959-60 1/48 $50-60
White, silver-gray, clear plastic. U. S. Space Force decals. Four crew figures—three suspended on wires. Side cargo door opens. Willy Ley designed transport and workshop. Reissued as PS194 (1969), 6870 (1970). Box art by R. Price.

**PS46** **Orbital Rocket** 1959-60 1/193 $90-110
White, blue, clear plastic. Air Force decals. Five figures. Landing gear on booster rocket retract. Booklet by Willy Ley. Also issued as civilian version PS47 (1959) with different orbiter. Box art by R. Price.

**PS47** **Passenger Rocket** 1959-60 1/193 $75-90
White, red, clear plastic. Five figures. Trans Space Lines decals. Landing gear on booster rocket retract. Willy Ley booklet explains how you can fly from New York to London in one hour. Also issued as military version PS46 (1959) with different orbiter. Box art by Tom Kowal.

**PS193** **Apollo-Saturn** 1968-70 1/144 $35-45
White, gray, yellow plastic launch pad. USA decals. Thirty inch tall model. Eight stages twist apart. Adapter stage opens to release Lunar Module. Launch pad base. Three launch figures. Monogram based this model on preliminary data released by NASA. Box art by Locher. Reissued as 6869 (1970), 6051 (1983), 5903 (1986).

**PS194** **Space Buggy** 1969-70 1/48 $25-35
White, clear plastic. Chrome plated astronauts and end cages. Reissue of PS45 (1959). Reissued as 6870 (1970).

**PS221** **U. S. Space Missiles** 1969-70 1/128 $60-70
White, blue plastic. This kit is a modified reissue of PD40 (1958). It contains thirty-six missiles. The Matador, Regulus, Snark, Vanguard and Jupiter C from PD40 were deleted. Ten new missiles were added. Two figures. Booklet. Reissued as 6871 (1970), 6055 (1983).

**1014** **Shuttle Enterprise** (snap) 1978-86 1/200 $4-6
White Plastic. Decals for Enterprise, Columbia, Atlantis, Discovery, and Challenger. Astronaut figure. Cargo doors open to show Spacelab. Has landing gear. Reissued as 1014 Challenger (1983), 1110 (1985), 5905 (1986).

**1110** **Space Shuttle** 1985-86 1/200 $4-6
White plastic. NASA decals. Young Astronauts. Reissue of 1014 with stand added and landing gear removed.

**5503** **First Lunar Landing** 1979 1/48 $15-20
Tenth anniversary edition. Reissue of 6872 (1970) without pre-painted base.

**5702** **Enterprise Space Shuttle** 1979 1/72 $20-25
White, clear plastic. Decals for Enterprise, Columbia, Discovery, Challenger, Atlantis. Two crew figures. Cargo doors open to show three different payloads. This is a big twenty-inch long model.
Reissued as 5702 (1981), 5900 (1986), 5904 (1986).

**5702** **NASA Space Shuttle** 1981-86 1/72 $20-25
White, clear plastic. Decals. In 1982 some kits were sold with a "Contains Columbia decals" sticker on the box. In 1983 the name on the box became Challenger. Reissue of 5702 (1979).

**5900** **Space Shuttle/Fuel Cluster** 1986 1/72 $45-55
White, black base plastic. Decals. Young Astronaut Series. Launch pad display stand. Reissue of 5702 (1979) with new fuel tank and booster rockets added. This is a huge model.

**5901** **First Lunar Landing** 1986 1/48 $15-20
Young Astronaut Series. Box art by Locher. Reissue of 6872 (1970).

**5902** **Apollo Command Module** 1986 1/32 $45-55
Young Astronaut Series. Box art by Locher. Reissue of 6873 (1970).

**5903** **Apollo Saturn V** 1986 1/144 $35-45
White, gray, yellow plastic. Decals. Young Astronaut Series. Box art by Locher. Reissue of PS193 (1968).

**5904** **NASA Space Shuttle** 1986 1/72 $25-35
White, clear plastic. Young Astronaut Series. Decals for Enterprise, Columbia, Discovery, Challenger, Atlantis. Reissue of 5702 (1979).

**5905** **Space Shuttle** (snap) 1986 1/200 $4-6
White plastic. NASA decals. Young Astronaut Series. Reissue of 1014 (1978).

**5906** **Eagle Lunar Explorer** 1986 1/72 $25-35
Young Astronauts series. This 1/144 scale space shuttle transforms into a fictional patrol-landing vehicle. Hasegawa's Operation Omega tooling was used to manufacture this model.

**6019** **US/USSR Missiles** 1984-86 1/144 $20-30
White, dark green plastic. Decals. Twenty missiles on a display base.

**6051** **Apollo Saturn** 1983 1/144 $20-30
White, gray, yellow plastic. Decals. Heritage Collection. Reissue of PS193.

**6055** **U. S. Space Missiles** 1983 1/128 $20-30
White, dark blue base plastic. Decals. Reissue of PS221 (1969).

**6060** **First Lunar Landing** 1984-85 1/48 $15-20
White, gray plastic. NASA decals. Heritage Collection. Box art by Locher. Reissue of 6872 (1970).

**6061** **Apollo Spacecraft** 1984-85 1/32 $45-55
White, silver, clear plastic. NASA decals. Heritage Collection. Box art by Locher. Reissue of 6873 (1970).

**6869** **Apollo Saturn V** 1970-71 1/144 $35-45
White, silver plastic. USA decals. Renumber of PS193 (1969).

**6870** **Space Buggy** 1970-71 1/48 $25-35
White, clear plastic. Chrome space men. Reissue of PS45 (1959).

**6871** **U. S. Space Missiles** 1970-71 1/128 $50-60
Renumber of PS221 (1969).

**6872** **First Lunar Landing** 1970-71 1/48 $25-35
White, gray plastic. Gold foil for thermal blanket on LEM. Base includes footprints in the dust and pre-painted recessed "shadows" for all the LEM and all the various accessories, such as the flag and camera. Figures of Neil Armstrong and Edwin Aldren. Box art by Locher. Reissued as 5503 (1979), 6060 (1984), 5901 (1986).

**6873** **Command/Service Modules** 1970-71 1/32 $45-55
White, silver, clear, gold plated plastic. Three crew figures. Decals. Apollo command and service modules. Clear panels show interiors of both modules. Box art by Locher. Reissued as 6061 (1984), 5902 (1986).

## Ship Models

**P3/PB3** **Racing Speedboat** 1954-64 $50-70
Tan, brown plastic. Driver figure. *Dipsy Doodle*. Based on Mat Wyza's Class B hydroplane powered by a ten horsepower Mercury engine. In the mid-1950s Kellogg's offered this kit in ivory or blue plastic as a premium that could be purchased for fifty cents and one box top.

**P16/PB16** **Racing Yacht** 1956-64 1/30 $40-60
Red, white plastic. Thin pliable polyethylene sail for actual pond sailing. Skipper and sailor figures. *Sea Breeze*. Star class racing yacht. 15 1/2 inches long.

**P17/PB17** ***Water Devil* Runabout** 1956-60 $60-70
Orange, white, blue, chrome plastic. Skipper and lady guest figures. Mahogany deck decal. Flag pendant. Can be powered by rubber band or electricity. Rudders can be moved to set course. Reissued as PB217M (1960). 12 1/4 inches long.

**P18/PB18** ***Wanderlust* Sloop** 1956-64 1/55 $45-55
Blue, white, tan, brown plastic. Four figures. Thin pliable polyethylene sail for actual pond sailing. 11 1/2 inches long. Reissued as PB183 (1968), 6857 (1970).

**PB48** **Frogmen and LCP(R) Boat** 1959-66 1/35 $80-100
Gray, black, yellow plastic. Boat, raft, five frogmen. One-piece hull to insure flotation. Frogmen float just below surface. This is the first box art Tom Kowal painted for Monogram. Reissued as PB182 (1967).

**PB179** **River Assault Rag Boat** 1967-69 1/48 $15-20
Gray plastic. Four crew figures. One piece hull. Box art by Korta. Reissued as 8299 (1973).

**PB180** **Swift Patrol Boat** 1967-69 1/48 $15-20
Gray plastic. One crew figure. One piece hull. Reissued as 8297 (1973).

**PB181** **Command Junk** 1967-69 1/48 $15-20
Gray plastic. Vacuum-formed sails. One crew figure. One piece hull. Can be built with masts lowered. Reissued as 8298 (1973).

**PB182** **Navy Frogmen UDT** 1967-69 1/35 $50-60
Reissue of PB48 (1959).

**PB183** ***Voyager* Sloop** 1968-70 1/55 $35-45
Brown, white sails. Four crew. Vacuum-formed sails. Reissue of P18 *Wanderlust* (1956). Reissued as 6857 (1970).

**PB217M** ***Water Devil* Runabout** 1960-63 $65-75
Orange, white, blue, chrome plastic. Skipper and lady guest figures. Mahogany deck decal. Flag pendant. Reissue of PB17 (1956) with electric motor.

**PB234** **USS *Kennedy*** 1970 16" $15-20
Gray plastic. Decals. Monogram's sixteen inch ship models were intended to be easy-to-build kits for younger modelers to play with. Reissued as 6854 (1970), 8295 America (1973).

**PB235** **USS *Brooke*** 1970 16" $20-30
Gray plastic. Decals. Guided missile destroyer. Tartar missiles, ASROC anti-sub missile, Kaman UH-2A copter. Turning the range finder turns both gun turret and missile launcher. Reissued as 6855 (1970), 6855 Ramsey (1973).

**PB236** **USS *Halsey*** 1970 16" $20-30
Gray plastic. Decals. Guided missile frigate. Reissued as 6856 (1970), 8296 Leahy (1973).

**1020** **USS *Kitty Hawk*** (snap) 1979-84 8 3/4" $4-6
Gray plastic. Decals. Also issued as 1021 (1979).

**1021** **USS *Constellation*** (snap) 1979-85 8 3/4" $4-6
Gray plastic. Decals. Also issued as 1020 (1979).

**1022** **USS *John F. Kennedy*** (snap) 1979-85 8 3/4" $4-6
Gray plastic. Decals.

**1035** **USS *Missouri*** (snap) 1982-85 16" $8-10
Gray plastic. Decals. Reissue of 3000 (1976).

**1036** **USS *Iowa*** (snap) 1982-84 16" $8-10
Gray plastic. Decals. Reissue of 3000 (1976).

**1037** **USS *New Jersey*** (snap) 1982-85 16" $8-10
Gray plastic. Decals. Reissue of 3000 (1976).

**3000** **USS *Missouri*** 1976-83 16" $12-15
Gray plastic. Decals. Also issued as 3001 (1976), 3006 (1978), 1035 (1982). John Steel box art.

**3001** **USS *New Jersey*** 1976-86 16" $12-15
Gray plastic. Decals. Also issued as 3000 (1976). John Steel box art.

**3002** **USS *Chicago*** 1976-79 16" $30-35
Gray plastic. Decals. When range directors are turned, the missile launchers also turn. Also issued as 3003 (1976). John Steel box art.

**3003** **USS *Columbus*** 1976-79 16" $30-35
Gray plastic. Decals. Also issued as 3002 (1976). John Steel box art.

**3004** **USS *Nimitz*** 1977-86 16" $8-10
Gray plastic. Decals. Fifteen planes on deck. Also issued as 3005. John Steel box art.

**3005** **USS *Eisenhower*** 1977-83 16" $8-10
Gray plastic. Decals. Also issued as 3004. John Steel box art.

**3006** **USS *Wisconsin*** 1978-79 16" $8-10
Gray plastic. Decals. Reissue of 300 (1976).

**3007** **USS *Kitty Hawk*** 1978-86 16" $8-10
Gray plastic. Decals. John Steel box art.

**3008** ***Bismarck*** 1977-79 16" $8-10
Gray plastic. Decals. Also issued as 3009 (1977).

**3009** ***Tirpitz*** 1977-86 16" $8-10
Gray plastic. Decals. Also issued as 3008 (1977).

**3101** **USS *Skipjack*** (Aurora) 1979-81 1/228 $10-15
Gray plastic. Decals.

**3102** **Wolfpack U-Boat** (Aurora) 1979-81 1/209 $10-15
Gray plastic. Decals.

**3103** **Japanese I-19 Sub** (Aurora) 1979-81 1/275 $10-15
Gray plastic. Decals.

**3500** ***Cutty Sark*** 1977-86 16" $8-10
Black, tan plastic. Vacuum-formed sails. Paper flag sheet. Decal. Rigging thread. Masts and yardarms are molded in one piece for easy assembly.

**3501** **USS *Constitution*** 1977-86 16" $8-10
Black, tan plastic. Vacuum-formed sails. Paper flag sheet. Decal. Rigging thread. Also issued as 3502 (1977).

**3502** **USS *United States*** 1977-86 16" $8-10
Black, tan plastic. Vacuum-formed sails. Paper flag sheet. Decal. Rigging thread. Also issued as 3501 (1977).

**3503** **USS *Independence*** (Aurora) 1978-86 1/600 $20-30
Gray, white plastic. The ex-Aurora carriers were twenty-one inches long—compared to Monogram's standard sixteen inches.

**3504** **USS *Forrestal*** (Aurora) 1978-86 1/600 $20-30
Gray, white plastic.

**3505** **USS *Saratoga*** (Aurora) 1978-86 1/600 $20-30
Gray, white plastic.

**3700** **USS *Enterprise*** (Aurora) 1978-86 1/400 $60-70
Gray, black plastic. Nuclear-powered supercarrier. Large three-foot long model.

**3701** ***Cutty Sark*** 1979-80 1/120 $20-30
Black, tan, brown, white plastic. Vacuum-formed sails. Paper flag sheet. Rigging thread. Molded in Morton Grove from Imai mold. 28 inches long.

**3702** **USS *Susquehanna*** (Imai) 1979-80 1/150 $30-40
Black, tan, brown plastic. Vacuum-formed sails. Paper flag sheet. Rigging thread. Molded at Morton Grove from Imai mold. The *Susquehanna* was the flagship of Commodore Perry's fleet that "opened" Japan to foreign trade. 28 inches long.

**3703** **USS *Constitution*** (Imai) 1979-80 1/120 $20-30
Black, tan, white plastic. Vacuum-formed sails. Paper flag sheet. Rigging thread. Molded at Morton Grove from Imai mold. 29 inches long. Reissued as 3704 (1980), 3705 (1981), 3706 (1981).

**3704** **USS *United States*** (Imai) 1980 1/120 $30-40
Black, tan, white plastic. Vacuum-formed sails. Paper flag sheet. Rigging thread. Molded at Morton Grove from Imai mold. 29 inches long. Reissue of 3703 (1981).

**3705** **USS *Constitution*** (Imai) 1981-84 1/120 $20-30
Black, tan, white plastic. Vacuum-formed sails. Paper flag sheet. Rigging thread. Molded at Morton Grove from Imai mold. 29 inches long. Reissue of 3703 (1979).

**3706** **USS *United States*** (Imai) 1981-84 1/120 $30-40
Black, tan, white plastic. Vacuum-formed sails. Paper flag sheet. Rigging thread. Molded at Morton Grove from Imai mold. 29 inches long. Reissue of 3704 (1980).

**6032** **The Final Countdown** 1980 $20-30
This gift set contains two models of the ship and aircraft used in the movie *The Final Countdown* starring Kirk Douglas and Martin Sheen. USS *Nimitz* (3004, 1977) and F-14 Tomcat (5992, 1971). Both molded in gray plastic. Box art is from a movie poster painted by Revell artist Jack Leynnwood.

**6039** **Rambo Attack Set** 1986 1/48 $30-35
Contains Rambo Combat Chopper 6809 (1970) in olive plastic and RAG River Patrol Boat PB179 (1967) in gray plastic.

**6854** **USS *John F. Kennedy*** 1970-78 16" $12-15
Gray plastic. Decals. Renumber of PB234 (1970).

**6855** **USS *Brooke*** 1970-78 16" $20-30
Gray plastic. Decals. Renumber of PB235 (1970).

**6856** **USS *Halsey*** 1970-78 16" $20-30
Gray plastic. Decals. Renumber of PB236 (1970).

**6857** ***Voyager* Cruising Sloop** 1970 1/55 $20-30
White, brown plastic. Vacuum-formed sails. Renumber of P18 *Wanderlust* (1956) with vacuum-formed sails.

**8294** **USS *Ramsey*** 1973-78 16" $20-30
Gray plastic. Decals. Reissue of PB235 *Brooke* (1970).

**8295** **USS *America*** 1973-78 16" $12-15
Gray plastic. Decals. Reissue of PB234 *Kennedy* (1970).

**8296** **USS *Leahy*** 1973-78 16" $20-30
Gray plastic. Decals. Reissue of PB236 *Halsey* (1970).

**8297** **Swift Boat** 1973-75 1/48 $10-15
Gray plastic. Decals. Reissue of PB180 (1967).

**8298** **Coastal Junk** 1973-75 1/48 $20-30
Gray plastic. Decals. Reissue of PB181 (1967).

**8299** **River Patrol Boat** 1973-75 1/48 $10-15
Gray plastic. Decals. Reissue of PB179 (1967).

## Military Vehicles

**MGP-1** **Military Wheels** 1957-63 1/35 $400-500
This gift set contains: PM21 Jeep & Gun, PM22 Truck, PM23 Half Track, PM24 Amphibious Weasel.

**PM21** **Jeep & Gun** 1957-65 1/35 $40-50
Olive brown plastic. Clear sheet of acetate for windshield. Polyethylene tires. Three figures. Decals. Windshield folds down. Jeep tows M3 37mm gun. Korta box art. Reissued as PD38 (1958), PM153 (1966), 6864 (1970), 8211 (1972), 6302 (1982).

**PM22** **Army Cargo Truck** 1957-65 1/35 $40-50
Olive brown plastic. Clear sheet of acetate for windshield. Five figures. Decals. Tail gate folds down. 2 1/2 ton 6 x 6 Eager Beaver Truck. Reissued asPM154 (1966), 6884 (1970), 8214 (1972), 6400 (1982).

**PM23** **Armored Half Track** 1957-65 1/35 $40-50
Olive brown plastic. Clear sheet of acetate for windshield. Five figures. Decals. Vinyl tires and tracks. Doors open, turret rotates, .50 anti-aircraft guns elevate. Reissued as PM155 (1966), 6885 (1970), 8215 (1972), 6401 (1982).

**PM24** **Army Weasel** 1957-65 1/35 $20-30
Olive brown plastic. Clear sheet of acetate for windshield. Four figures. Decals. Reissued as PM156 (1966), 6886 (1970), 8212 (1972), 6303 (1982).

**PM34** **Personnel Carrier** 1958-65 1/35 $40-50
Olive brown clear plastic. Decals. Nine figures. Black vinyl tires and tracks. Revision of PM23 Half Track modified to serve as a personnel carrier. Fred T box art. Reissued as PM157 (1966), 6887 (1970), 8216 (1958).

**PM35** **Military Figures** 1958-65 1/35 $30-40
Olive brown plastic. Eighteen figures. Reissued as PM158 (1966), 6888 (1970), 8213 (1972), 6304 (1982).

**PM37** **M48A2 Patton Tank** 1958-65 1/35 $35-45
Olive brown, black plastic. Polyethylene tracks. Decals. Four figures. Reissued as PM159 (1966), 6863 (1970), 8217 (1972), 6501 (1983).

**PM153** **Jeep & Gun** 1966-70 1/35 $20-30
Olive brown plastic. Decals. Reissue of PM21 (1957).

**PM154** **Eager Beaver Truck** 1966-70 1/35 $20-30
Olive brown plastic. Decals. Reissue of PM22 (1957).

**PM155** **Armored Half Track** 1966-70 1/35 $20-30
Olive plastic. Decals. Reissue of PM23 (1957).

**PM156** **Amphibious Weasel** 1966-70 1/35 $20-25
Olive plastic. Black vinyl tracks. Decals. Reissue of PM24 (1957).

**PM157** **Personnel Carrier** 1966-70 1/35 $20-30
Olive plastic. Decals. Reissue of PM34 (1958).

**PM158** **Military Figures** 1966-70 1/35 $20-25
Olive plastic. Reissue of PM35 (1958).

**PM159** **Patton Tank** 1966-70 1/35 $20-25
Olive plastic. Black vinyl tracks. Decals. Reissue of PM37 (1958).

**PM230** **German Panzer IV** 1970 1/32 $20-30
Tan plastic. Rust colored vinyl tracks. Decals. The chassis of this model is also used on PM233 (1970). Renumbered 6859 (1970), 8218 (1972).

**PM233** **German Flak Panzer IV** 1970 1/32 $20-30
Tan plastic. Decals. Rust colored vinyl tracks. The chassis of this model is also used on PM230 (1970). Renumbered 6860 (1970), 8219 (1972).

**1006** **Army Half Track** (snap) 1976-85 1/32 $8-10
Olive plastic.

**1007** **Jeep & Cycle** (snap) 1976-85 1/32 $8-10
Olive plastic.

**4100** **M-8 Armored Car** 1976-77 1/32 $10-15
Olive plastic. (No vinyl tires.) Decals. This M-8 has a cannon in a turret. Also issued as 4101 (1976).

**4101** **M-20 Armored Car** 1976-78 1/32 $10-15
Olive plastic. Decals. Two figures. (No vinyl tires.) This M-20 has a machine gun on a ring mount. Also issued as 4100 (1976).

**4200** **Sherman Screamin' Mimi** 1975-82 1/32 $15-25
Olive plastic. Gray vinyl tracks. Three figures. Decals for two options. Can be built as stock M4 or with T-34 rocket launcher. Hull is textured to represent iron. Also issued as 4201 (1975). Reissued as 6500 (1983).

**4201** **Sherman M4 Hedge Hog** 1975-82 1/32 $15-25
Olive plastic. Decals. Can be built as standard M4 or with Cullin Cutter on front, sandbags on hull, wooden planks on turret. Also issued as 4200 (1975).

**6034** **Ground Attack** 1984 1/48 $15-25
Diorama scene with ground terrain base and ex-Aurora Sherman tank (olive brown plastic) and 6804 FW-190 (olive green, black plastic). Don Greer box art.

**6035** **Tank Hunter** 1984 1/48 $15-25
Diorama scene with ground terrain base and ex-Aurora Panther tank (tan plastic) and 6806 P-51B (silver plastic). P-51 has optional spinner with no propeller blades. Don Greer box art.

**6302** **Jeep & Gun** 1982-86 1/35 $10-15
Olive plastic. Reissue of PM21 (1957).

**6303** **Attack Weasel** 1982-86 1/35 $10-15
Olive plastic. Reissue of PM24 (1957).

**6304** **U. S. Figures** 1982-86 1/35 $10-15
Olive plastic. Reissue of PM35 (1958).

**6400** **2 1/2 Ton Truck** 1982-86 1/35 $15-20
Olive plastic. Reissue of PM22 (1957).

**6401** **Armored Half Track** 1982-86 1/35 $15-20
Olive plastic. Reissue of PM23 (1957).

**6402** **M-8 Armored Car** 1982-86 1/32 $10-15
Olive plastic. Reissue of 4100 (1976).

**6500** **Sherman Screamin' Mimi** 1983-85 1/32 $15-20
Olive plastic. Reissue of 4200 (1975).

**6501** **Patton Tank** 1983-86 1/35 $15-20
Olive plastic. Reissue of PM37 (1958).

**6502** **Lee Tank** 1983-85 1/32 $15-20
Olive plastic. Reissue of 7536 (1973).

**6503** **Panzerkampfwagen** 1983-85 1/32 $15-20
Tan plastic. Reissue of 7581 (1974).

**6859** **German Panzer IV** 1970-72 1/32 $20-30
Tan plastic. Rust colored vinyl treads. Reissue of PM230 (1970). All of Monogram's German tanks use the same chassis.

**6860** **German Flak Panzer IV** 1970-72 1/32 $20-30
Tan plastic. Reissue of PM233 (1970).

**6861** **German Assault Tank** 1970-72 1/32 $20-30
Tan plastic. Box art by Bill Koster. Reissued as 8220 (1972).

**6863** **Patton Tank** 1970-72 1/35 $20-25
Olive plastic. Reissue of PM37 (1958).

**6864** **Jeep & Gun** 1970-72 1/35 $10-15
Olive plastic. Reissue of PM21 (1957).

**6884** **Eager Beaver Truck** 1970 1/35 $15-20
Olive plastic. Reissue of PM27 (1957).

**6885** **Armored Half-Track** 1970-71 1/35 $15-20
Olive plastic. Reissue of PM23 (1957).

**6886** **Amphibious Weasel** 1970-71 1/35 $10-15
Olive plastic. Reissue of PM24 (1957).

**6887** **Personnel Carrier** 1970 1/35 $15-20
Olive plastic. Reissue of PM34 (1958).

**6888** **Military Figure Set** 1970 1/35 $15-20
Olive plastic. Reissue of PM35 (1958).

**6970** **Radio Controlled Tank** 1978 12" $25-35
Olive plastic. Made from the Asahi mold. Motorized and radio controlled. A switch on the tank sets it rolling, and buttons on the controller turn it right or left. A Leopard Tank.

**7505** **Panzerjager IV** 1973-78 1/32 $20-25
Tan plastic. Uses same chassis as 8219 (1972). Optional parts for external armor skirting, two of which have battle damage holes.

**7506** **Sturmpanzer 43** 1973-77 1/32 $20-25
Tan plastic. Two crew figures. Optional side skirt armor. Uses same chassis as 8219 (1972).
**7535** **Grant Tank M3** 1973-78 1/32 $20-25
Tan plastic. Two crew figures. Decals for British North African tank. Also issued as 7536 (1973).
**7536** **Lee Tank M3** 1973-78 1/32 $20-25
Olive plastic. Two crew figures. Decals for several US and one Russian unit. Reissued as 6502 (1983).
**7578** **M-48A2 Patton Tank** (snap) 1974-85 1/48 $8-10
Olive plastic. Stick-on decals. Molded-in tracks.
**7579** **Tiger I Tank** (snap) 1974-85 1/48 $8-10
Gray plastic. Stick-on decals.
**7581** **Panzerspahwagen SDK** 1974-78 1/32 $20-25
Tan, clear plastic. Three figures for camp diorama. Vinyl tires. Decals for four units. Engine compartment door can be built open.
**7582** **Ostwind Flakpanzer IV** 1974-79 1/32 $20-25
Tan plastic. Three figures. Uses same chassis as 8219 (1972).
**8211** **Jeep & 37mm Gun** 1972-78 1/35 $10-15
Olive plastic. Reissue of PM21 (1957).
**8212** **Amphibious Weasel** 1972-78 1/35 $10-15
Olive plastic. Reissue of PM24 (1957).
**8213** **Infantry Figures** 1972-78 1/35 $15-20
Olive plastic. Reissue of PM35 (1958).
**8214** **2 1/2 Ton Truck** 1972-78 1/35 $15-20
Olive plastic. Reissue of PM22 (1957).
**8215** **Armored Half Track** 1972-78 1/35 $15-20
Olive plastic. Reissue of PM23 (1957).
**8216** **Personnel Carrier** 1972-78 1/35 $15-20
Olive plastic. Reissue of PM34 (1958).
**8217** **Patton Tank** 1972-82 1/35 $15-20
Olive plastic. Reissue of PM37 (1958).
**8218** **Panzerkampfwagen IV** 1972-77 1/32 $20-25
Olive plastic. Two crew figures. Reissue of PM230 (1970).
**8219** **Flakpanzer Tank** 1972-77 1/32 $20-25
Olive plastic. Two crew figures. Reissue of PM233 (1970).
**8220** **Sturmgeschuetz IV** 1972-78 1/32 $20-25
Olive plastic. Two crew figures. Assault tank. Reissue of 6861 (1970).

## PC Car Models--- 1954-1969

**MGP-8** **Auto Racing Trio** $400-500
Gift set containing PC1 Midget Racer, PC2 Hot Rod, PC12 Indy Racer. Includes tube of cement.
**P1/PC1** **Midget Racer** 1954-64 1/20 $40-60
Red, clear plastic. The earliest issue had no decals, but a decal sheet was soon added in later issues. First issue box has just the Monogram name on the box lid; second issue has the Four Star logo. Hood removes to show Offenhauser engine. In the mid-1950s Kellogg's offered P1 as a mail-in premium for 50 cents and a box top from breakfast cereals. Reissued as PC110 (1965).
**P2/PC2** **Hot Rod** 1954-59 1/24 $65-75
Blue, cream, plastic. Some PC2 issues appeared in off-white plastic or combinations of blue and off-white. The earliest issue had no decals, but a decal sheet was soon added in later issues. First issue box has just the Monogram name on the box lid; second issue has the Four Star logo. '32 Ford with a Mercury engine. In the mid-1950s Kellogg's offered P2 as a mail-in premium. Reissued as PC55 (1959), PC114 (1965), 6718 (1970).
**P4** **'55 Cadillac Convertible** 1955 1/20 $120-130
Blue, off-white, clear plastic. Metal axles. Rubber tires. Husband, wife, boxer dog figures. Also issued as P5 (1955). P4 and P5 are the first kits to bear the Four Star Monogram logo. Reissued as P13 (1956).
**P5** **'55 Cadillac Coupe** 1955 1/20 $120-130
Yellow, off-white, clear plastic. Metal axles. Rubber tires. Also issued as P4 (1955).
**P12/PC12** **Indy Racer** 1956-64 1/24 $70-80
Off-white plastic. Plastic tires. #9 racing decals. Hinged hood. Driver, mechanic figures. Tool box. Front wheels steer. Kurtis Kraft racer of Roger Ward. Reissued as PC212M (1960), PC111 (1965), 6715 (1970).
**P13/PC13** **'56 Cadillac Convertible** 1956-58 1/20 $120-130
Red, off-white, clear plastic. Reissue of P4 (1955).
**PC49** **Slingshot Dragster** 1959-64 1/22 $105-115
Blue, black, silver plastic. Driver figure. Can be powered by CO2 canister. Box art by Tom Kowal. Reissued as PC112 (1965), 6716 (1970).
**PC51** **Jet Firebolt** 1959-64 1/29 $95-105
Red, clear plastic. Black plastic wheels. Driver figure. Decals. CO2 cartridge fits in opening in rear to power car. Box art by Bob Korta. Reissued as PC113 (1965), 6717 (1970).
**PC55** **'32 Ford Roadster** 1959-64 1/24 $95-105
Purple, silver, plastic. Driver figure. Flame decals. Box art by Korta. Redesigned issue of P2 (1954). Reissued as PC114 (1965), 6718 (1970).
**PC57** **'32 Ford Sport Coupe** 1959-64 1/21 $180-200
Red, black, clear, chrome plastic. Decals. Box art by Tom Kowal. Reissued as PC257M (1960).
**PC59** **Long John Dragster** 1960-64 1/22 $95-105
Red, silver plastic. Vinyl tires. Decals. Model of Calvin Rice's "Hot Rod Magazine Special." Box art by Bob Korta. Reissued as PC259M (1960), PC115 (1965), 6719 (1970).
**PC60** **Black Widow** 1960-70 1/24 $105-115
Black, off-white, clear, chrome plastic. Moon disk wheel covers. Three options of decals. Ford '26 T pickup hot rod. Reissued as PC260M (1960), 6723 (1970).
**PC61** **Green Hornet** 1960-70 1/24 $70-80
Green, clear, chrome plastic. Vinyl tires. Decals. Ford '23 T hot rod based on Geraghty & Crawford's "Grasshopper." Removable top, fenders, body. Uses the oversize engine from PC57. Box art by Tom Kowal. Reissued as 6724 (1970).
**PE62** **Customizing Engine** 1960-64 1/8 $80-90
Red, black, silver, clear, chrome plastic. Chevy 283 V-8 engine. Snap-assembly to convert into many variations. Can be motorized. A modified version of this engine was used in the 1/8 scale hot rods: PC78, PC84, PC85, PC86. Reduced to 1/24 scale for use in the PC68 '36 Ford.
**PC63** **Quarter Midget Racer** 1961-66 1/24 $80-90
Chrome plated body. Driver figure. Decals. Vinyl tires. Box art by Clement Fraser. Reissued as PC178 (1967), 6730 (1970).
**PC64** **Customizing Ford A** 1961-64 1/24 $85-95
Tan, black, clear, chrome plastic. '30 Ford Phaeton. Reissued as PC75 (1962), PC116 (1965), 8279 (1973).
**PC65** **Customizing Dragster** 1961-64 1/20 $155-165
Orange, silver, gray, clear plastic. Vinyl tires. Decals. Optional Chevy and Chrysler engines. Builds six ways. Box art by Tom Kowal. Reissued as PC117 Sizzler (1965).
**PC68** **Customizing '36 Ford** 1961-64 1/24 $95-105
Tan, black, clear, chrome plastic. Decals. Six-way customizing kit. Options include stock three-window coupe and stock cabriolet convertible with operating rumble seat. Reissued as PC118 (1965), 7554 (1974), 7570 (1974), 2721 (1985).
**PC71** **Customizing '30 Ford** 1962-64 1/24 $95-105
Green, black, white, clear, chrome plastic. Decals. Optional Ford or Chevy engines. One of six versions has opening rumble seat. Box art by Tom Kowal. Reissued as PC120 (1965), 7551 (1974), 7552 (1974).
**PC72** **Customizing '34 Ford** 1962-64 1/24 $95-105
Maroon, black, clear, chrome plastic. Builds three-window coupe, convertible, or four other ways. Optional Ford and Pontiac engines. Rumble seat opens. Reissued as PC119 coupe (1965), 8281 coupe (1973), 2201 convertible (1975).
**PC75** **Red Chariot Custom** 1962-68 1/24 $95-105
Red, white, clear, chrome plastic. Decals. '30 Ford Phaeton hot rod. Chevy engine. Decals. Box art by Clement Fraser. Reissue of PC64 (1961) with no custom options.
**PC76** **Yellow Jacket Roadster** 1962-68 1/24 $120-130
Yellow, black, chrome plastic. No clear parts. Vinyl tires. Optional rumble seat, fenders, racing slick rear tires. Decals. '30 Ford hot rod with Chevy V-8. Never reissued. Box art by Clement Fraser.
**PC78** **Big "T" Custom Roadster** 1962-70 1/8 $115-125
Red, white, silver, black, clear, chrome plastic. Uses simplified version of PE62 Chevy 283 V-8 engine. Reissued as 6772 (1970), 7507 (1975), 2604 (1978), 2609 (1985).
**PC81** **'34 Duesenberg SJ Phaeton** 1963-70 1/24 $30-40
Tan, black, clear, chrome plastic. Hood removes to show straight eight engine. Box art by Locher. Reissued as 6764 (1970), 8201 (1972).
**PC83** **Customizing '55 Chevrolet** 1963-69 1/24 $125-135
Mandarin red or teal blue body, cream, clear, chrome plastic. Optional parts for two stock and any custom variation. Convertible or hardtop. Starbird styling. Blue body is more rare.
**PC84** **Big Drag '24 T Roadster** 1963-68 1/8 $250-270
Blue, white, black, chrome plastic. Uses PE62 Chevy 283 V-8 engine. Starbird styling. Based on PC78 (1962).
**PC85** **Big Rod '24 T Bucket** 1963-69 1/8 $250-270
Yellow, white, black, clear, chrome plastic. Uses PE62 Chevy 283 V-8 engine. Starbird styling. Based on PC78 (1962).
**PC86** **Big Tub '24 T Touring** 1963-69 1/8 $250-270
Orange, white, black, silver, clear, chrome plastic. Uses PE62 Chevy 283 V-8 engine. Starbird styling. Based on PC78 (1962).
**PC87** **'37 Mercedes Benz 540K** 1963-70 1/24 $30-40
Red, white, black, clear, chrome plastic. Hood removes. Box art by Al Lasack. Reissued as 6765 (1970), 8202 (1972), 2304 (1978), 2306 (1982).
**PC88** **Big Deuce** 1963-68 1/8 $120-130
Yellow or Red, off-white, black, transparent red, clear, chrome plastic. Hot rod decals. Pre-painted whitewall vinyl tires. '32 Ford. A model of the full size car Darryl Starbird built for Monogram. Reissued as 2602 (1977).
**PC89** **Customizing Thunderbird** 1964-69 1/24 $125-135
Black, clear, chrome plastic. Introduced in boxes with optional colors: red, yellow, blue, ivory. Yellow, blue, ivory are the rarest colors found today. Doors open. 1958 Ford Thunderbird. Builds four ways: stock hardtop, stock convertible, custom hardtop, futuristic bubble top. Starbird styling. Box art by Walt Pozdro. Reissued as 7550 (1974).
**PC91** **Customizing '40 Ford Pickup** 1964-69 1/24 $95-105
Light blue, white, black, clear, chrome plastic. Build stock or customize. Doors open, hood opens, tailgate lowers, side windows can be raised and lowered. Starbird styling. Box art by Locher. Reissued as 8282 (1973), 2265 (1980), 2720 (1985).
**PC92** **Little "T"** 1964-69 1/24 $95-105
Red, white, clear, chrome plastic. Decals. Steerable wheels. '24 Ford T. 283 Chevy engine.

Builds three versions. Starbird styling. The plastic parts from the Big T were used as the pattern for this model. Reissued as 6756 (1970), 2200 (1975).

**PC93** **Blue Beetle ’29 Ford Pickup** 1964-69 1/24 $120-130
Blue, white, clear, chrome plastic. Plastic white inserts for whitewalls. Cadillac engine. Surfboard, scuba diving equipment. Starbird styling. Box art by Walt Pozdro. Reissued as PC242 Boss “A” Bone (1970), 6755 (1970), 7555 (1974).

**PC94** **Li’l Coffin** 1964-70 1/24 $75-85
Burgundy, white, clear, chrome plastic. Skeleton figure. Larry Faber’s ’32 Ford sedan show rod. Reissued as PC250 (1970), 6749 (1970) in raspberry plastic, 2705 (1985) in red plastic.

**PC95** **Predicta** 1964-69 1/24 $70-80
Red, white, clear, chrome plastic in first issue. An early run of the kits used metallic pearl red plastic, but difficulty in mixing the metallic component led to its discontinuation. Bubble top opens, front wheels steer. Real car was built by Starbird and purchased by Monogram.

**PC98** **Jaguar XK-E GT Coupe** 1964-70 1/8 $95-105
Red, white, clear, chrome plastic. Textured plastic for upholstery. Wires for engine. Racing decals. Doors open, windows crank up and down, front wheels steer, working suspension, front end tilts open to show six-cylinder engine. Box art by Locher. Reissued as 6773 (1970), 2601 (1976).

**PC99** **Porsche 904 GTS** 1964-70 1/32 $25-35
Silver, clear, chrome plastic. Vinyl tires. #50 racing decals. Body has attachments for conversion to slot car use. Box art by Morgan. Reissued as 6712 (1970).

**PC100** **Cooper-Ford** 1964-70 1/32 $35-45
Metallic blue, clear, chrome plastic. Vinyl tires. Racing decals. Body has attachments for conversion to slot car use. Reissued as 6713 (1970).

**PC101** **Ferrari 250 GTO** 1964-70 1/32 $35-45
Red, clear, chrome plastic. Vinyl tires. #30 decals. Body has attachments for conversion to slot car use. Box art by Al Lasack. Reissued as 6714 (1970).

**PC102** **Ferrari 275P** 1964-69 1/24 $35-45
Red, clear, chrome plastic. Racing decals. Vinyl tires. Body has attachments for conversion to slot car use.

**PC103** **Woody Wagon** 1965-70 1/24 $85-95
Red, tan, clear, chrome plastic. Reissued as 6725 (1970), 7553 (1974).

**MM104** **Super Fuzz** 1965 $180-200
White plastic. Transparent blue plastic for helmet light, posable eyeballs, and chin drool. Stan “Mouse” Miller’s character Fred Flypogger as a policeman in a T-rod police car. Includes small mouse figure.

**MM105** **Flip Out** 1965 $200-220
White plastic. Transparent blue plastic for chin drool and posable eyeballs. Fred as a surfer. Includes small mouse figure.

**MM106** **Speed Shift** 1965 $200-220
White plastic. Transparent blue chin drool and posable eyeballs. Fred riding a set of rear wheels with 8-ball shifter in his hand. Includes small mouse figure.

**PC108** **Futurista** 1965-70 1/24 $135-145
Yellow, red, clear, chrome plastic. Darryl Starbird designed the full-size car for Monogram. VW engine can be removed and displayed on a stand. Reissued as 6726 (1970).

**PC109** **’31 Rolls Royce Phantom II** 1965-70 1/24 $25-35
Black, silver, clear, chrome plastic. Front wheels steer. Doors and rumble seat open. Removable hood. Box art by Locher. Reissued as 6766 (1970), 8203 (1972), 2307 (1982).

**PC110** **Midget Racer** 1965-68 1/20 $65-75
Red, clear plastic. Decals. Reissue of PC1 (1954).

**PC111** **Indianapolis Racer** 1965-70 1/24 $70-80
Reissue of PC12 (1956).

**PC112** **Slingshot Dragster** 1965-70 1/22 $105-115
Reissue of PC49 (1959).

**PC113** **Firebolt** 1965-70 1/29 $95-105
Red, black, clear plastic. Decal. New box art by Bob Korta. Reissue of PC51 (1959).

**PC114** **Deuce Hot Rod** 1965-70 1/24 $90-105
Maroon (later issues red), black plastic. Early maroon issues are more valuable. Box art by Bob Korta. Reissue of PC55 (1959) with no part changes.

**PC115** **Long John Dragster** 1965-70 1/22 $95-105
Reissue of PC59 (1960).

**PC116** **’30 Ford Phaeton** 1965-69 1/24 $85-95
Tan, black, clear, chrome plastic. Reissue of PC64 (1961).

**PC117** **Sizzler Dragster** 1965-69 1/20 $200-225
Orange, silver, clear, chrome plastic. Vinyl tires. Optional bodies for rail, streamliner, or ’32 Bantam coupe. 392 Chrysler Hemi and 327 Chevy motors. Racing decals. Box art by Tom Morgan. Reissue of PC65 (1961).

**PC118** **’36 Ford Coupe** 1965-69 1/24 $85-95
Tan, black, clear, chrome plastic. Box art by Charles Spear. Reissue of PC68 (1961).

**PC119** **’34 Ford Coupe** 1965-69 1/24 $85-95
Reissue of PC72 (1962).

**PC120** **’30 Ford Coupe** 1965-69 1/24 $85-95
Green, black, white, clear, chrome plastic. Reissue of PC71 (1962).

**PC124** **Scarab** 1965-69 1/24 $35-45
Blue, clear, chrome plastic. #14 racing decals. Body has attachments for conversion to slot car use. Box art by Tom Morgan.

**PC125** **Lola GT** 1965-70 1/32 $45-55
Blue, clear plastic. Racing decals. Body has attachments for conversion to slot car use. Reissued as 6720 (1970).

**PC126** **Corvette Sting Ray** 1965-70 1/8 $145-155
Blue, black, clear, chrome plastic. Headlights retract, hood opens, steerable front wheels. Reissued as 6774 (1970), 2600 (1976), 2724 (1985).

**PC127** **Porsche 904 GT** 1965-69 1/24 $35-45
Vinyl tires. Racing decals. Body snaps on to chassis. A simplified model intended for double duty as a slot car. Body has attachments for conversion to slot car use. Box art by Morgan.

**PC128** **Ferrari 275P** 1965-70 1/32 $35-45
Red, clear, chrome plastic. Racing decals. Vinyl tires. Body has attachments for conversion to slot car use. Reissued as 6721 (1970).

**PC130** **’37 Cord 812 Convertible** 1966-70 1/24 $25-35
Off-white, black, clear, chrome plastic. Hood opens. Headlights in open or closed position. Optional top up or top down parts. Reissued as 6767 (1970), 8204 (1972), 2233 (1978).

**PC131** **Orange Hauler** 1966-70 1/24 $70-80
Orange, white, clear, chrome plastic. Starbird built the full-size custom car for Monogram. Front wheels steer. Reissued as 6727 (1970).

**PC132** **Little Deuce ’32 Ford** 1966-69 1/24 $85-95
White, clear, chrome plastic. Pontiac engine. Starbird styling. The plastic parts were used as the pattern for this model. Reissued as PC241 (1970), 6754 (1970), 8280 (1973), 2718 (1985).

**PC133** **’27 Bugatti 35B** 1966-70 1/24 $35-40
Blue, silver, clear, chrome plastic. Simulated leather straps for hood and spare tire. With hay bales, guard rails, nameplate, grass base. Reissued as 6768 (1970), 8205 (1972), 2234 (1978).

**PC134** **Uncertain “T”** 1966-70 1/24 $190-210
White, clear sheet of acetate, chrome plastic. Award-winning show rod with display platform, gold rope, trophy, nameplate, and pretty girl. A model of Steve Scott’s show rod. Renumbered 6733 (1970). Photo box art.

**PC137** **Ferrari GP** 1966-70 1/32 $45-55
Red plastic. No vinyl tires. #7 racing decals. Renumbered 6700 (1970). Also issued as a slot car.

**PC138** **FI Lotus 33** 1966-70 1/32 $45-55
Renumbered 6701 (1970). Also issued as a slot car.

**PC139** **Boss ’40 Willys** 1966-70 1/32 $55-65
Orange, clear plastic. No vinyl tires. #25 decals. Renumbered 6702 (1970). Also issued as a slot car. Box art by Morgan.

**PC140** **’34 Ford Coupe** 1966-70 1/32 $55-65
Green, clear plastic. No vinyl tires. Decals. Renumbered 6703 (1970). Also issued as a slot car. Box art by Morgan.

**PC141** **’37 Hemi Fiat** 1966-70 1/32 $55-65
Blue, clear, chrome plastic. No vinyl tires. Drag decals. Renumbered 6704 (1970). Also issued as a slot car. Box art by Morgan.

**PC142** **Chaparral 2D Coupe** 1966-70 1/24 $45-55
White, clear, chrome plastic. Racing decals. Driver figure. Movable rear spoiler. Renumbered 6728 (1970).

**PC167** **’59 Corvette** 1967-70 1/35 $45-55
Box art by Bob Korta with background added. Reissue of PC404 (1960).

**PC168** **’59 MGA 1600** 1967-70 1/32 $45-55
Red, clear, chrome plastic. Plastic tires. Racing decals. Box art by Locher. Reissue of PC405 (1960).

**PC169** **’50 Austin Healey Sprite** 1967-70 1/26 $35-45
Light blue, clear plastic. Plastic tires. Racing decals. Reissue of PC406 (1960).

**PC170** **Ford “T” Pick-Up** 1967-70 1/32 $55-65
Yellow, clear plastic. Reissue of 410 (1961).

**PC171** **Deuce Roadster** 1967-70 1/32 $55-65
Red, clear, plastic. Box art by Kowal with added background. Reissue of PC412 (1961).

**PC172** **Slingshot Dragster** 1967-70 1/32 $85-95
Box art by Kowal with added background. Reissue of PC411 (1961).

**PC173** **Super Modified Sportsman** 1967-70 1/24 $45-55
White, clear, chrome, plastic. Decals. Driver figure. Snap-in whitewalls for tires. Renumbered 6729 (1970).

**PC174** **’41 Lincoln Continental** 1967-70 1/24 $20-25
Metallic blue, white, clear, chrome plastic. Hood removes. Box art by Locher. Reissued as 6769 (1970), 8206 (1972).

**PC175** **Hurst Hairy Olds** 1967-70 1/24 $20-30
White, clear, chrome plastic. ’67 Olds 442. Joe Schubeck’s twin-engine car. Box art by Morgan. Reissued as 6734 (1970), 2218 (1977).

**PC178** **Hot Shot Midget** 1967-70 1/24 $70-80
Red, chrome plastic. Driver figure. Reissue of PC63 (1961).

**PC185** **Duesenberg Town Car** 1968-70 1/24 $30-40
Black, clear, chrome plastic. Redesign of PC81 (1963). Box art by Morgan. Reissued as 6770 (1970), 7549 (1974).

**PC188** **Boot Hill Express** 1967-70 1/24 $45-55
Orange, clear, chrome plastic. Skeleton in Stetson hat and “Boot Hill Express” tombstone. Model of show rod of Ray Farhner & Sons of Kansas City that used a real 1800s vintage hearse. Reissued as 6735 (1970), 2703 (1985).

**PC212M** **Indy Racer** (Motorized) 1959-63 1/24 $70-80
Off-white, clear plastic. Also in gray plastic. Racing decals. Reissue of PC12 (1956).

**PC223** **Bathtub Buggy** 1969-70 1/24 $135-145
White, brass chrome plastic. Transparent yellow acetate sheet. Decals. Based on a George Barris full-size show rod with a 289 Mustang V-8. Renumbered 6744 (1970).

**PC250** **Li'l Coffin** 1970 1/24 $65-75
Burgundy, white, clear, chrome plastic. Reissue of PC94 (1964).
**PC257M** **Sports Coupe** (Motorized) 1960-63 1/21 $95-105
Blue, white, clear, chrome plastic. Reissue of PC57 (1959).
**PC259M** **Long John** (Motorized) 1960-63 1/22 $95-105
Red, silver plastic. Reissue of PC59 (1960).
**PC260M** **Black Widow** (Motorized) 1960-63 1/24 $105-115
Black, off white, clear, chrome plastic. Reissue of PC60 (1960).
**P404** **1959 Corvette** 1960-66 1/35 $35-45
White, clear plastic. No chrome parts. Plastic wheels. Racing decals. Forty Niner 49 cent kit. Box art by Bob Korta. Reissued as PC167 (1967), 6705 (1970).
**P405** **'59 MGA-1600** 1960-66 1/32 $45-55
Red, clear, chrome plastic. Plastic tires. Decals. Forty Niner. Box art by Locher. Reissued as PC168 (1967), 6706 (1970).
**P406** **'58 Austin-Healey Sprite** 1960-66 1/26 $45-55
Light blue, clear, chrome plastic. Plastic tires. Racing decals. Forty Niner. Reissued as PC169 (1967), 6707 (1970).
**P410** **Pick-Up** 1961-66 1/32 $45-55
Yellow, clear plastic. Decals. Removable top. '26 T Roadster. Forty Niner. Box art by Tom Kowal. Reissued as PC170 (1967), 6708 (1970).
**P411** **Rail Dragster** 1961-66 1/32 $85-95
Blue, clear plastic. Decals. Forty Niner. Box art by Tom Kowal. Reissued as PC172 (1967) 6710 (1970).
**P412** **'32 Ford Roadster** 1961-66 1/32 $55-65
Red, clear plastic. Decals. Forty Niner. Box art by Tom Kowal. Reissued as PC171 (1967) 6709 (1970).

## Custom Accessories

| | | | | |
|---|---|---|---|---|
| **AK201** | **Six Carburetor Set** | 1963-64 | 1/8 | $25-30 |
| **AK202** | **Oval Gas Tank Set** | 1963-64 | 1/8 | $25-30 |
| **AK203** | **Racing Set** | 1963-64 | 1/8 | $25-30 |
| **AK204** | **GMC Blower Set** | 1963-64 | 1/8 | $25-30 |
| **AK205** | **Chrome Wheel Set** | 1963-64 | 1/8 | $20-25 |
| **AK206** | **Whitewall Drag Slick Set** | 1963-64 | 1/8 | $20-25 |
| **AK207** | **Whitewall Tire Set** | 1963-64 | 1/8 | $20-25 |

## 1970-1979 Cars

**1004** **Toyota Pick-Up** (snap) 1976-82 1/32 $15-20
Orange, yellow, clear, black plastic. Decals. All Snap-Tite 1/32 scale cars have black plastic tires. Reissued as 1012 (1977).
**1005** **Datsun Pick-Up** (snap) 1976-82 1/32 $15-20
Yellow or orange, black, clear, chrome plastic. Decals. Reissued as 1013 (1977).
**1010** **Dodge Police Van** (snap) 1976-83 1/32 $20-25
White, black, clear plastic. Police decals. Reissue of 1000 (1975).
**1011** **Chevy Emergency Van** (snap) 1976-83 1/32 $20-25
Off-white, black, clear plastic. Ambulance decals. Reissue of 1001 (1975).
**1012** **Toyota Pick-Up/cycle** (snap) 1977-83 1/29 $20-25
White body, red interior or Red body, white interior, black, clear plastic. Decals. With Husqvarna 125 dirt bike. Reissue of 1004 (1976).
**1013** **Datsun Camper** (snap) 1977-83 1/32 $20-25
Red, off-white, black, clear plastic. Decals. Reissue of 1005 (1976).
**1016** **'78 Corvette** (snap) 1978-86 1/32 $15-20
Orange, black, clear plastic. Decals. Reissued as 1040 (1981).
**1017** **'78 Trans Am** (snap) 1978-86 1/32 $15-20
Red, black, clear plastic. Decals. Reissued as 1039 (1981), 1047 (1982).
**1018** **'55 Chevy** (snap) 1978-86 1/32 $15-20
Light blue, black, clear plastic. Decals.
**1019** **'78 Camaro** (snap) 1978-86 1/32 $10-15
Yellow, black, clear plastic. Decals. Reissued as 1046 (1982).
**1200** **GMC General** (snap) 1978-86 1/32 $15-20
Red, black, clear, chrome plastic. Decals.
**1201** **Chevy Bison** (snap) 1978-86 1/32 $15-20
Black, red, clear chrome plastic. Decals. Reissued as 1301 (1980).
**1202** **Freightliner Conventional** (snap) 1978-83 1/32 $25-30
White, black, clear, chrome plastic. Decals. Reissued as 1300 (1980).
**1203** **Freightliner Cabover** (snap) 1978-83 1/32 $45-55
Black, clear, chrome plastic. 1979 release in blue plastic. Decals.
**2000** **'65 Mustang 2 + 2** (Aurora) 1978-82 1/32 $20-25
Off-white, clear, chrome plastic.
**2001** **Mako Shark** (Aurora) 1978-82 1/32 $20-25
Blue, clear plastic. '68 Corvette.
**2002** **'65 Pontiac GTO** (Aurora) 1978-83 1/32 $20-25
Red, clear, chrome plastic.
**2003** **'65 Barracuda** (Aurora) 1978-82 1/32 $20-25
Orange, clear, chrome plastic.

**2101** **Porsche 911 Carrera** 1976-79 1/24 $15-25
Yellow, clear, chrome plastic. Decals. No engine, seats molded into interior part. Reissued as 2107 (1978), 2119 (1981).
**2102** **Mercedes 450SL** 1976-79 1/24 $15-25
Blue, clear, chrome plastic. Decals. Reissued as 2109 (1978).
**2103** **'76 Midnight Capri II S** 1976-79 1/24 $15-25
Black, clear, gold chrome plastic. Pinstripe decals. Reissued as 2108 (1978), 2120 (1981).
**2104** **Datsun 280Z** 1976-79 1/24 $15-25
Red, clear, chrome plastic. Decals. Reissued as 2110 (1978), 2118 (1981).
**2105** **Triumph TR-7 Wedge** 1977-79 1/24 $15-25
Yellow, clear, chrome plastic. Decals. Textured roof to simulate vinyl. Reissued as 2111 (1980), 2115 (1981).
**2106** **Porsche 924** 1977-79 1/24 $15-25
Red, clear, chrome plastic. Decals. Reissued as 2112 (1980), 2114 (1980), 2117 (1981).
**2107** **Porsche Carrera RSR** 1978-80 1/24 $15-25
Orange, clear, chrome plastic. Decals. Reissue of 2101 (1976).
**2108** **'76 Capri Group II** 1978-80 1/24 $15-25
Blue, clear, chrome plastic. Decals. Reissue of 2103 (1976).
**2109** **Mercedes 450 Rally** 1978-80 1/24 $15-25
White, clear, chrome plastic. Race decals. Reissue of 2102 (1976).
**2110** **Datsun SCCA Rally** 1978-80 1/24 $15-25
Yellow, clear chrome plastic. Decals. Reissue of 2104 (1976).
**2111** **Triumph TR-7 Racer** 1978-80 1/24 $15-25
Black, clear, chrome plastic. Decals. Reissue of 2105 (1977).
**2112** **Porsche 924 Group 4** 1978-80 1/24 $15-25
White, clear, chrome plastic. Decals. Reissue of 2106 (1977).
**2200** **Street "T" Early Iron** 1975-79 1/24 $20-30
Red, clear, chrome plastic. With two wheel trailer. Chevy 283 engine. Reissue of PC92 Little T (1964).
**2201** **'34 Ford Rag Top** 1975-78 1/24 $20-30
Red, black, clear, chrome plastic. Decals. Early Iron. '61 Pontiac engine, mag wheels. Reissue of PC72 (1962).
**2203** **'57 Chevy** 1976-79 1/24 $25-35
Red, black, clear, chrome plastic. "Wildfire" decals. Funny car. Reissue of 8284 Outcast (1973).
**2204** **'72 El Camino** 1975-78 1/24 $30-40
Yellow, clear, chrome plastic. "Hornet" decals in 1975 release; "Desperado" decals in 1977 release. Funny car. Reissue of 8283 Troublemaker (1973).
**2205** **'70 Plymouth 'Cuda** 1975-78 1/24 $25-35
White body, yellow interior and chassis. First release has "Great White Cuda" decals. Second release (1977) has black body and yellow chassis. "Black Magic" decals. Reissue of 6762 (1971).
**2206** **Plymouth Duster** 1975-78 1/24 $25-35
Lime green body, dark olive chassis, clear plastic. First release has "Duster's Last Stand" decals designed by Dick Locher. Second release (1977) has "Super Duster" decals. Reissue of 6763 (1971).
**2211** **'55 Chevy Street Machine** 1975-86 1/24 $10-15
Black, clear, chrome plastic. Flame decals. Hood opens to show 350 V-8 Chevy engine. Goodyear rally GT tires. Reissue of PC229 Badman (1969).
**2212** **'70 Corvette Hatchback SS** 1976-81 1/24 $25-35
Yellow, black, clear plastic. Decals. Hood opens. Clear panels on roof. Reissue of 7504 (1973).
**2216** **Chevy Street Van** 1977-81 1/24 $25-30
Black, clear, chrome plastic. "Black Gold" decal. Three options for side windows. Optional roof vent, sun roof. Detailed interior. Also issued as 2224 (1977), 2232 (1978).
**2217** **'77 Chevy LUV Stepsider** 1977-80 1/24 $15-20
Orange, clear, chrome plastic. Decals. Hood opens. Reissue of 2213 (1976).
**2218** **Oldsmobile 4-4-2** 1977-79 1/24 $20-25
Yellow, clear, chrome plastic. Decals. Reissue of PC175 (1967).
**2219** **'66 Malibu SS** 1977-86 1/24 $10-15
Black, clear, chrome plastic. Flame decals. Hood opens to show 427 engine. Reissued as 2229 (1978).
**2220** **'69 Chevy Camaro Z28** 1977-86 1/24 $10-15
Off-white, clear, chrome plastic. Pinstripe decals. Reissued as 2230 (1978), 2201 (1983), 2725 (1986).
**2223** **'78 Jeep CJ-7 Renegade** 1977-83 1/24 $10-15
Blue, clear, chrome plastic. Hood opens. Removable top, doors. Reissued as 2231 (1978), 2402 (1980), 2261 (1980), 2405 (1981).
**2224** **Chevy Off-Road Van** 1977-81 1/24 $20-25
Red, clear, chrome plastic. Decals. Also issued as 2216 (1977).
**2225** **'57 Chevy Hardtop** 1977-86 1/24 $10-15
Red, clear, chrome plastic. Flame decals.
**2226** **'55 Ford F-100 Panel Truck** 1977-81 1/24 $10-15
Orange, clear, chrome plastic. Bad Creature decals. Customized version only. Reissued as 2242 pick-up (1978).
**2227** **'57 Vette** 1977-83 1/24 $10-15
Red, clear, chrome plastic. Decals. Build stock or custom with hood scoops, roll bar.
**2228** **Chevy Sport Pick-Up** 1977-83 1/24 $20-25
Black, clear, chrome plastic. Decals. '75 Chevy Stepside 4 x 4. Reissued as 2264 (1980).
**2229** **'66 Chevy Malibu** 1978-86 1/24 $15-20
Red, clear, chrome plastic. Decals. Street rod. Reissue of 2219 (1977).

**2230** **'69 Chevy Street Camaro** 1978-83 1/24 $15-20
Orange, clear, chrome plastic. Decals. Hood opens. Reissue of 2220 (1977).

**2231** **'78 Jeep CJ-7 Off Road** 1978-82 1/24 $10-15
Yellow, clear, chrome plastic. Bald eagle decals. Reissue of 2223 (1977).

**2232** **Chevy Van "Vanpire"** 1978-81 1/24 $25-30
Black, clear, chrome. Decals. Reissue of 2216 (1977).

**2233** **Cord 812 Convertible** 1978-79 1/24 $20-25
Burgundy, black, clear, chrome plastic. Reissue of PC130 (1966).

**2234** **Bugatti Type 35B** 1978-79 1/24 $15-20
Blue, silver, clear, chrome plastic. Reissue of PC133 (1966).

**2235** **'57 Chevy Nomad** 1978-81 1/24 $15-20
Yellow, clear, chrome plastic. Build stock or custom with hood scoops, roof spoiler, roll bar.

**2236** **'75 GMC Sport Pick-Up** 1978-82 1/24 $35-40
Red, clear, chrome plastic. Hood opens. Off road version. Reissued as 2248 (1979), 2273 (1981).

**2237** **'53 Chevy 2 Door Hardtop** 1978-83 1/24 $15-20
Light blue, clear, chrome plastic. Hood opens. Builds as stock or hot rod.

**2238** **'75 Chevy Blazer** 1978-83 1/24 $25-30
Maroon, clear, chrome plastic. Reissued as 2249 (1980), 2295 (1982), 2420 (1984), 2421 (1984).

**2239** **'56 Chevy Hardtop** 1978-86 1/24 $15-20
Light blue, clear, chrome plastic. Also issued as 2255 (1978).

**2240** **'39 Chevy Panel** 1978-81 1/24 $15-20
Lime green, clear, chrome plastic. Reissued as 2256 coupe (1979).

**2241** **'78 El Camino** 1978-81 1/24 $15-20
Black, clear, chrome plastic. Royal Knight decals. Also issued as 2252 (1978).

**2242** **'55 Ford F-100 Pick-Up** 1978-80 1/24 $15-20
Yellow, clear, chrome plastic. Reissue of 2226 panel (1977). Reissued as 2285 (1981).

**2243** **XK-E** (Aurora) 1978-80 1/25 $15-20
White, black, clear, chrome plastic. Front end tilts open.

**2244** **'63 Ferrari GTO** (Aurora) 1978-80 1/25 $15-20
Red, black, clear, chrome plastic. Hood, doors open.

**2245** **Maserati 3500** (Aurora) 1978-80 1/25 $20-25
Maroon, tan, clear, chrome plastic. Hood, doors, trunk open.

**2246** **Aston Martin DB4** (Aurora) 1978-80 1/25 $20-25
Silver, black, clear, chrome plastic. Hood, doors, trunk open.

**2247** **'79 Trans Am** 1979-83 1/24 $15-20
Black, clear plastic. Firebird decals. Removable clear roof panels. Reissued as 2258 (1980), 2270 (1980), 2716 (1985).

**2248** **'75 GMC Jimmy** 1979-81 1/24 $20-25
Off-white, clear, chrome plastic. Reissue of 2236 (1978).

**2250** **Mustang Hatchback** 1979-81 1/24 $20-25
Silver, clear plastic. '79 Indy pace car decals. Hood opens. Sun roof. Reissued as 2260 (1980), 2276 (1981).

**2251** **'80 Chevy LUV Pickup** 1979-81 1/24 $15-20
Off-white, clear plastic. Camper top. Reissue of 2213 (1976).

**2252** **El Camino Camper** 1978-81 1/24 $15-20
Red, clear, chrome plastic. Hood, tailgate open. Also issued as 2241 (1978).

**2253** **Corvette Pace Car** 1978-83 1/24 $15-20
Black, clear, chrome plastic. '78 Indy pace car decals. Hood opens. Clear roof panels. Silver anniversary Corvette. Reissued as 2259 (1980).

**2254** **Camaro Z-28** 1978-84 1/24 $15-20
Yellow, clear, chrome plastic. Reissued as 2266 (1980), 2717 (1985).

**2255** **Super Charged '56 Chevy** 1978-86 1/24 $10-15
Black, clear, chrome plastic. Hood opens. Flame decals. Also issued as 2239 (1978).

**2256** **'39 Chevy Coupe** 1979-81 1/24 $10-15
Maroon, clear, chrome plastic. Street rod without a stock option. Reissue of 2240 panel (1978). Reissued as 2719 (1985).

**2257** **Mazda RX-7** 1978-82 1/24 $10-15
Red, clear, chrome plastic. Wankel Roatry engine. Reissued as 2277 (1981).

**2300** **'30 Packard Speedster** 1975-80 1/24 $15-20
Russet brown, avocado, clear, chrome plastic. Hood removes. Top can be built up or down. Also issued as 2301 (1975).

**2301** **'30 Packard Boattail** 1975-86 1/24 $15-20
Pacific coral, russet brown, clear, chrome plastic. Also issued as 2300 (1975).

**2302** **Duesenberg SJ Roadster** 1976-86 1/24 $15-20
Wine red, black, clear, chrome plastic.

**2303** **'31 Rolls Royce Phaeton** 1978-86 1/24 $15-20
Maroon, gray, clear, chrome plastic. Hood lifts off, steerable front wheels. Based on the only surviving example of the two of these cars that were built.

**2304** **Mercedes 540K Coupe** 1978-83 1/24 $15-20
Maroon, black, clear, chrome plastic. New body on the chassis of PC87 (1963).

**2400** **'26 Mack Dump Truck** 1976-77 1/24 $20-25
Green, black, clear plastic. Decals. Bed dumps, tailgate swings open. Reissue of 7537 (1973).

**2401** **'26 Mack Log Hauler** 1976-77 1/24 $20-25
Red, black, clear plastic. Brown plastic logs held in place with metal chains. Decals. Reissue of 7537 (1973).

**2600** **'65 Corvette Sting Ray** 1975-81 1/8 $70-80
Red, black, clear, chrome plastic. Reissue of PC126 (1965).

**2601** **Jaguar XK-E** 1976-79 1/8 $70-80
Yellow, black, silver, transparent red, clear, chrome, plastic. Reissue of PC98 (1964).

**2602** **'32 Ford Roadster** 1977-83 1/8 $150-160
Black, beige, off-white, clear, chrome plastic. Reissue of PC88 (1963).

**2603** **'78 Corvette** 1978-81 1/8 $100-110
Orange, black, beige, transparent red, clear, chrome plastic. Decals for Indy pace car. T roof panels remove. Hood opens. Reissued as 2606 (1982).

**2604** **Street "T" Rod** 1978-81 1/8 $70-80
Red, beige, black, clear plastic. Reissue of PC78 (1962).

**5694** **Snake Rail Dragster** 1972-75 1/24 $60-70
White, chrome plastic. Hot Wheels decals. Front engine rail. Also issued as 5695.

**5695** **Mongoose Rail Dragster** 1972-75 1/24 $60-70
Blue, chrome plastic. Hot Wheels decals. Front engine rail. Also issued as 5694.

**5990** **Goin' Buggy** 1971-72 1/12 $60-70
Yellow, lime green, black, clear chrome plastic. Decals. Custom Volksrods. Street customized bug body has opening rear hood to show engine. Custom Shalako dune buggy body fits on same chassis as bug body.

**6003** **Dr. Pepper Car in a Bottle** 1976-77 1/36 $25-35
Lime green, black, clear, chrome plastic. Rail dragster.

**6100** **'53 Corvette** 1977-81 1/24 $15-20
Die-cast metal body. Red plastic interior, chassis. Clear, chrome plastic. Reissued in all plastic as 2291 (1982).

**6101** **'56 T-Bird** 1977-81 1/24 $15-20
Die-cast metal body. Reissued in all plastic as 2289 (1982).

**6102** **'50 MG-TC** 1977-81 1/24 $15-20
Die-cast metal body. Reissued in all plastic as 2290 (1982).

**6103** **'53 Street Jaguar XK-120** 1978-81 1/24 $15-20
Die-cast metal body.

**6200** **Duesenberg SJ Bobtail** 1978-81 1/24 $15-20
Die-cast metal body.

**6201** **Packard D Cowl Phaeton** 1978-81 1/24 $15-20
Die-cast metal body. 1931 Packard.

**6700** **Ferrari GP** 1970-71 1/32 $35-40
Red, clear plastic. Decals. Renumber of PC137 (1966).

**6701** **Lotus 33 GP** 1970-71 1/32 $35-40
Renumber of PC138 (1966).

**6702** **Boss '40 Willys** 1970-78 1/32 $45-55
Orange, clear plastic. Decals. Renumber of PC139 (1966).

**6703** **Ford Screamer** 1970-78 1/32 $35-40
Green, clear plastic. Decals. Renumber of PC140 (1966).

**6704** **'37 Hemi Fiat** 1970-78 1/32 $35-40
Blue, clear, chrome plastic. Decals. Dragster. Renumber of PC141 (1966).

**6705** **'59 Corvette** 1970-78 1/32 $30-35
Yellow, clear plastic. Number 16 racing decals. Renumber of PC404 (1960).

**6706** **'59 MGA 1600** 1970-71 1/32 $30-35
Renumber of PC168 (1967).

**6707** **'58 Austin Healy Sprite** 1970-71 1/32 $30-35
Renumber of PC169 (1967).

**6708** **Ford T Pickup** 1970-78 1/32 $35-40
Yellow, clear, chrome plastic. Renumber of PC170 (1967).

**6709** **Deuce Roadster** 1970-78 1/32 $35-40
Red, clear, chrome plastic. Decals. Renumber of P412 (1961).

**6710** **Slingshot Dragster** 1970-72 1/32 $55-65
Blue, clear plastic. Decals. Renumber of PC172 (1967).

**6712** **Porsche 904 GTS** 1970-75 1/32 $30-35
Silver, clear, chrome plastic. Racing decals. Renumber of PC99 (1964).

**6713** **Cooper-Ford** 1970-75 1/32 $35-40
Light blue, clear, chrome plastic. Decals. Renumber of PC100 (1964).

**6714** **Ferrari 250 GTO/LM** 1970-71 1/32 $30-35
Red, clear, chrome plastic. Decals. Renumber of PC101 (1964).

**6715** **Indianapolis Racer** 1970-75 1/24 $30-35
White plastic. Renumber of PC111 (1965).

**6716** **Slingshot Dragster** 1970-75 1/22 $55-65
Renumber of PC112 (1965).

**6717** **Firebolt** 1970-72 1/29 $55-65
Red, black, clear plastic. Decal. Renumber of PC113 (1965).

**6718** **'32 Ford Deuce Roadster** 1970-75 1/24 $35-40
Red, black plastic. Renumber of PC114 (1965).

**6719** **Long John Dragster** 1970-72 1/22 $55-65
Box art by Morgan. Renumber of PC115 (1965).

**6720** **Lola GT** 1970-71 1/32 $30-35
Renumber of PC125 (1965).

**6721** **Ferrari 275P** 1970-75 1/32 $30-35
Red, clear, chrome plastic. Racing decals. Renumber of PC128 (1965).

**6723** **Black Widow** 1970-72 1/24 $90-100
Black, off white, clear, chrome plastic. Decal. Renumber of PC60 (1960).

**6724** **Green Hornet** 1970-72 1/24 $35-40
Green, off white, clear, chrome plastic. Decal. Renumber of PC61 (1960).

**6725** **Woody Wagon** 1970-71 1/24 $35-40
Red, tan, clear, chrome plastic. White inserts for whitewall tires. Renumber of PC103 (1965).

**6726** **Futurista** 1970 1/24 $105-115
Yellow, red, clear, chrome plastic. Renumber of PC108 (1965).
**6727** **Orange Hauler** 1970-72 1/24 $35-40
Orange, white, clear, chrome plastic. Renumber of PC131 (1966).
**6728** **Chaparral 2D Coupe** 1970-72 1/24 $25-30
White, clear, chrome plastic. Racing decals. Renumber of PC142 (1966).
**6729** **Super Modified Sportsman** 1970-72 1/24 $30-35
White, clear, chrome plastic. Decals. Renumber of PC173 (1967).
**6730** **Hot Shot Midget Racer** 1970-72 1/24 $30-35
Red, chrome plastic. Racing decals. Renumber of PC178 (1967).
**6733** **Uncertain T** 1970-72 1/24 $140-160
White, clear, chrome plastic. Renumber of PC134 (1966).
**6734** **Hurts Hairy Olds** 1970-73 1/24 $25-30
White, clear, chrome plastic. Hurst decals. Renumber of PC175 (1967).
**6735** **Boot Hill Express** 1970-78 1/24 $25-30
Orange, clear, chrome plastic. Renumber of PC188 (1967).
**6744** **Bathtub Buggy** 1970-73 1/24 $100-120
White, brass chrome plastic. Decals. Renumber of PC223 (1969).
**6749** **L'il Coffin** 1970-76 1/24 $25-30
Raspberry, white, clear, chrome plastic. Renumber of PC250 (1970). Collector trading cards.
**6762** **The Snake** 1971-75 1/24 $30-35
Yellow body, bright blue plastic chassis, chrome plastic. Some rare late production chassis in gray. Blue-tinted clear plastic in early releases; changed to smoke-tint in later releases. Hot Wheels decals. Don Prudhomme's '70 Plymouth Barracuda. 426 hemi engine. Box art by Morgan. Reissued as 2205 (1975).
**6763** **The Mongoose** 1971-75 1/24 $30-35
Red body, blue chassis, chrome plastic. Blue-tinted clear plastic in early releases; changed to smoke-tint in later releases. Hot wheels decals. Tom McEwen's '70 Plymouth Duster. Box art by Morgan. Reissued as 2206 (1975).
**6764** **'34 Duesenberg Phaeton** 1970-71 1/24 $15-20
Tan, black, clear, chrome plastic. Renumber of PC81 (1963).
**6765** **'37 Mercedes-Benz** 1970-71 1/24 $15-20
Red, white, black, clear, chrome plastic. Renumber of PC87 (1963).
**6766** **'31 Rolls Royce Phantom II** 1970-71 1/24 $15-20
Black, silver, clear, chrome plastic. Renumber of PC109 (1965).
**6767** **'37 Cord 812** 1970-71 1/24 $15-20
Off white, black, clear, chrome plastic. Renumber of PC130 (1966).
**6768** **'24 Bugatti 35B** 1970-71 1/24 $15-20
Blue, silver, clear, chrome plastic. Renumber of PC133 (1966).
**6769** **'41 Lincoln Continental** 1970-71 1/24 $15-20
Metallic blue, white, clear, chrome plastic. Renumber of PC174 (1967).
**6770** **'34 Duesenberg Town Car** 1970-71 1/24 $15-20
Black, clear, chrome plastic. Renumber of PC185 (1968).
**6772** **Big "T" Show Rod** 1970 1/8 $90-110
Red, white, silver, black, clear, chrome plastic. Decal. Renumber of PC78 (1962).
**6773** **Jaguar XK-E** 1970 1/8 $70-80
Red, white, clear, chrome plastic. Renumber of PC98 (1964).
**6774** **Corvette Sting Ray** 1970 1/8 $80-90
Blue, black, clear, chrome plastic. Renumber of PC126 (1965).
**7507** **Big "T" Street Rod** 1973-76 1/8 $100-110
Yellow, beige, black, clear, chrome plastic. Wide Goodyear street slicks on chrome mag wheels. Decals. Reissue of PC78 (1962).
**7528** **Snake Rear Engine** 1973-76 1/24 $25-30
Yellow, chrome plastic. Silver vinyl fuel, ignition lines. Decals. Don Prudhomme's rail dragster. Body shell removes. Christmas tree start lights. Track official figure with hands over ears. Also issued as 7529 (1973).
**7529** **Mongoose Rear Engine** 1973-76 1/24 $25-30
Red, chrome plastic. Silver vinyl fuel, ignition lines. Decals. Some rare kits are in orange plastic. Tom McEwen's rail dragster. Body shell removes. Christmas tree start lights. Track official figure. Also issued as 7528 (1973).
**7537** **'26 Mack Stake Truck** 1973-77 1/24 $20-25
Yellow, black, clear plastic. Decals for Tidewater Trucking and Ringling Brothers Circus, which was then owned by Mattel. Hood, tailgate open.
**7539** **Mack Tank Truck** 1974-77 1/24 $20-25
Red, black, clear plastic. Texaco decals. Storage compartments on side open. Instructions for World War I camouflage pattern. Reissue of 7537 (1973).
**7544** **Elegant Beetle** 1974-75 1/16 $65-75
Black, clear, chrome plastic. Rolls front end on VW bug. Rear deck flips down to show chrome plated engine. Goodyear street slicks. Redesign of 6659 Smug Bug (1972).
**7547** **7-Up Car in a Bottle** 1975-77 1/36 $25-30
Yellow, black, green tinted clear, chrome plastic. 7-Up decals.
**7548** **Pepsi Car in a Bottle** 1975-77 1/36 $25-30
Red, black, clear, chrome plastic. Pepsi decals. A rail dragster.
**7549** **Duesenberg Town Car** 1974-80 1/24 $15-20
Lime green, black, clear, chrome plastic. Reissue of PC185 (1968).
**7550** **'58 T-Bird** 1974-78 1/24 $35-40
Red, black, clear, chrome plastic. White plastic inserts for whitewall tires. Reissue of PC89 (1964).
**7551** **'30 Ford Coupe** 1974-79 1/24 $20-25
Lime green, black, silver, chrome, clear plastic. Decals. Reissue of PC71 (1962).
**7552** **'30 Ford Cabriolet** 1974-78 1/24 $20-25
Yellow, black, clear, chrome plastic. Decals. Convertible top up or down. Reissue of PC120
**7553** **'30 Ford Woody** 1974-77 1/24 $15-20
Yellow, tan, clear, chrome plastic. Optional panels for van version. Tailgate opens. Chevy 6 engine. "Early Iron" series. Reissue of PC103 (1965).
**7554** **'36 Ford Coupe** 1974-78 1/24 $20-25
Red, black, clear, chrome plastic. Reissue of PC68 (1961).
**7555** **'29 Ford Roadster Pick-Up** 1974-86 1/24 $15-20
Yellow, black, clear, chrome plastic. Decal. Early Iron series. Added "wooden" extensions for sides of bed wall. Reissue of PC93 (1964).
**7570** **'36 Ford Convertible** 1974-78 1/24 $15-20
Yellow, black, clear, chrome plastic. Early Iron series. Goodyear street slicks on mag wheels. Merc flathead engine. Reissue of PC68 (1961).
**8201** **'34 Duesenberg SJ Phaeton** 1972-83 1/24 $15-20
Yellow, black, clear, chrome plastic. Reissue of PC81 (1963).
**8202** **'39 Mercedes-Benz 540-K** 1972-80 1/24 $15-20
Silver, black, clear, chrome plastic.
**8203** **'31 Rolls Royce Phantom II** 1972-79 1/24 $15-20
Black, silver, clear, chrome plastic. Reissue of PC109 (1965).
**8204** **'37 Cord 812 Phaeton** 1972-75 1/24 $15-20
Red, black, clear, chrome plastic. Reissue of PC130 (1966).
**8205** **'27 Bugatti Type 35B** 1972-75 1/24 $20-25
Blue, clear plastic. Reissue of PC133 (1966).
**8206** **'41 Lincoln Continental** 1972-78 1/24 $15-20
Black, tan, clear plastic. Plastic whitewall inserts. Convertible. Reissue of PC174 (1967).
**8279** **'30 Ford Early Iron** 1973-77 1/24 $15-20
Red black, clear, chrome plastic. "Early Iron" decals. New wide Goodyear street slicks on chrome mag rims. 283 Chevy engine. Ford Touring. Reissue of PC116 (1965).
**8280** **'32 Ford Roadster** 1973-78 1/24 $20-25
Black, white, clear, chrome plastic. "Early Iron" decals. New wide Goodyear street slicks on chrome mag rims. Ford Roadster. Reissue of PC132 (1966).
**8281** **'34 Ford Coupe Early Iron** 1973-78 1/24 $25-30
Lime green, black, clear, chrome plastic. "Early Iron" decals. New wide Goodyear street slicks on chrome mag rims. Reissue of PC72 (1962).
**8282** **'40 Ford Pickup Early Iron** 1973-79 1/24 $15-20
Orange, black, clear, chrome plastic. "Early Iron" decals. New wide Goodyear street slicks on chrome mag rims. Chrome hood scoop. Reissue of PC91 (1964).

## Tom Daniel Cars

**PC189** **Beer Wagon** 1967-69 1/24 $65-75
Yellow, chrome plastic. Decals. Tom Daniel's first design for Monogram. Mack Bulldog truck with eight chrome stacks, racing slicks, and a chrome beer keg gas tank. Beer barrels in truck bed. Renumbered 6736 (1970), reissued as 2732 (1986). Box art by Tom Daniel.
**PC190** **T'Rantula** 1968-69 1/24 $100-125
Green, clear, chrome plastic. Optional drag chute. Clear prop to tilt car into wheelie posture. Spider web decals. STP decals in early production runs, changed to Juice Box in later runs. Includes small spider figure with two metal parts to make a tie tack. Includes mail-in order slip for T'Rantula T shirt. Daniel called this "one of my favorite designs." Renumbered 6737 (1970), reissued as 2744 (1986). Box art by Daniel.
**PC192** **Pie Wagon** 1968-70 1/24 $100-125
Burgundy purple, clear, chrome and brass chrome plastic. Lighter purple plastic is later kit runs. "Mother's Pies" decal. Optional "Pizza Wagon" and "Taco Wagon" decals. Rear door of this C-cab opens to show rack of pies. Renumbered 6738 (1970), reissued as 2745 (1986). Box art by Daniel.
**PC205** **Red Baron** 1968 1/24 $125-150
Red, chrome plastic. Decals. T-bucket with German surfer helmet. World War I vintage Mercedes-Benz aircraft motor, two side-mounted machine guns. Reissued as PC212 (1968). Box art by Daniel.
**PC206** **Garbage Truck** 1968-69 1/24 $75-95
White, chrome plastic. Decals. Rear opens to reveal rock band inside. Design originated at Monogram, and Daniel added some touches, such as the band. Renumbered 6739 (1970).
**PC212** **Red Baron with Triplane** 1968-69 1/24 $75-95
Red, chrome plastic. This reissue of the Red Baron added a very nice 1/87 scale triplane. World War I model historian Brad Hansen noted: "Even when Monogram is goofing around, they do a better job than most." Reissue of PC205 (1968). Renumbered 6740 (1970), reissued as 6050 (1970), 2704 (1985). Box art by Daniel.
**PC217** **Paddy Wagon** 1968-69 1/24 $65-75
Dark blue, clear, chrome plastic. Daniel recommended a driver and sergeant figure hanging on back. These were not developed for the original kit, but were included in the Special Edition 1997 reissue. "Monogram did a super job on it. I was always proud of it." Some PC217 editions from 1970 have a Hot Wheels diecast Paddy Wagon car included. ($180-200) Renumbered 6741 (1970), reissued as 2733 (1986). Box art by Daniel.
**PC219** **Big Red Baron** 1969-69 1/12 $175-200
Red, chrome plastic. Decals. Includes same 1/87 scale triplane as in PC212 and a small skull with a German World War I spiked helmet. Renumbered 6778 (1970), reissued as 2506 (1986). Box art by Daniel.
**PC220** **Ghost of the Red Baron** 1969-69 1/5 $350-450
Bone white, chrome plastic. Yellow tinted pre-cut acetate lenses for skull's glasses. Black peel-

n-stick decal for iron cross base. Skull mounted on Iron Cross stand. Snap assembly. Rubber band mount makes it a bobbing head. Renumbered 6742 (1970). Box art by Daniel.

**PC222** **Tijuana Taxi** 1969-69 1/24 $250-300
Orange, clear, chrome plastic. Decals. Starfish mag wheels, chicken coop on roof. Daniel says this model was inspired by the taxis he saw on the streets of Tijuana and by the popularity of musician Herb Alpert and his Tijuana Brass. Renumbered 6743 (1970). Box art by Daniel.

**PC224** **King Chopper** 1969 1/8 $275-350
Purple, clear, chrome plastic. Vinyl tubing for brake lines and spark plug wires. Vulture perched on sissy bar. Decals. Trike based on a '74 Harley-Davidson. Builds to a fifteen inch long model. Renumbered 6782 (1970), reissued as 7542 Satan's Cycle (1974). Box art by Daniel.

**PC225** **Rommel's Rod** 1969 1/24 $250-325
Tan, clear , chrome plastic. Decals. With two skeleton figures. Hood removes to show engine. Daniel mated the front end of Monogram's Mercedes 540K to the rear end of a halftrack to create a "Krazy Kommand Kar." Renumbered 6745 (1970). Box art by Daniel.

**PC228** **Dragon Wagon** 1969 1/24 $250-325
Yellow, clear, chrome plastic. Decals—including "See Daring Dave." Renumbered 6746 (1970), reissued as 2208 Hangman (1975). Box art by Daniel.

**PC229** **'55 Chevy Badman** 1969 1/24 $75-100
Yellow, red tinted clear, chrome plastic. STP decals. "Adios Mother" decal on back. Dragster. Redesign of PC83 Customizing '55 Chevy (1963). Renumbered 6747 (1970), reissued as 2211 (1975). Box art by Daniel. Collector trading cards.

**PC231** **Sand Crab** 1969 1/24 $125-150
Lime green, green tinted clear, chrome plastic. Sand dune base. Green tinted clear prop to pose car doing a wheelie off the dune. Flower Power decals. VW 1600 engine. Steerable front wheels. Renumbered 6748 (1970), reissued as 7532 Li'l Van (1973). Box art by Daniel.

**1000** **Dodge Van** (snap) 1975-83 1/32 $20-25
Lime green, yellow, black, clear, chrome plastic. Molded with lime green body/yellow interior or yellow body/lime green interior. "Vanana Split" decals. Custom van with porthole side windows, dual roof scoops, and sidepipes. Reissued as 1010 (1976).

**1001** **Chevy Van** (snap) 1975-83 1/32 $20-25
Yellow, lime green black, clear, chrome plastic. Molded with lime green body/yellow interior or yellow body/lime green interior. Custom van with porthole side windows, vent window on roof, sidepipes, and louvered hood. "Streeto Vandito" decals. Reissued as 1001 (1976).

**2202** **Quicksilver Chevy Delivery** 1975-79 1/24 $100-125
Silver, clear, chrome plastic. Yellow felt for interior carpeting. Silver foil decals. Reissue of 6752 (1970).

**2207** **Sand Shark** 1975-77 1/24 $25-45
Yellow, clear, chrome plastic. Shark decals. Redesign of 5986 Dog Catcher (1971) with shark fin on top of cab and fins for running boards. Daniel began reworking design as a "sand dragster," but someone at Monogram finished the work and it came out as Sand Shark. Issued in same year as movie *Jaws*.

**2208** **Hangman** 1975-77 1/24 $75-95
Black, clear, chrome plastic. Redesign of PC228 Dragon Wagon (1969) as gallows tow truck. Daniel liked the tow truck concept, but in later years, as the Dragon Wagon became rare and collectible, he regretted its loss.

**2209** **Stinger** 1975-77 1/24 $25-30
Orange, clear, chrome plastic. Decals. Redesign of 6054 Trick "T" (1971) with added rear spoiler, clear canopy for driver, and no open drag chute option. Front wheels updated to Centerlines.

**2210** **Rattler** 1975-77 1/24 $125-150
Lime green, clear, chrome plastic. Snake decals. Redesign of 5987 Horn Toad (1971). Has the three-spoke wheels and street tires of the 1973 yellow-edition Horn Toad. New louvers in top and sides of body and an enclosed panel cab with a large open sun roof.

**2213** **Mojave Mule** 1976-78 1/24 $30-40
Yellow, clear, chrome plastic. Chevy '77 LUV pickup. Tom Daniel's final design for Monogram. Reissued as 2217 (1977), 2251 (1979), 2280 (1981).

**2214** **Vanbulance** 1976-78 1/24 $30-35
Reissue of 6657 (1972). Not a Tom Daniel design.

**2215** **Firebomb Van** 1976-78 1/24 $50-75
Red, clear, chrome plastic. Flame decals. '65 Volkswagen. Reissue of 6757 Baja Bandito (1970). This redesign was done by the staff of Monogram, not Daniel. Sirens, emergency lights, water nozzle added. Ladder replaces surf board on roof rack.

**2221** **Pinto Street Rod** 1977-78 1/24 $25-30
Lime green, clear, chrome plastic. Reissue of 6654 (1972). Redesign by Monogram.

**2222** **Vega Minivan** 1977-78 1/24 $25-30
Orange, clear, chrome plastic. Woodgrain body decal. Reissue of 6655 (1972). Redesign by Monogram.

**2267** **Bad Actor Chevy Delivery** 1980-81 1/24 $25-35
Off-white, clear, chrome plastic. Decals. Clear roof in rear was replaced by sunroof in front. Reissue of 6752 Street Fighter (1970). Redesign by Monogram.

**2506** **Big Red Baron** 1986 1/12 $70-80
Red, chrome plastic. No clear parts. Decals. Includes triplane and skull. Reissue of PC219.

**2704** **Red Baron Show Car** 1985-86 1/24 $20-25
Red, chrome plastic. Reissue of PC205 (1968). Does not have the triplane.

**2732** **Beer Wagon** 1986 1/24 $15-20
Yellow plastic. Brown plastic beer barrels. Decals. Reissue of PC189 (1967).

**2733** **Paddy Wagon** 1986 1/24 $20-25
Black, clear, brass chrome plastic. Reissue of PC217 (1968). This reissue stayed in the Monogram until 2000.

**2745** **Pie Wagon** 1986 1/24 $20-25
Brownish-red, clear, chrome, brass chrome plastic. Decals. Reissue of PC192 (1968).

**2746** **Bad Medicine** 1986 1/24 $30-35
Black, white, chrome plastic. Decals. Reissue of 6055 (1971).

**5093** **Ice "T"** 1970 1/24 $200-225
Yellow, clear, chrome plastic. Decals. Blocks of ice with ice tongs in back. This issue includes a Hot Wheels diecast Ice "T" car. The yellow "Hot Wheels" sticker was printed on the box, not stuck on later. Also issued as 6757 (1970).

Construction equipment Snap Draggin's model bodies were randomly molded in either red, yellow, orange, or lime green. Accessory parts came in black and silver plastic. There are no chrome or clear parts on the construction equipment Snap Draggin's. Each has a value of $75-100.

**5690** **Boss Bulldozer** (snap) 1972-73 Snap Draggin's
Wild lunging bulldozer on rocky mountain base.

**5691** **Extreme Shovel** (snap) 1972-73 Snap Draggin's
Super cool steam shovel with working boom and blown steamer motor. Mounded on earthen base.

**5692** **Mountain Mover** (snap) 1972-73 Snap Draggin's
Tough dump truck with blown motor and tilting payload full of rocky earth. Mounted on earthen base.

**5693** **Screamin' Skipshovel** (snap) 1972-73 Snap Draggin's
Fierce front-loader with blown motor in the rear, lunging forward on earth base.

**5697** **Groovy Grader** 1972-75 1/24 $75-100
Yellow, chrome plastic. Decals. Road grader rail dragster with a rear-mounted, rear-facing engine. Super-wide dual rear slicks.

**5698** **Unreal Roller** 1972-75 1/24 $150-175
Grape purple, chrome plastic. Wild road roller with mostly chrome parts and mod blown motor.

**5985** **Firecracker** 1971-72 1/24 $125-150
Red, clear, brass chrome plastic. Fire truck with fire hose, Ford Cobra V-8, and hose header side pipes. Uses the same super-wide tires as the Groovy Grader, Horn Toad, Honest Engine, and others. Daniel said, "One of my better box art efforts." Reissued as 7530 Fire Iron (1973). Box art by Daniel.

**5986** **Dog Catcher** 1971-72 1/24 $175-200
Orange, orange tinted clear, chrome plastic. Gray vinyl screen for cage. (Tint in the clear parts became smoked in later runs.) Decals. Dog driver figure. Reissued as 5986 (1973), 2207 Sand Shark (1975). Box art by Locher.

**5986** **Dog Catcher** 1973-74 1/24 $225-300
Black, clear, chrome plastic. (Some rare kits came in red plastic.) Gray vinyl screen for cage. Decals. Super-wide rear slicks are replaced by Goodyear slicks on snowflake mag rims. Reissue of 5986 (1971).

**5987** **Horn Toad** 1971-72 1/24 $175-200
Lime green, smoke tinted clear plastic. Red lizard scale decals. Pontiac 6 engine is tilted to one side. One-piece windshield and doors unit tilts forward to open. Rear deck cover flips open to show chromed gas tank. Super-wide tires and unique wheel hubs with long points. Box art by Daniel. Reissued as 5987 (1973).

**5987** **Horn Toad** 1973-74 1/24 $225-275
Yellow, clear, chrome plastic. Gold lizard scale decals. Super-wide tires and horned wheels replaced with Goodyear street tires and three-spoke mag wheels. Reissue of 5987 (1971). Reissued as 2210 Rattler (1975).

**5988** **Low Blow** 1971-72 1/8 $50-75
Blue, clear, chrome plastic. Red vinyl tubing for throttle cables and spark plug wires. *Easy Rider* inspired decals. Extended front wheel, knobby tires, high rise handlebars. Mini-bike aimed at younger modelers. Reissued as 7534 Popper Chopper (1973).

**5989** **Devil Chopper** 1971-72 1/8 $225-250
Red, clear, red-tinted chrome plastic. Vinyl tubing. Front forks are bones with horns at the top. Chrome skull dangles from bony hand at top of rear sissy bar. Pointy high rise seats. Box art by Morgan. Reissued as 7541 Grim Reaper (1974).

**5991** **Super Digger** 1971-75 1/12 $350-400
Red, silver, clear plastic. Decals. Driver figure. An AA rail dragster mounted on a base containing a battery-powered electric motor that makes engine sound and activates the model. Rear wheels spin, dragster lifts up, falls back down, and the drag chute pops. Locher box art.

**6050** **Red Baron** 1970 1/24 $200-225
Red, chrome plastic. Decals. In 1970 Mattel included a 1/64 diecast Hot Wheels Red Baron in with the plastic model kit. An orange day-glow 6050 sticker was pasted over the PC212 kit number.

**6054** **Trick "T"** 1971-75 1/24 $125-150
Silver gray, orange tinted clear, chrome plastic. Later releases have smoked clear and then clear plastic. Some rare circa 1973 kits are molded in orange plastic. Decals. With dual open drag chutes. T-bucket dragster with the engine back in the driver compartment and the driver up where the engine should be. In 1973 the box art and decals change. Reissued as 2209 Stinger (1975). Box art by Daniel.

**6055** **Bad Medicine** 1971-76 1/24 $100-125
Grape purple, white, chrome plastic. Some kits were issued in red, blue, or orange plastic in the early 1970s. Decals. C-cab rail dragster with skeleton driver in coffin-shaped seat holding a scythe brake lever in one hand and the steering wheel in the other. Cow skull nose ornament. Reissued as 2746 (1986). Box art by Daniel.

**6650** **Li'l Red Baron** (snap) 1972-76 1/32 $100-125
Red, silver, black plastic. Caricature of the Red Baron car lunging wildly from an Iron Cross base. Photo box art.

**6651** **T'Rantula** (snap) 1972-76 1/32 $100-125
Lime green, black, silver plastic. Caricature of T'Rantula doing wheelie off a spider wed base. Tom Daniel declared: "Design-wise, it was even MORE radical than its 'big brother' 1/24 scale kit." Photo box art.

**6652** **Leap Hog ATV** (snap) 1972-76 1/32 $75-100
Lime green, silver, black, red plastic. Three-wheel all terrain vehicle with jumbo tires mounted in wheelie pose on its shadow display base. Driver figure is modeled on Daniel's oldest son Kelly. Photo box art.

**6653** **Roar 'n Peace Chopper** 1972-76 1/32 $75-100
Lime green, silver, red, black plastic. (snap) Chopper with extended forks. Driver makes the peace sign while pulling a wheelie from a display base. Photo box art.

**6654** **Poison Pinto** 1972 1/24 $125-150
Lime green, smoke tinted clear, chrome plastic. Decals. Daniel designed the skull and cross-cylinders decal. Intended to be matched with 6655 Rat Vega. Reissued as 6654 (1973), 2221 (1977). Photo box art.

**6654** **Poison Pinto** 1973-76 1/24 $150-175
Red, clear, chrome plastic. Decals. New slotted mag wheels/street tires replace original starfish mags/slicks. Reissue of 6654 (1972). Photo box art.

**6655** **Rat Vega** 1972 1/24 $125-150
Black, smoke-tinted clear, chrome plastic. Decals. Hood with smoked-clear scoop lifts off to show engine. Panel wagon. Reissued as 6655 (1973), 2222 (1977). Photo box art.

**6655** **Rat Vega** 1973-76 1/24 $75-100
Yellow, clear, chrome plastic. Decals. (Some kits are molded in red plastic.) Starfish mags/ street tires replace first issue's five-spoke mags/slicks. Photo box art.

**6656** **Honest Engine** 1972-75 $125-150
Red, brass chrome plastic. Old-time locomotive with V-8 Chrysler engine, wide racing slicks, and gas tank, drag chute in coal car. Daniel, a self-confessed train nut, enjoyed designing this model, but observed: "Some of the modeling 'purists' out there think I had lost it with this one." Photo box art.

**6657** **Vandal** 1972-80 1/24 $75-100
Black, clear, chrome plastic. Decals. Miniature groovy posters printed on cardboard, intended to be cut out and installed in back. Asymmetrical '73 Chevy van with engine where the front passenger seat should be. Side door opens to show plush interior. Motorbike on rear bumper is a model of a full-size bike designed by Daniel. Reissued as 2214 Vanbulance (1976). Photo box art.

**6658** **Draggin' Fly** 1972-73 1/24 $150-175
Yellow, chrome plastic. Decals. Rubber band. Three-wheel airplane/drag bike with driver figure. Rubber-band powered pusher propeller in back.

**6659** **Smug Bug** 1972 1/16 $125-150
Blue, black, smoke-tinted clear, chrome plastic. VW with a Hemi V-8 in back. Front and rear ends tilt open to show interior. Reissued as 7543 Muscle Bug (1974). Redesigned as 7544 Elegant Beetle (1974).

**6660** **Top Chop** 1972 1/12 $100-125
Yellow, clear, chrome plastic. Vinyl tubing. Rainbow stripe decals. Three-wheel trike with transverse-mounted Hemi motor behind driver's seat. Reissued as 7545 Vampire (1974).

**6736** **Beer Wagon** 1970-77 1/24 $50-75
Yellow, chrome plastic. Decals. Renumbering of PC189 (1967). Collector trading cards.

**6737** **T'Rantula** 1970-76 1/24 $50-75
Green, clear, chrome plastic. Decals. Renumbering of PC190 (1968). Collector trading cards.

**6738** **Pie Wagon** 1970-75 1/24 $75-100
Burgundy purple, clear, chrome and brass plastic. Renumbering of PC192 (1968). Collector trading cards.

**6739** **Garbage Truck** 1970-73 1/24 $50-75
White, chrome plastic. Decals. Renumbering of PC206 (1968).

**6740** **Red Baron** 1970-77 1/24 $50-75
Red, chrome plastic. Decals. Renumbering of PC212 (1968). Collector trading cards.

**6741** **Paddy Wagon** 1970-77 1/24 $65-75
Dark blue, clear, chrome plastic. 1973-1974 releases in bright blue plastic. Some 1970 releases included a Hot Wheels diecast Paddy Wagon car in a box marked with a yellow sticker. ($175-200) Renumbering of PC217 (1968). Collector trading cards.

**6742** **Ghost of the Red Baron** 1970-72 1/5 $350-450
Bone white, chrome plastic. Sheet of yellow tinted acetate. Rubber bands. Stick-on decal. Renumbering of PC220 (1969).

**6743** **Tijuana Taxi** 1970-75 1/24 $250-300
Orange, clear, chrome plastic. Decals. Renumbering of PC222 (1969). Collector trading cards.

**6745** **Rommel's Rod** 1970-76 1/24 $250-300
Tan, clear, chrome plastic. Decals. Later releases in lighter tan plastic. Renumbering of PC225 (1969). Collector trading cards.

**6746** **Dragon Wagon** 1970-73 1/24 $250-300
Yellow, clear, chrome plastic. Renumbering of PC228 (1969). Collector trading cards.

**6747** **'55 Chevy Badman** 1970-86 1/24 $50-75
Yellow, red-tinted clear, chrome plastic. Some early 1970s issues in orange plastic. Red-tinted clear parts changed to smoked tint, then to clear. STP decals change to Juice Box around 1971-1972. Painted box art changed to photo box art in later releases. Renumbering of PC229 (1969).

**6748** **Sandcrab** 1970-72 1/24 $125-150
Lime green, green tinted clear, chrome plastic. Green tinted clear becomes smoke-tinted in later production run. Renumbering of PC231 (1969). Collector trading cards.

**6752** **Street Fighter** 1970-72 1/24 $125-250
Orange, red tinted clear, chrome plastic. "Bad News" and STP decals. 1960 Chevy sedan delivery wagon with full glass roof over rear. Front end tilts to show 228 Camaro engine. Reissued as 7531 Quicksilver (1973), 2202 Quicksilver (1975), 2267 Bad Actor (1980). Two box art versions by Daniel: First, side view of race with lime green Barracuda. Second, three-quarter view of race with purple Barracuda and purple box lettering. Second is more rare. Collector trading cards.

**6754** **Son of Ford** 1970-72 1/24 $100-125
Orange, clear, chrome plastic. Decals. '32 Ford hot rod with 302 Mustang engine. Uses same starfish mag wheels as Tijuana Taxi. Redesign of PC132 (1966). Box art by Daniel. Collector trading cards.

**6755** **Boss A Bone** 1970-72 1/24 $100-125
Red, black, clear, chrome plastic. Decals. '29 Model A Ford pickup with Olds V-8 engine. Redesign of Blue Beetle PC93 (1964). Box art by Daniel. Collector trading cards.

**6756** **Sweet "T"EE** 1970-72 1/24 $100-125
Dark Yellow, black, clear, chrome plastic. Later production runs had lighter yellow plastic. 327 Chevy engine with GMC blower. Redesign of PC92 Little T (1964). Box art by Daniel. Collector trading cards.

**6757** **Ice "T"** 1970-76 1/24 $50-75
Yellow, clear, chrome plastic. Some releases in the early 1970s were molded in lime green plastic. Concealed headlights flip open, two blocks of ice with tongs in cargo space. First kit to have Monogram's wrinkled slicks. Box art by Daniel. Collector trading cards. Issued as 5093 (1970) with a Hot Wheels diecast car included.

**6759** **Baja Bandito** 1970-72 1/24 $125-150
Orange, red-orange tinted clear, chrome plastic. "Love" decals. '65 Volkswagen van with 327 Chevy engine at mid-body. Peace sign in place of VW symbol on front. Clamshell side doors fold up and down to show trail bike and surf board inside. Daniel: "The hippie invasion was in full swing. Flower power and love and all that good stuff." Reissued as 7527 Baja Beast (1973), 2215 Firebomb (1976). Collector trading cards.

**6761** **Cherry Bomb** 1970-79 1/24 $100-125
Red, green tinted clear, chrome plastic. Later releases with smoked clear and then just clear plastic. Bubble top tilts up. Futuristic turbine-powered rod pulls a surfboard-shaped trailer with Harley-powered bike with cherry bomb shaped gas tank. Box art by Daniel. Later releases with photo box art. Collector trading cards.

**6775** **Mean Maverick** 1970-75 1/12 $325-375
Orange, gray, yellow, purple tinted clear, chrome plastic. Decals. Separate foot pedal activates a battery powered motor to lift funny car body, showing chassis and Ford 427 engine. Drag chute can be built packed or open. Box art by Daniel.

**6778** **Big Red Baron** 1970-72 1/12 $200-225
Red, clear, chrome plastic. Renumbering of PC219 (1969).

**6781** **S'Cool Bus** 1970-72 1/24 $125-150
Yellow, silver, chrome plastic. Orange tinted sheets of clear acetate for windows and sun roof. Side and rear windows have line drawings of kids done by Daniel. Decals. One-piece bus body is hinged to tilt up revealing two Chrysler engines and driver's seat in rear end. Hood is the one Daniel originally designed for GM's 1962 trucks. "I snuck that in there." Daniel box art. Some 1970 issues contained a Hot Wheels diecast S'Cool Bus car. Reissued as 8290 (1973). Collector trading cards.

**6782** **King Chopper** 1970-72 1/12 $275-325
Purple, clear, chrome plastic. Vinyl tubing for brake lines and spark plug wires. Vulture perched on sissy bar. Decals. Based on a '74 Harley-Davidson. Builds to a fifteen inch long model. Box art by Daniel. Renumbering of PC224 (1969).

Snap Draggins were made from two molds, with each mold producing four bodies (6783-6785 and 6786-6898). Runs of four bodies were molded in yellow, blue, red, and lime green plastic. Thus each body can be found in any of four standard colors. Rarely some bodies appear in orange plastic, and around 1973 one run of olive drab plastic cars was made. The clear parts are tinted green (rarely blue) in early releases, smoked in later releases, and finally just clear. Chassis and trim are molded in black and silver. Stick-on decals. Each is valued at $75-100.

**6783** **Thunderbug** (snap) 1970-76 Snap Draggin's.
Volkswagen with Iron Cross wheels and Iron Cross on roof with spike. Mounted on shadow display base. This is the first in the "Snap-Draggin's" series of comic, distorted cars. Collector trading cards.

**6784** **Dune Rat** (snap) 1970-76 Snap Draggin's.
No clear parts. Stick-on decals. Dune buggy with rat tail. Mounted on shadow base. Collector trading cards.

**6785** **Screamin' Vette** (snap) 1970-76 Snap Draggin's.
"Mister T" stick-on decal in honor of the man who sold Tom Daniel his first Corvette. Mounted on shadow display base. Collector trading cards.

**6786** **Boss Mustang** (snap) 1970-76 Snap Draggin's.
Lunging pony car mounted on shadow display base. Collector trading cards.

**6895** **Hemi Semi** (snap) 1971-73 Snap Draggin's.
Scrunched-up tractor-trailer on a shadow display base.

**6896** **Super Taxi** (snap) 1971-73 Snap Draggin's.
Chevy Nova mounted on base in wheelie pose.

**6897** **Roarin' Rail** (snap) 1971-73 Snap Draggin's.
Rail digger with driver in enclosed body mounted in wheelie position on shadow base.

**6898** **Street Cleaner** (snap) 1971-73 Snap Draggin's.
'70 Camaro Z-28 pulling a wheelie on a shadow base.

**6899** **Jinx Express** 1971-72 1/24 $100-125
Silver, green tinted clear, chrome plastic. Later releases with smoked clear plastic. Decals. Brinks armored truck with a pig snout front end. The model serves as a piggy bank: slot in top for coins, combination lock to open vault door in rear. Box art by Morgan. Reissued as 7533 Fast Buck (1973).

**7500** **Cop Out** 1973-83 1/24 $50-75
Black, clear, chrome plastic. Plymouth Duster police cruiser funny car. Body same as 6763 Mongoose Duster (1971). Body tilts up to reveal same chassis used in 8284 '57 Chevy Outcast (1973) and 6762 Snake Barracuda (1971).

**7503** **Flapjack** (snap) 1973-83 $75-100
Silver, black, clear plastic. Battery powered motor spins the prop, flaps the wings, and advances-retracts the machine guns. Wisniewski designed working mechanisms. Daniel designed the shell, base, and bouncy wire arm holding the plane. Monogram marketed it to "junior model buffs," but it cost $4.00. Nevertheless, Daniel declared: "It really worked out great . . . and was a terrific seller too."

**7504** **'70 California Street Vette** 1973-82 1/24 $100-125
Orange, black, clear, chrome plastic. Hood opens. A model of Daniel's personal car. Large louvers on hood, top, rear window. Reissued as 2212 stock (1976).

**7527** **Baja Beast** 1973-78 1/24 $25-35
Yellow, clear, chrome plastic. Decals. Metal wire for flag aerial. Reissue of 6759 Baja Bandito (1970) with new off-road lights and new decals. Front symbol changed from peace sign to hand making the peace sign.

**7530** **Fire Iron** 1973-76 1/24 $50-75
Red, clear, and brass chrome plastic. Decals. Reissue of 5985 Firecracker (1971) with new starfish mag wheels and the less extreme Goodyear tires used on most Monogram show car models at this time.

**7531** **Quicksilver** 1973-75 1/24 $100-125
Silver, clear, chrome plastic. Silver foil decals. Sheet of yellow felt for interior carpeting. Reissue of 6752 Street Fighter (1970) with added hood scoop, new grille and quad headlights.

**7532** **Li'l Van** 1973-76 1/24 $50-75
Yellow, clear, chrome plastic. Some kits molded in orange or lime green. Metal wire for antenna flag. Decals. Reissue of PC231 Sand Crab (1969) with added cab in rear, windshield, off-road lights. This revision of the Sand Crab was built in to the original mold as a planned future release. Does not include the sand dune base of Sand Crab.

**7533** **Fast Buck** 1973-76 1/24 $50-75
Blue, clear, chrome plastic. Decals. Reissue of 6899 Jinx Express (1971) with no parts modifications, but new decals. Photo box art.

**7534** **Popper Chopper** 1973-76 1/8 $50-75
Yellow, clear, chrome plastic. Decals. Reissue of 5988 Low Blow (1971) with modified driver's seat, new padded headrest. Still includes driver's helmet. Photo box art.

**7541** **Grim Reaper** 1974-75 1/8 $225-250
Black, clear, chrome plastic. Vinyl tubing. Major redesign of 5989 Devil Chopper (1971) with dual rectangular headlights in place of round headlight, rectangular forks in place of the bone forks, new seat, handle bars, coffin shaped gas tank, added Iron Cross on back.

**7542** **Satan's Cycle** 1974-75 1/8 $275-350
Red, clear, chrome plastic. Vinyl tubing. Decals. Reissue of PC224 King Chopper (1969) with dual rectangular headlights replacing the original single round headlight.

**7543** **Muscle Bug** 1974-75 1/16 $175-200
Red, black, clear, chrome plastic. Decals. Reissue of 6659 Smug Bug (1972). New decals feature muscle-building insect showing off his biceps and shouting "Hemi Power!"

**7545** **Vampire** 1974-75 1/12 $125-150
White, clear, chrome plastic. Vinyl tubing. Decals. Reissue of 6660 Top Chop (1972) with no mold changes and new purple and red flame scallops.

The following four compact funny cars have stretched bodies that were produced from the same mold. Runs were molded in yellow and red—thus each car can be found in both yellow and red. Also silver and black plastic parts. They share the same motor, chassis, and wheels as the 1974 issues of 8275-8278. Bodies tilt up to show interior.

**7571** **'75 Vega Funny Car** (snap) 1974-82 1/32 $25-35
"Earthquake" decals.

**7572** **'75 Pinto Funny Car** (snap) 1974-82 1/32 $25-35
"Shut Out" decals. Some bodies are in orange plastic.

**7573** **'72 Gremlin Funny Car** (snap) 1974-78 1/32 $25-35
"GRRemlin" decals.

**7574** **'75 Mustang II FC** (snap) 1974-82 1/32 $25-35
"Mustang II Stampede" decals.

The following four funny cars have bodies that were produced by the same mold and were molded in yellow and dark orange. Thus each car can be found in both yellow and orange. (Later releases were molded in orange and lime green.) They share the same interior, chassis, motor, and wheels. Interiors of the original 1973 releases are molded in silver with an air scoop that protrudes through the hood.

The motor is a blown hemi with four upward-facing injectors. In 1974 the motor received a three-hole injector scoop, the interior part was deleted, and small fin spoilers were added to attach to the body over the rear wheels. Wheels are molded in black plastic.

Windows are smoked clear. Some rare kits have been found with pale yellow, red, and olive green plastic bodies, and chassis parts in white and blue. The stretched bodies tilt up to show the interior.

**8275** **Fake Out** (snap) 1973-82 1/32 $25-35
'72 Mustang. Decals.

**8276** **Whiplash** (snap) 1973-82 1/32 $25-35
'72 Camaro. Decals.

**8277** **Rip Off** (snap) 1973-82 1/32 $25-35
'72 Plymouth Duster funny car. Decals.

**8278** **Fiend** (snap) 1973-78 1/32 $25-35
Dodge Charger funny car. Decals.

**8283** **Troublemaker** 1973-75 1/24 $50-75
Red, smoked clear, chrome plastic. Some rare releases in yellow plastic. Later releases with clear windows. Decals. Stretched '72 Chevy El Camino with rear end that tilts to show injected motor in back. Chromed intake pipes and exhaust headers. Reissued as 2204 Hornet (1975), 2204 Desperado (1977).

**8284** **Outcast** 1973-75 1/24 $125-150
Blue, black, smoke-tinted clear, chrome plastic. Decals. Chopped and modified '57 Chevy funny car. Body tilts up to show same chassis/motor as in 7500 Cop Out (1973) and 6762 The Snake (1971). Reissued as 2203 Wildfire (1975), 2203 Chevy Funny Car (1977).

**8290** **S'Cool Bus** 1973-77 1/24 $75-100
Yellow, silver-gray, clear, chrome plastic. Clear acetate for windows (without the orange tint or pictures of kids). Decals changed to standard GMC truck grille in front, replacing the original bared-teeth design. Reissue of 6781 (1970) with the body part cut in two at the cowl so that it would fit into a standard size car kit box.

## 1980-1985 Car Models

**1023** **Jeep CJ-7 Renegade** (snap) 1980-84 1/32 $10-15
Blue, black, clear, chrome plastic. Reissued as 1033 (1981).

**1024** **Ford Bronco XLT** (snap) 1980-84 1/32 $10-15
Red, black, silver, clear, chrome plastic. Removable hardtop. Reissued as 1034 (1981), 1041 (1981).

**1027** **'80 Mustang Coupe** (snap) 1980-86 1/32 $10-15
Off white, clear plastic. Decals. Reissued as 1038 (1981).

**1028** **Datsun 280ZX** (snap) 1980-84 1/32 $10-15
Lime green, black, clear plastic. Reissued as 1048 (1982).

**1029** **'68 Pontiac GTO** (snap) 1981-83 1/32 $15-20

**1030** **'70 Mustang Mach I** (snap) 1981-83 1/32 $10-15
Reissued as 1049 (1982).

**1031** **'82 Malibu Police Car** (snap) 1981-84 1/32 $10-15
White, black, clear, chrome plastic.

**1032** **'69 Camaro Z-28** (snap) 1981-85 1/32 $10-15
Yellow, black, clear chrome plastic.

**1033** **Off Road Jeep** (snap) 1981-84 1/32 $10-15
Yellow, black, clear, chrome plastic. Reissue of 1023 (1980).

**1034** **Off Road Bronco** (snap) 1981-83 1/32 $10-15
Blue, black, clear, chrome plastic. Reissue of 1024 (1980).

**1038** **'80 Turbo Mustang** (snap) 1981-84 1/32 $10-15
Yellow, clear plastic. Hot Wheels. Includes Mattel offer of a free die-cast Hot Wheels car with the purchase of three Hot Wheels model kits. Reissue of 1027 (1980).

**1039** **Hot Firebird** (snap) 1981-85 1/32 $10-15
Hot Wheels. Reissue of 1017 (1978).

**1040** **'82 Corvette Sting Ray** 1981-85 1/32 $10-15
Orange, black, clear, chrome plastic. (snap) Hot Wheels. Reissue of 1016 (1978).

**1041** **Bronco 4 Wheeler** (snap) 1981-84 1/32 $10-15
Bucking bronco decal. Hot Wheels. Reissue of 1024 (1980)

**1042** **Snake Pepsi Challenger** 1982-85 1/32 $15-20
White, black, clear, chrome plastic. (snap) Body tilts up. Don Prudhomme's Trans Am funny car.

**1043** **Blue Max Ford EXP** (snap) 1982-85 1/32 $15-20
Blue, black, clear, chrome plastic. Raymond Beadle's funny car. Also issued as 1044, 1045.

**1044** **Dodge Fabrege Super** (snap) 1982-84 1/32 $15-20
Metallic green, black, clear, chrome plastic. Al Segrini's Dodge Omni funny car.

**1045** **Mercury Budweiser** (snap) 1982-85 1/32 $15-20
Red, black, clear, chrome plastic. Kenny Bernstein's '82 Mercury LN7 funny car. Also issued as 1043.

**1046** **Custom Camaro** (snap) 1982-84 1/32 $10-15
Reissue of 1019 (1978).

**1047** **Trans Am Street** (snap) 1982-84 1/32 $10-15
White, black, clear, chrome plastic. Reissue of 1017 (1978).

**1048** **Datsun 280Z Coupe** (snap) 1982-84 1/32 $10-15
Yellow, black, clear, chrome plastic. Reissue of 1028 (1980).

**1049** **'70 Boss Mustang** (snap) 1982-84 1/32 $10-15
Red, clear plastic. Flame decals. Reissue of 1030 (1981).

1204 **Peterbilt 359** (snap) 1980-85 1/32 $15-20
Yellow, black, clear, chrome plastic. Orange decals. A conventional. Reissued as 1302 (1981).

1205 **Kenworth W900** (snap) 1980-85 1/32 $35-40
Blue, red, clear, chrome plastic. Decals. An Aerodyne conventional. Reissued as 1303 (1981).

1206 **Fruehauf Van** (snap) 1980-84 1/32 $15-20
White, black plastic. Birdseye decal. Refrigerator van. Rear doors open. Also issued as 1207 without the refrigerator unit.

1207 **Fruehauf Van** (snap) 1980-83 1/32 $15-20
Gray, black plastic. Harley-Davidson decal. Also issued as 1206.

1208 **Peterbilt Cabover** (snap) 1981-83 1/32 $20-25
Red, clear, chrome plastic. Decals.

1209 **Kenworth Cabover** (snap) 1981-86 1/32 $15-20
Red, black, clear, chrome plastic. Decals. Kenworth Aerodyne Cabover. Reissued as 1304 (1982).

1210 **Mack Conventional** (snap) 1982-86 1/32 $20-25
Red, black, clear, chrome plastic. Decals.

1211 **Tanker Trailer** (snap) 1982-83 1/32 $15-20
Silver, black plastic. Union decals. Also issued as 1212.

1212 **Tanker Trailer** (snap) 1982-84 1/32 $15-20
Silver, black plastic. Texaco decals. Also issued as 1211.

1213 **Mack Fire Pumper** (snap) 1982-86 1/32 $15-20
Red, black, clear, chrome plastic. "Morton Grove" decals. Reissued as 1214.

1214 **Mack Fire Truck** (snap) 1982-86 1/32 $15-20
Yellow, black, clear, chrome plastic. "Glenview" decals. Reissue of 1213.

1300 **Freightliner Rig** (snap) 1980-81 1/32 $25-30
Off-white, white, black, clear, chrome plastic. "Dairy Queen" decal. Reissue of 1202 (1978) with reefer trailer.

1301 **Chevy Bison Rig** (snap) 1980-81 1/32 $25-30
Black, silver, clear, chrome plastic for truck. Gray plastic trailer. "Cracker Jack" decal. Reissue of 1201 (1978) with van trailer.

1302 **Peterbilt Rig** (snap) 1981-82 1/32 $25-30
Yellow, white, clear, chrome plastic. "Eskimo Pie" decals. Reissue of 1204 (1980) and 1206 (1980).

1303 **Kenworth Rig** (snap) 1981-83 1/32 $25-30
Blue, black, white, clear, chrome plastic. With 1207 van. "Sea-Land" decals. Reissue of 1205 (1980).

1304 **Kenworth Coe/Van** (snap) 1982-84 1/32 $25-30
Black, clear, chrome plastic. With 1207 van. "Faberge" decals. Reissue of 1209 (1981), 1207 (1980).

1305 **Mack/Tanker** (snap) 1982-84 1/32 $25-30
Blue, black, silver, clear, chrome plastic. Mack conventional. With tanker. "Gulf" decals. Reissue of 1210 (1982).

1400 **Pontiac Trans Am** (snap) 1981-83 1/24 $10-15
Yellow, clear, chrome plastic. Vinyl tires. Hood opens to show detailed engine.

1401 **'81 Corvette** (snap) 1981-83 1/24 $10-15
Red, clear, chrome plastic. Hood lifts off. Engine block is molded into the body part.

1402 **'79 Datsun Pickup** (snap) 1981-85 1/24 $10-15
Off-white, clear, chrome plastic. Reissued as 1412 (1985).

1403 **Camaro Z-28** (snap) 1981-83 1/24 $10-15
Orange, clear, chrome plastic. Hood opens.

1404 **'83 Z-28 Camaro** (snap) 1982-85 1/24 $10-15
Red, clear, chrome plastic.

1405 **'83 Corvette** (snap) 1982-85 1/24 $8-10
Red, smoked clear, chrome plastic. Listed as an '84 Corvette in the 1983 Monogram catalog. Reissued as 1410 (1985).

1406 **'82 Dodge Charger** (snap) 1982-85 1/24 $8-10
Yellow, clear, chrome plastic. Decals. Reissued as 1411 (1985).

1407 **Simon & Simon Camaro** 1983-86 1/24 $20-25
Red, clear, chrome plastic. (snap) Reissued as 1409 (1985).

1408 **Barbie Corvette** (snap) 1984 1/24 $15-20
Silver, smoked clear plastic. "Barbie" decal. Reissue of 1401 (1981).

1409 **'85 Camaro Z-28E** (snap) 1985-86 1/24 $10-15
Yellow reissue of 1407 (1983) with new skirting, grille, hood louvers.

1410 **'85 Corvette** (snap) 1985-86 1/24 $10-15
Red, smoked clear plastic. Decals. Reissue of 1405 (1982).

1411 **Shelby Charger Turbo** 1985-86 1/24 $8-10
Metallic blue '85 Dodge Charger. (snap) Reissue of 1406 (1982).

1412 **'79 Datsun Pick-Up** (snap) 1985-86 1/24 $10-15
Off white, clear, chrome plastic. Miller beer decals. Reissue of 1402 (1981).

1413 **'85 Dodge Daytona** (snap) 1986 1/24 $12-15
Black, smoked clear plastic. Decals. Hood opens. Turbo-Z.

1414 **'82 Collectors' Vette** (snap) 1986 1/24 $12-15
Silver, smoked clear, chrome plastic. Decals. Hood opens.

1500 **Peterbilt Conventional** 1982-86 1/25 $15-20
Yellow, black, clear, chrome plastic. Decal. (snap) Monogram broke with its standard 1/24 scale for these kits so that they would be compatible with the 1/25 scale trailers of AMT and MPC. Reissued as 2422 (1985), 2423 (1985).

1501 **Kenworth Conventional** 1982-86 1/25 $15-20
Silver, black, clear plastic. Decals. (snap)

1502 **Red "Animal" 4 x 4** 1985-86 1/24 $15-20
Red, black, silver, clear plastic. Decals. As wheels turn, claws reach out from tires and then retract as they reach the road surface. Also issued as 1503.

1503 **Black "Animal" 4 x 4** 1985-86 1/24 $15-20
Yellow, black, silver, clear plastic. Decals. Also issued as 1502.

2004 **'82 Chevy Camaro Z/28** 1982-85 1/32 $10-15
Red, clear plastic. Decals. Reissued as 2013 (1983).

2005 **'82 Ford Escort Sport** 1981-83 1/32 $10-15
Yellow, black, clear plastic. Reissued as 2008 (1982).

2006 **'69 Chevy Nova SS** 1981-85 1/32 $15-20
Yellow, clear, chrome plastic. Decal. Reissued as 2011 (1982).

2007 **'69 Dodge Hemi Charger** 1981-83 1/32 $15-20
Red, black, clear, chrome plastic. Flame decals. Reissued as 2010 (1982).

2008 **'82 Mercury LN-7** 1982-83 1/32 $10-15
Reissue of 2005 (1981).

2009 **'71 Trans Am Firebird** 1982-85 1/32 $10-15
White, clear, chrome plastic. Vinyl tires. Reissued as 2013 (1983).

2010 **'69 Hemi Street Charger** 1982-85 1/32 $15-20
Reissue of 2007 (1981) with added blower.

2011 **Street '69 Nova** 1982-85 1/32 $15-20
Yellow, clear, chrome plastic. Reissue of 2006 (1981).

2012 **Trans Am Street Machine** 1983-84 1/32 $10-15
Reissue of 2009 (1982).

2013 **Camaro Midnight Streaker** 1983-84 1/32 $10-15
Reissue of 2004 (1982).

2113 **Ferrari 308 GTB** 1980-81 1/24 $15-20
Red, clear, chrome plastic. Reissued as 2116 (1981).

2114 **Porsche 924 Turbo** 1980-81 1/24 $10-15
Black, clear, chrome plastic. Reissue of 2106 (1977).

2115 **Triumph TR-8** 1981 1/24 $15-20
Silver, clear, chrome plastic.

2116 **Ferrari 308 Racer** 1981 1/24 $15-20
Yellow, clear, chrome plastic. Reissue of 2113 (1980).

2117 **Porsche 924 Rally** 1981 1/24 $10-15
Orange, clear, chrome plastic. Reissue of 2106 (1977).

2118 **Datsun 280Z Rally** 1981 1/24 $10-15
Red, clear, chrome plastic. Reissue of 2104 (1976).

2119 **Porsche Carrera 911 Rally** 1981-82 1/24 $10-15
Light blue, clear, chrome plastic. Reissue of 2101 (1976).

2120 **Capri II Rally** 1981 1/24 $15-20
Yellow, clear, chrome plastic. Racing decals. Reissue of 2103 (1976).

2200 **'70 Chevelle High Roller** 1983 1/24 $20-25
Black, clear, chrome plastic. Decal. Reissue of 2268 (1980).

2201 **'69 Camaro High Roller** 1983-86 1/24 $20-25
Red, clear, chrome plastic. Decals. Reissue of 2220 (1977).

2202 **'83 Black Trans Am** 1982-84 1/24 $10-15
Black, clear, chrome plastic. Decals.

2204 **Buick Regal Grand National** 1983-84 1/24 $20-25
White, clear, chrome plastic. "Mountain Dew" decals. '82 Buick. Darrell Waltrip's #11 car. Box art by David Lord. Also issued as 2205 (1983), 2298 (1984), 2707 (1985).

2205 **Buick Grand National Uno** 1983 1/24 $20-25
Red, clear, chrome plastic. "Uno" decals. Buddy Baker's #1 car. Box art by David Lord. Also issued as 2204.

2206 **'83 T-Bird Grand National** 1983-84 1/24 $20-25
Yellow, clear, chrome plastic. "Wrangler" decals. Dale Earnhardt's #15 car. Box art by David Lord. Also issued as 2207.

2207 **'83 T-Bird Grand National** 1983 1/24 $20-25
White, clear plastic. "Melling" decals. Bill Elliott's #9 car. Box art by David Lord. Also issued as 2206.

2208 **'68 Pontiac GTO** 1984-85 1/24 $10-15
Orange, clear plastic. Decals.

2209 **'85 Corvette** 1984-86 1/24 $10-15
Red, smoked clear, chrome plastic. Hood opens.

2210 **'84 Thunderbird Pro Stock** 1984-86 1/24 $10-15
White, clear, chrome plastic. Bob Glidden's dragster. 7-Eleven decals. Don Hardy chassis. Box art by David Lord. Also issued as 2218 (1984), 2727 (1986), 2738 (1986).

2213 **'71 Plymouth Satellite** 1984-86 1/24 $15-20
Black, clear, chrome plastic. Decals.

2214 **'70 Dodge 340 Challenger** 1983-86 1/24 $10-15
Dark metallic red, clear plastic. Reissued as 2729 (1986).

2215 **'69 Dodge 440 Six Pack** 1983-86 1/24 $10-15
Metallic blue, clear, chrome plastic. Decals. Super Bee Dodge Coronet.

2216 **Reher & Morrison Camaro** 1984-85 1/24 $20-25
White, clear, chrome plastic. Decals. Pro Stock dragster. Don Ness chassis. Also issued as 2217.

2217 **Iaconio '83 Camaro** 1984-85 1/24 $20-25
Yellow, clear, chrome plastic. Frank Iaconio's Pro Stock dragster. Don Ness chassis. Also issued as 2216.

2218 **Smith '84 Thunderbird** 1984-85 1/24 $10-15
Rickie Smith's Pro Stock dragster. Don Hardy chassis. Also issued as 2210 (1984).

**2222** **'83 Mustang Convertible** 1983-84 1/24 $15-220
Red, clear, chrome plastic. Decal. GT.

**2224** **'85 Pontiac Trans Am** 1984-86 1/24 $10-15
Black, clear, chrome plastic. Firebird decal. Hood opens.

**2233** **NFL American Conf. Van** 1983 1/24 $30-35
White, smoked clear plastic. Decals for all American Conference teams. Chevy van. Also issued as 2234.

**2234** **NFL National Conf. Van** 1983 1/24 $30-35
White, smoked clear plastic. Decals for all National Conference teams. Chevy van. Also issued as 2233.

**2242** **'85 Pontiac Fiero GT** 1984-86 1/24 $10-15
Red, clear, chrome plastic.

**2243** **'85 Mustang SVO** 1984-86 1/24 $15-20
Red, clear, chrome plastic. Hood opens.

**2244** **Elliot Coors '85 T-Bird** 1984-86 1/24 $10-15
Red, clear, chrome plastic. Bill Elliott's #9 car.

**2245** **Budweiser '84 Monte Carlo** 1984 1/24 $15-20
White, clear, chrome plastic. Decals for both the #11 Waltrip car and #12 Bonnett car. Box art by David Lord. Also issued as 2299 (1984), 2706 (1985).

**2249** **Sheriff's '75 Blazer** 1980-83 1/24 $20-25
Orange, clear, chrome plastic. Hood opens. Reissue of 2238 (1978).

**2258** **Trans Am Street Machine** 1980-83 1/24 $10-15
Off-white, clear, chrome plastic. '79 Trans Am.

**2259** **Corvette Street Machine** 1980-83 1/24 $10-15
Light blue, clear, chrome plastic. Hood opens. Fender extensions, rear spoiler. Reissue of 2253 (1978).

**2260** **'79 Mustang Cobra** 1980-83 1/24 $15-20
Red, clear, chrome plastic. Mustang II. Hood opens, removable sun roof. Reissue of 2250 (1979).

**2261** **Mork & Mindy Jeep** 1980 1/24 $20-25
Blue, clear, chrome plastic. Hood opens. Reissue of 2223 (1977).

**2262** **'80 Ford F-150 Ranger** 1980-83 1/24 $15-20
Red, clear, chrome plastic. Reissued as 2274 (1981), 2418 (1984), 2419 (1984).

**2263** **'80 Dodge Ramcharger** 1980-81 1/24 $40-45
Off-white, clear, chrome plastic. Pinstripe decals. Hood opens. Reissued as 2272 (1981).

**2264** **Chevy 4 x 4 Pickup** 1980-82 1/24 $15-20
Yellow, clear, chrome plastic. '75 Stepside. Reissue of 2228 (1977).

**2265** **'40 Ford Pickup** 1980-81 1/24 $10-15
Yellow, clear, chrome plastic. "Lemon Crate" decals. '48 Merc flathead engine. Hood, doors, windows, tailgate open. Reissue of PC91 (1964).

**2266** **Camaro Street Machine** 1980-83 1/24 $10-15
Red, clear, chrome plastic. "Street Stalker" decals. Z-28. Wire wheels, rear fender flairs, hood opens. Reissue of 2254 (1978).

**2268** **'70 Chevy Malibu SS454** 1980-86 1/24 $8-10
Red, clear, chrome plastic. Reissued as 2284 (1981), 2200 (1983), 2715 (1985).

**2269** **Corvette America** 1980-83 1/24 $20-25
Orange, clear, chrome plastic. Four seat, four door Corvette. California Custom Coach of Pasadena customized a '70 coupe.

**2270** **'81 Trans Am Turbo** 1980-83 1/24 $8-10
Red, clear, chrome plastic. Firebird decal. Reissue of 2247 (1979).

**2271** **'80 Ford Bronco XLT** 1981-82 1/24 $10-15
Black, clear, chrome plastic. Fabric-textured plastic on camper top. Reissued as 2286 (1981).

**2272** **'80 Ramcharger High Roller** 1981-86 1/24 $15-20
Off white, clear, chrome plastic. Charging ram decal. Hood opens. Reissue of 2263 (1980).

**2273** **'77 GMC High Roller PU** 1981-85 1/24 $15-20
Orange, clear, chrome plastic. Reissue of 2236 (1978).

**2274** **'80 Ford F-150 High Roller** 1981-86 1/24 $15-20
Blue, clear, chrome plastic. Decals. Reissue of 2262 (1980).

**2275** **BMW 635** 1981-82 1/24 $10-15
Red, clear, chrome plastic. Also issued as 2287 (1981).

**2276** **'79 Mustang Cafe Racer** 1981-83 1/24 $15-20
Yellow, clear, chrome plastic. Racing decals. Reissue of 2250 (1979).

**2277** **Mazda Cafe Racer** 1981-83 1/24 $15-20
Blue, clear, chrome plastic. Racing decals. Reissue of 2257 (1978).

**2278** **'81 Chevy Sport X** 1981-83 1/24 $8-10
Yellow, clear, chrome plastic. Also issued as 2288 (1981).

**2279** **'81 Land Rover** 1981-83 1/24 $25-35
Off-white, clear plastic. No chrome parts.

**2280** **'80 Chevy LUV 4WD** 1981-83 1/24 $15-20
Light blue, black, clear, chrome. Decal. High roller. Reissue of 2213 (1976).

**2281** **'82 Trans Am** 1981-82 1/24 $10-15
Red, smoked clear, chrome plastic.

**2282** **'70 Boss Mustang 429** 1981-86 1/24 $10-15
Orange, clear, chrome plastic.

**2283** **Corvette Street Machine** 1981-86 1/24 $8-10
Black, clear, chrome plastic. Flame decals. '57 Corvette.

**2284** **'70 Chevelle Malibu** 1981-85 1/24 $8-10
Orange, clear, chrome plastic. Reissue of 2268 (1980). Major decal treatment for this street machine version.

**2285** **Ford F-100 Stroh Pickup** 1981-83 1/24 $10-15
Red, clear, chrome plastic. Stroh decals. '55 Ford. Beer barrels in back. Reissue of 2242 (1978).

**2286** **Ford Bronco High Roller** 1981-83 1/24 $15-20
Red, clear, chrome plastic. '80 Bronco. Reissue of 2271 (1981).

**2287** **BMW Rally** 1981-83 1/24 $10-15
Added spoiler. Reissue of 2275 (1981).

**2288** **'81 X Citation Rally** 1981-83 1/24 $10-15
Black, clear, chrome plastic. Also issued as 2778 (1981).

**2289** **'56 T-Bird** 1982-86 1/24 $8-10
Red, clear, chrome plastic. Reissue of 6101 metal body (1977).

**2290** **'50 MG-TC** 1982-86 1/24 $10-15
White, red, clear, chrome. Reissue of 6102 metal body (1977).

**2291** **'53 Corvette** 1982-86 1/24 $8-10
White, red, clear, chrome plastic. Reissue of 6100 metal body (1977).

**2292** **'71 Hemi Cuda** 1982-85 1/24 $10-15
Orange, clear, chrome plastic. Funny car. Reissued as 2701 (1985).

**2293** **'70 Plymouth GTX** 1982-85 1/24 $10-15
Green, clear, chrome plastic. Reissued as 2730 (1986).

**2294** **'69 Pontiac GTO Judge** 1982-86 1/24 $8-10
Off-white, clear chrome plastic. Decals.

**2295** **Chevy Blazer Pull Dozer** 1982-83 1/24 $15-20
High roller. Reissue of 2238 (1978).

**2296** **Miller '81 Mustang IMSA** 1982-84 1/24 $10-15
White, clear, chrome plastic. Miller Brewing decals. Also issued as 2297.

**2297** **Ford Motorsport Mustang** 1982-86 1/24 $10-15
White, clear, chrome plastic. Blue racing stripe, #16 decals. '81 Mustang. IMSA. Also issued as 2296.

**2298** **Allison Miller '84 Buick** 1984-85 1/24 $15-20
White, clear plastic. Bobby Allison's #22 Regal. Box art by David Lord. Reissue of 2204 (1983).

**2299** **Labonte Piedmont Chevy** 1984-85 1/24 $10-15
'84 Chevy Monte Carlo. Terry Labonte's #44 car. Box art by David Lord. Also issued as 2245 (1984).

**2305** **'32 Cadillac V-16 Phaeton** 1980-86 1/24 $15-20
Off-white, black, clear, chrome plastic.

**2306** **Mercedes Convertible** 1982-86 1/24 $25-30
White, black, clear, chrome plastic. Reissue of PC87 (1963).

**2307** **Rolls Royce Roadster** 1982-86 1/24 $10-15
Lime green, silver, clear, chrome plastic. Reissue of PC109 (1965).

**2402** **Jeep CJ-7 Renegade** 1980-82 1/20 $15-20
Red, black, clear, chrome. Hood opens. Reissued as 2405 (1981).

**2403** **'80 Camaro Z/20 Turbo** 1980-83 1/20 $15-20
Black, red, clear plastic. Clear roof panels. Reissued as 2413 (1982).

**2404** **'80 Corvette Coupe** 1980-81 1/20 $15-20
Yellow, beige, clear, chrome plastic. T-top removes, hood opens to show 305 V-8 engine, fastback opens. Reissued as 2406 (1981), 2408 (1982).

**2405** **Jeep CJ-7 Off Road** 1981-83 1/20 $15-20
Lime green, black, clear, chrome plastic. Hood opens. Roll cage. Reissue of 2402 (1980).

**2406** **Custom Corvette** 1981-83 1/20 $15-20
Fender extensions, rear spoiler, custom wheels. Reissue of 2404 (1980).

**2407** **'81 Trans Am Firebird** 1981-83 1/20 $15-20
White, red, clear, chrome plastic.

**2408** **'82 Collectors Corvette** 1982-83 1/20 $20-25
Silver, smoked clear plastic. Decals. Reissue of 2404 (1980).

**2413** **Ultra Z Camaro** 1982-83 1/20 $45-50
Silver, black, smoked clear, chrome plastic. Reissue of 2403 (1980).

**2418** **The Krusher Ford 4 x 4** 1984-86 1/24 $10-15
Red, white, clear, chrome plastic. Decals. Hood opens. '80 Ford F-150. Monster truck with giant tires. Reissue of 2262 (1980).

**2419** **Quadzilla 4 x 4 Ford** 1984-86 1/24 $10-15
Black, white, clear, chrome plastic. Decals. Hood opens. '80 Ford F-150. Monster truck with giant tires. Reissue of 2262 (1980).

**2420** **Monster Mash 4 x 4 Chevy** 1985-86 1/24 $10-15
Red, white, clear, chrome plastic. Decals. Hood opens. Monster truck with giant tires. Box art by Elmore. Reissue of 2238 (1978).

**2421** **Hammerhead 4 x 4 Chevy** 1985-86 1/24 $10-15
Dark blue, white, clear, chrome plastic. Decals. Hood opens. Monster truck with giant tires. Box art by Parkinson. Reissue of 2238 (1978).

**2422** **Devastator 6 x 6** 1985-86 1/32 $8-10
Black, white, clear, chrome plastic. Decals. Monster truck with giant tires. Reissue of 1500 (1982).

**2423** **Intimidator 6 x 6** 1985-86 1/32 $8-10
Red, white, clear, chrome plastic. Decals. Monster truck with giant tires. Reissue of 1500 (1982).

**2500** **Peterbild 359 Tractor** 1980-86 1/16 $75-85
Yellow, black, clear, chrome plastic. Decal. Hood tilts forward to show engine.

**2501** **Kenworth Conventional** 1981-86 1/16 $135-140
Red, black, clear, chrome plastic. Decals. Reissued as 2502 (1982).

**2502** **Kenworth Conventional** 1982-86 1/16 $135-140
Dark metallic blue, black, clear, chrome plastic. Decals. Molded in "Metal Glow" plastic and includes Turtle Wax to polish the finish. Reissue of 2501 (1981).

**2503 Flatbed Trailer** 1983-86 1/16 $35-45
Orange plastic. When pulled from the molding machine the plastic of the bed tended to warp—by coincidence giving the bed just the rise in the middle of an unloaded flatbed.

**2605 '80 Pontiac Trans Am** 1980-85 1/8 $90-100
Black, tan, translucent red, tinted clear plastic. Firebird decal. Hood opens to show 301 turbo V-8, roof t-panels remove, front wheels steer.

**2606 '82 Corvette** 1982-86 1/8 $90-100
Silver, black, clear, chrome plastic. Roof panels remove. Hood opens to show engine. Molded in "Metal Glow" plastic and includes Turtle Wax to polish the finish. Revised reissue of 2603 (1978).

**2607 '82 Z-28 Camaro** 1982-85 1/8 $90-100
Maroon, black, blue, tan, smoked clear, chrome plastic. Molded in "Metal Glow" plastic and includes Turtle Wax to polish the finish. Ken Merker rated this the best of the 1/8 car models. "The parts fit together well—just click, click, click." Reissued as 1610 (1985).

**2608 '85 Corvette** 1984-86 1/8 $90-100
Red, tan, black, clear, chrome plastic. Hood tilts forward to show engine.

**2609 Golden "T" Street Rod** 1985-86 1/8 $90-100
Black, metallic charcoal interior, clear, gold chrome plastic. Pinstripe decals. Cardboard "street" base. Reissue of PC78 (1962).

**2610 Camaro Iroc-Z** 1985-86 1/8 $90-100
Black, tangerine orange, smoked clear, chrome plastic. IROC-Z decal. Revision of 1607 (1982).

**2700 '65 Mustang Shelby GT-350** 1985-86 1/24 $8-10
White, clear, chrome plastic. Blue racing stripe decals. Also issued as 2713 (1985), 2736 (1986).

**2701 '71 Plymouth 'Cuda** 1985-86 1/24 $10-15
Black, clear, chrome plastic. Flame decals. Street machine. Hood opens to show 426 Hemi engine. Reissue of 2292 (1982).

**2702 '33 Ford ZZ Top Eliminator** 1985-86 1/24 $10-15
Red, clear, chrome plastic. Decals. '33 Ford coupe with radically chopped top. Comes with three rock band figures.

**2703 Boot Hill Express** 1985-86 1/24 $35-40
Yellow, clear, chrome plastic. Reissue of PC188 (1967).

**2705 Li'l Coffin Show Rod** 1985-86 1/24 $10-15
Red, white, clear, chrome plastic. Reissue of PC94 (1964).

**2706 Skoal Bandit '85 Chevy** 1985-86 1/24 $15-20
Harry Gant's #33 car. Decals. Reissue of 2245 (1984).

**2707 '84 Valvoline Buick Regal** 1985-86 1/24 $10-15
White, clear, chrome plastic. Decals. Ron Bouchard's #47 car. Box art by David Lord. Reissue of 2204 (1983).

**2708 '86 Mustang GTP** 1985-86 1/24 $8-10
White, clear, chrome plastic. Ford Motors decals. Also issued as 2709.

**2709 '86 Mustang GTP 7-Eleven** 1985-86 1/24 $8-10
White, clear, chrome plastic. 7-Eleven decals. Also issued as 2708.

**2710 7-Eleven Mustang FC** 1985-86 1/24 $15-20
White, clear, chrome plastic. Decals. Funny car. All three funny cars share the same chassis and Keith Black 500 cc engine. Billy Meyer's car.

**2711 Wendy/Pepsi Trans Am FC** 1985-86 1/24 $20-25
White, clear, chrome plastic. Decals. '85 Pontiac Trans Am funny car. Don Prudhomme's car.

**2712 Miller Warrior Trans Am** 1985-86 1/24 $20-25
Red, clear, chrome plastic. Miller decals. '85 Pontiac Trans Am funny car. Dale Pulde's car.

**2713 '65 Mustang 2 + 2** 1985-86 1/24 $15-20
Red, clear, chrome plastic. Decals. Also issued as 2700 (1985).

**2714 '64 Pontiac GTO Coupe** 1985-86 1/24 $8-10
Red, clear, chrome plastic. Transparent red plastic tail lights. *Model Car Journal*'s (November 1985) Dennis Doty declared this model superior to AMT's.

**2715 '70 Chevelle Street Machine** 1985-86 1/24 $8-10
Blue metalflake, clear, chrome plastic. Decals. 3 'n 1 kit. Parts to build three versions, including three sets of wheels. Reissue of 2268 (1980).

**2716 '78 Trans Am Street Machine** 1985-86 1/24 $8-10
Black, clear, chrome. "Warbird" decals on side panels. 3 'n 1 kit. Parts to build three versions, including three sets of wheels. Reissue of 2247 (1979).

**2717 '78 Camaro Street Machine** 1985-86 1/24 $8-10
Black, clear, chrome plastic. Decals. "Midnight Z" decals. Parts to build three versions, including ten wheels. Reissue of 2254 (1978).

**2718 '32 Ford Roadster** 1985-86 1/24 $8-10
Yellow, clear, chrome plastic. Flame decals. Street rod. Reissue of PC132 (1966).

**2719 '39 Chevy Coupe** 1985-86 1/24 $10-15
Dark red, clear, chrome plastic. Flame decals. Street rod. Reissue of 2256 (1979).

**2720 '40 Ford Pickup Street Rod** 1985-86 1/24 $8-10
Red, black, clear, chrome plastic. Flame decals. Reissue of PC91 (1964).

**2721 '36 Ford Coupe Street Rod** 1985-86 1/24 $8-10
Dark red, black, clear, chrome plastic. Flame decals. Reissue of PC68 (1961).

**2722 #43 '85 Pontiac Grand Prix** 1986 1/24 $15-20
Light blue, clear, chrome plastic. STP decals. Richard Petty's #43 car.

**2723 Motorcraft'86 Thunderbird** 1986 1/24 $15-20
White, clear, chrome plastic. Motorcraft decals. Ricky Rudd's #15 car.

**2724 '65 Vette "Black Rat"** 1985-86 1/24 $12-15
Black, clear, chrome plastic. Reissue of PC126 (1965).

**2725 '69 Camaro** 1986 1/24 $12-15
Yellow, clear, chrome plastic. Elaborate "Rampage" decals. Reissue of 2220 (1977).

**2726 Budweiser Funny Car** 1986 1/24 $15-20
Red, clear, chrome plastic. Decals. Kenny Bernstein's '85 Ford Tempo. Stretched body tilts up to show chassis, engine, driver's cage.

**2727 Budweiser/Motorcraft FC** 1986 1/24 $15-20
Red, clear, chrome plastic. Motorcraft/Budweiser decals. '85 Thunderbird. Frank Iaconio's pro stock funny car. Reissue of 2210 (1982).

**2728 Boss Mustang 429 2 'n 1** 1986 1/24 $15-20
White, clear, chrome plastic. Decals. Extra wheels, hood, engine parts for stock or street version.

**2729 '70 Dodge Challenger 2 'n 1** 1986 1/24 $15-20
Red, clear, chrome plastic. Decals. Build street or dragster version. Reissue of 2214 (1983).

**2730 '70 Plymouth GTX 2 'n 1** 1986 1/24 $10-15
Metallic Blue, clear, chrome plastic. Two decal sheets. Reissue of 2293 (1982).

**2731 '86 Chevy Monte Carlo SS** 1986 1/24 $10-15
Black, clear, chrome plastic.

**2734 Folger's '86 Monte Carlo SS** 1986 1/24 $10-15
Dark red, clear, chrome plastic. Decals. Tim Richmond's #25 car.

**2735 Thunderbird Turbo Coupe** 1986 1/24 $12-15
Red, clear plastic. '87 Thunderbird. Optional panels, wheels for custom version.

**2736 '65 Mustang GT-350H** 1986 1/24 $15-20
Black, clear, chrome. Gold racing stripe decals. Reissue of 2700 (1985).

**2737 Miami Vice Daytona Spyder** 1986 1/24 $10-15
Black, chrome, clear plastic. A Ferrari body and interior on Monogram's Corvette chassis (7504).

**2738 Pro/Street '86 T-Bird** 1986 1/24 $10-15
Red, smoked clear, chrome plastic. Decals. Reissue of 2210 (1984).

**2739 Pro/Street '84 Camaro** 1986 1/24 $15-20
Black, smoked clear, gold chrome plastic. Elaborate decals. "Mean and Nasty." Reissue of 2216 (1984).

**2800 '57 Chevy Coupe** 1986 1/12 $20-25
Black, red, chrome, clear plastic. Decals. Vinyl tires. Hood opens. Optional parts. Fuzzy dice for rear view mirror.

## Motorcycles

Monogram purchased and then sold just one shipment of motorcycle kits from the small Japanese company Union.

| | | | | |
|---|---|---|---|---|
| **2409** | **Yamaha XS11** | 1982-83 | 1/15 | $45-55 |
| **2410** | **Honda CBX** | 1982-83 | 1/15 | $45-55 |
| **2411** | **Kawasaki Z1-R** | 1982-83 | 1/15 | $45-55 |
| **2412** | **Kawasaki 2400 FX** | 1982-83 | 1/15 | $45-55 |
| **2414** | **Honda Road Racer** | 1982 | 1/15 | $45-55 |
| **2415** | **Harley Davidson FXS-80** | 1982 | 1/15 | $45-55 |
| **2416** | **Kawasaki Police 1000** | 1982 | 1/15 | $45-55 |
| **2417** | **Kawasaki 2550 Custom** | 1982 | 1/15 | $45-55 |

## Locomotives

**1105 Hudson** (snap) 1982-86 1/87 $10-15
Black plastic. New York Central decals. Coal tender car. Railroad track base. Made in HO scale to fit in with HO electric train layouts. Also issued as 1106, 1107.

**1106 Hudson** (snap) 1982-86 1/87 $10-15
Black plastic. Chelsea & Ohio decals. Also issued as 1105, 1107.

**1107 Hudson** (snap) 1982-86 1/87 $10-15
Black plastic. Santa Fe decals. Also issued as 1105, 1106.

**1600 Big Boy** (snap) 1984-86 1/87 $10-15
Black plastic. Union Pacific decals. Also issued as 1601, 1602.

**1601 Big Boy** (snap) 1984-86 1/87 $10-15
Black plastic. Baltimore & Ohio decals. Also issued as 1600, 1602.

**1602 Big Boy** (snap) 1984-86 1/87 $10-15
Black plastic. Duluth, Missabe & Iron Range decals. Also issued as 1600, 1601.

## Snoopy

**5696 Snoopy Ice Hockey** 1972-77 $75-100
Mustard, white, red plastic. Pre-painted details. Snap assembly. Snoopy vs. Woodstock table-top game.

**5902 Snoopy & His Motorcycle** 1971-75 $60-75
Yellow, white, silver plastic. Snoopy, with Woodstock in sidecar. Front wheel can be set to steer in a circle. Electric motor powered.

**5903** **Red Baron Fokker Tri Plane** 1971-75 $60-75
Red, white, black plastic. Pre-painted details. Decals. Electric motor spins prop.
**6661** **Snoopy High Wire** 1972-75 $75-100
White, red plastic. Snoopy and Woodstock ride high wire from ladder to dog house.
**6779** **Snoopy & Sopwith Camel** 1970-77 $60-75
Yellow, black, white plastic. Pre-painted details. Decals. Snap assembly. AA battery-powered motor spins prop. Mattel claimed, "It was the biggest selling plastic model kit ever created."
**6894** **Snoopy & His Bugatti** 1971-75 $60-75
Red, white plastic. Decals. Can be displayed on stand or set to zoom around room in circles on electric motor power.
**7502** **Snoopy is Joe Cool** 1973-75 $60-75
White, blue plastic. Decals for board, sunglasses, flowers on baggy swimsuit. Snoopy spins on one leg while riding surfboard over wave base.

## Science Fiction & Figure Kits

**CR101** **Zebras** 1961 $40-45
Off-white figures, black plastic frame. Pre-painted vacuum-formed background. 7 3/4 x 10 inch frame. Artorama.
**CR102** **Lions** 1961 $40-50
Off-white figures, black plastic frame. Pre-painted vacuum-formed background. 7 3/4 x 10 inch frame. Artorama.
**CR103** **Giraffes** 1961 $40-50
Off-white figures, black plastic frame. Pre-painted vacuum-formed background. 12 1/2 x 15 1/2 frame. Artorama.
**6007** **Frankenstein** (Aurora) 1983 1/8 $25-35
Black, glow plastic.
**6008** **Dracula** (Aurora) 1983 1/8 $15-25
Black, glow plastic.
**6009** **Wolfman** (Aurora) 1983 1/8 $15-25
Brown, glow plastic.
**6010** **Mummy** (Aurora) 1983 1/8 $15-25
Ivory, glow plastic.
**6011** **Flying Sub** (Aurora) 1979-80 $15-25
Yellow, gray, clear plastic. Top lifts off to show interior. Seven crew members. From the TV show *Voyage to the Bottom of the Sea*.
**6012** **The UFO** (Aurora) 1979-80 $25-35
Silver, transparent red plastic. Top lifts off to show interior. From the TV show *The Invaders*.
**6014** **Attak Track** 1983-85 $8-10
Orange, blue plastic. Masters of the Universe. Licensed from Mattel.
**6015** **Talon Fighter** 1983-85 $8-10
Red, yellow plastic. Masters of the Universe.
**6016** **Roton Combat** 1984-85 $8-10
Red, black plastic. Masters of the Universe.

## Shogun Warriors

The Shogun Warriors were made from the tooling borrowed from Japan.

**6020** **Dragon** 1978 $10-15
Red, yellow, silver plastic. These models can be snapped apart and reassembled. Spring-loaded "flying fists," rockets, and battle axe. 10 inches tall.
**6021** **Great Mazinga** 1978 $10-15
Blue, red, silver plastic. Flying fists, sword, dagger, jet wings. 9 inches tall.
**6022** **Raydeen** 1978 $10-15
Wrist spike, bow and arrows, opening face shield. 10 inches tall.
**6023** **Raider** 1978 $10-15
Red, blue, black plastic. Arm has claw, auger, spring-loaded rocket launcher options.
**6024** **Gaiking** 1978 $10-15
Bright green, dark green, black.
**6025** **Grandizer** 1978 $10-15
Maroon, silver, black plastic. Launches spring-loaded fists.
**6026** **Space Fighter Raider** 1978-80 $35-45
Gray plastic. Decals. Evil Cylon craft. Battlestar Galactica. All of the Galactica models are simple kits. Fires spring-loaded missiles from under wings. Eleven inches wide.
**6027** **Colonial Viper** 1978-80 $35-45
Gray plastic. Decals. Black decals to represent cockpit glass. Battlestar Galactica. Spring-loaded missile fires from nose pod. Eleven inches long.
**6028** **Battlestar Galactica** 1979-80 $50-60
Silver plastic. Decals. Mounted on a display stand with a "planet" base.
**6029** **Cylon Base Star** 1979-80 $50-60
Silver plastic. Decals. Eleven inches in diameter. Mounted on a stand.
**6030** **Buck Rogers Starfighter** 1979-80 $35-45
Off-white plastic.
**6031** **Buck Rogers Marauder** 1979-80 $35-45
Coral, transparent red plastic.
**6040** **Triceratops** (Aurora) 1979-80 $25-35
Dark green plastic. Includes base.
**6041** **Giant Woolly Mammoth** 1979-80 $25-35
Brown, white plastic. (Aurora)
**6042** **Spiked Dinosaur** 1979-80 $25-35
Tan plastic. Includes base.
**6043** **Tyrannosaurus** (Aurora) 1979-81 $50-60
Green, white plastic.
**6044** **Allosaurus** (Aurora) 1980-81 $25-35
Green plastic.
**6045** **Armored Dinosaur** (Aurora) 1980-81 $25-35
Tan plastic. Has only one of the original two Aurora base parts. Ankylosaurus.
**6046** **Dimetrodon** (Aurora) 1980-81 $25-35
Brown plastic. Includes base.
**6050** **Head Lite Skull** 1980-81 1/2 $20-30
Glow off-white plastic. Two D batteries power eye-socket flashlights or red glowing eyes. Squeeze hand grip and jaws open.
**6066** **Spay-C** 1984-85 $3-5
White plastic. NASA *Columbia* decals. GoBots. Three inch robot transforms into space shuttle. The GoBots were manufactured in Japan by Tonka and packaged by Monogram in the United States. Each has a pull-back motor and vinyl tires to propel them across the floor.
**6067** **Buggyman** 1984-85 $3-5
Red, blue-tinted clear plastic. Stick-on decals. Plastic wheels. GoBots. Three-and-a-half inch robot transforms into dune buggy.
**6068** **Royal-T** 1984-85 $3-5
White plastic. USAF and RAF decals. GoBots. Three inch robot transforms into Harrier fighter plane.
**6069** **Turbo** 1984-85 $3-5
Red, smoked clear plastic. Stick-on decals. GoBots. Four inch robot transforms into Ferrari sports car.
**6108** **Turbo Teen-Trans Am** 1985 1/32 $6-8
Red, blue tinted clear plastic. Firebird decal. Five inch robot-boy transforms into Trans-Am car. Also issued as 6109.
**6109** **Trans Am** 1985 1/32 $6-8
Black, clear plastic. Firebird decal. Also issued as 6108.
**6202** **Cy Kill** 1984-85 $6-8
Blue, white plastic. Seven inch robot
**6203** **Leader I** 1984-85 $6-8
Red, white plastic. Seven inch robot
**6300** **Godzilla** 1978 $40-50
Green, glow parts plastic. Ex-Aurora.
6301 Superman 1978 1/8 $20-30
Blue plastic. Ex-Aurora.